VOLUME 448   MARCH 1980

THE ANNALS

of The American Academy *of* Political
and Social Science

(ISSN 0002-7162)

RICHARD D. LAMBERT, *Editor*

ALAN W. HESTON, *Assistant Editor*

THE ACADEMIC PROFESSION

Special Editors of This Volume

PHILIP G. ALTBACH   SHEILA SLAUGHTER

Professor and Chairman   *Assistant Professor*
Department of Foundations   *of Education, Virginia*
of Education, and Professor of   *Polytechnic and*
Higher Education, State University   *State University*
of New York, Buffalo

PHILADELPHIA

Copy Editor

Kim Holmes, Ph.D.

The articles appearing in THE ANNALS are indexed in the
Book Review Index, the *Public Affairs Information Ser-
vice Bulletin, Social Sciences Index, Monthly Periodical
Index,* and *Current Contents: Behavioral, Social, Man-
agement Sciences* and *Combined Retrospective Index
Sets.* They are also abstracted and indexed in *ABC Pol
Sci, Historical Abstracts, United States Political Science
Documents, Social Work Research & Abstracts, Inter-
national Political Science Abstracts* and/or *America:
History and Life.*

International Standard Book Numbers (ISBN)

ISBN 0-87761-249-8, vol. 448, 1980; paper—$4.50
ISBN 0-87761-248-x, vol. 448, 1980; cloth—$5.50

*Issued bimonthly by The American Academy of Political and Social Science at 3937 Chestnut
St., Philadelphia, Pennsylvania 19104. Cost per year: $18.00 paperbound; $23.00 clothbound.
Add $2.00 to above rates for membership outside U.S.A. Second-class postage paid at Phila-
delphia and at additional mailing offices.*

*Claims for undelivered copies must be made within the month following the regular month
of publication. The publisher will supply missing copies when losses have been sustained in
transit and when the reserve stock will permit.*

Editorial and Business Offices, 3937 Chestnut Street, Philadelphia, Pennsylvania 19104.

CONTENTS

PREFACE ....*Philip G. Altbach* and *Sheila Slaughter*   vii

THE CRISIS OF THE PROFESSORIATE ....*Philip G. Altbach*   1

DIALECTIC ASPECTS OF RECENT CHANGE IN ACADEME ......*Logan Wilson*   15

CAREERS FOR ACADEMICS AND THE FUTURE PRODUCTION
    OF KNOWLEDGE ....*Robert T. Blackburn*   25

TEACHING, RESEARCH, AND ROLE THEORY ....*Michael A. Faia*   36

THE "DANGER ZONE": ACADEMIC FREEDOM AND
    CIVIL LIBERTIES ....*Sheila Slaughter*   46

IN BETWEEN: THE COMMUNITY COLLEGE TEACHER ...*Howard B. London*   62

FACULTY UNIONISM: THE FIRST TEN YEARS ....*Joseph W. Garbarino*   74

ACADEMIC TENURE: ITS RECIPIENTS AND ITS EFFECTS ....*Lionel S. Lewis*   86

AFFIRMATIVE ACTION AND THE
    ACADEMIC PROFESSION ....*Robert C. Johnson, Jr.*   102

UNTENURED AND TENUOUS: THE STATUS OF
    WOMEN FACULTY ....*Lilli S. Hornig*   115

AFRICAN ACADEMICS: A STUDY OF SCIENTISTS AT THE
    UNIVERSITIES OF IBADAN AND NAIROBI ....*Thomas Owen Eisemon*   126

THE INDIAN ACADEMIC: AN ELITE IN THE MIDST OF
    SCARCITY ....*Suma Chitnis*   139

BOOK DEPARTMENT...   151

INDEX...   207

iii

CONTENTS

BOOK DEPARTMENT

PAGE

INTERNATIONAL RELATIONS AND POLITICS

COHEN, WARREN I. *The Chinese Connection.* Carl F. Pinkele 151

DePORTE, A. W. *Europe between the Superpowers: The Enduring Balance.* Paul
L. Rosen 152

FISHER, GLEN. *American Communication in a Global Society.* Richard B. Kielbowicz 153

GELB, LESLIE H. and RICHARD K. BETTS. *The Irony of Vietnam: The System Worked.*
Justus M. Van Der Kroef 154

HENKIN, LOUIS. *The Rights of Man Today.* Osmond K. Fraenkel 155

JOYCE, JAMES AVERY. *The New Politics of Human Rights.* Osmond K. Fraenkel 155

MYTELKA, LYNN KRIEGER. *Regional Development in a Global Economy.* John B.
Adesalu 156

WHYNES, DAVID K. *The Economics of Third World Military Expenditure.* John B.
Adesalu 156

MOSHER, FREDERICK C. *The GAO: The Quest for Accountability in American Government.* Charles T. Barber 157

PAINTER, MARTIN and BERNARD CAREY. *Politics Between Departments: The Fragmentation of Executive Control in Australian Government.* Charles T. Barber 157

SHICHOR, YITZHAK. *The Middle East in China's Foreign Policy.* Albert L. Weeks 158

THORNTON, A. P. *Imperialism in the Twentieth Century.* S. G. Checkland 159

LISKA, GEORGE. *Career of Empire: American and Imperial Expansion over Land and
Sea.* S. G. Checkland 159

AFRICA, ASIA, AND LATIN AMERICA

ADAS, MICHAEL. *Prophets of Rebellion: Millenarian Protest Movements Against
European Colonial Order.* Peter Cocks 161

BATATU, HANNA. *The Old Social Classes and the Revolutionary Movements of Iraq.*
Louay Bahry 162

BINDER, LEONARD. *In a Moment of Enthusiasm: Political Power and the Second
Stratum in Egypt.* James B. Mayfield 163

DENG, FRANCIS MADING. *Africans of Two Worlds: The Dinka in Afro-Arab Sudan.*
John MacKenzie 164

SHAHRANI, M. NAZIF MOHIB. *The Kirghiz and Wakhi of Afghanistan: Adaptation to
Closed Frontiers.* Christopher J. Brunner 165

SOMJEE, A. H. *The Democratic Process in a Developing Society.* Richard S. Newell 166

TAYLOR, WILLIAM B. *Drinking, Homicide, and Rebellion in Colonial Mexican Villages.*
Sylvia Vatuk 167

TEIWES, FREDERICK C. *Politics and Purges in China: Rectification and the Decline of
Party Norms 1950–1965.* Robert P. Gardella 168

WOODS, RANDALL BENNETT. *The Roosevelt Foreign Policy Establishment and the
"Good Neighbor:" The United States and Argentina 1941–1945.* Donald G.
Bishop 169

CONTENTS   V

EUROPE   PAGE

BALFOUR, MICHAEL. *Propaganda in War 1939–1945: Organizations, Policies and Publics in Britain and Germany.* Norman D. Palmer 170

GRIGG, JOHN. *Lloyd George: The People's Champion, 1902–1911.* Neal A. Ferguson 170

MULLER, EDWARD N. *Aggressive Political Participation.* John S. Robey 171

PROTHERO, I. J. *Artisans and Politics in Early Nineteenth-Century London: John Gast and his Times.* Alfred F. Havighurst 172

ROTHROCK, GEORGE A. *The Huguenots: A Biography of a Minority.* David L. Schalk 173

SMITH, ANTHONY, ed. *Television and Political Life: Studies in Six European Countries.* Harvey W. Kushner 174

UNITED STATES HISTORY AND POLITICS

ANDERSON, KRISTI. *The Creation of a Democratic Majority, 1928–1936.* Donald B. Schewe 174

FINE, SIDNEY. *Frank Murphy: The New Deal Years.* Donald B. Schewe 174

BRAMS, STEVEN J. *The Presidential Election Game.* Frederick M. Finney 175

JONES, ROCHELLE and PETER WOLL. *The Private World of Congress.* Robert E. Gilbert 176

KORB, LAWRENCE J. *The Fall and Rise of the Pentagon: American Defense Policies in the 1970s.* Minoo Adenwalla 177

LIEBMAN, ARTHUR. *Jews and the Left.* Murray Smith 178

WILSON, WOODROW. *The Papers of Woodrow Wilson,* Vols. 29, 30: *1913–1914,* ed. Arthur S. Link et al. Louis Filler 179

STERN, PAULA. *Water's Edge: Domestic Politics and the Making of Foreign Policy.* Ghulam M. Haniff 180

STROUT, RICHARD L. *TRB: Views and Perspectives on the Presidency.* Fred Rotondaro ... 181

GOLDWATER, BARRY. *With No Apologies.* Fred Rotondaro 181

GERPEN, MAURICE VAN. *Priveleged Communication and the Press: The Citizen's Right to Know Versus the Law's Right to Confidential News Source Evidence.* Charles P. Elliot 182

FALLOWS, MARJORIE. *Irish Americans: Identity and Assimilation.* Laura L. Becker 183

WROBEL, PAUL. *Our Way: Family, Parish and Neighborhood in a Polish-American Community.* Laura L. Becker 183

SOCIOLOGY

ANDERSON, ANNELISE GRAEBNER. *The Business of Organized Crime: A Cosa Nostra Family.* William Kristol 184

BAHM, ARCHIE J. *The Philosopher's World Model.* Samuel J. Fox 185

BRAIN, JAMES LEWTON. *The Last Taboo: Sex and the Fear of Death.* James H. Frey .. 186

BURT, ROBERT A. *Taking Care of Strangers: The Rule of Law in Doctor-Patient Relations.* Joel S. Meister 186

vi   CONTENTS

                                                                          PAGE
COMSTOCK, GEORGE, et al. *Television and Human Behavior.* Robert Schmuhl   187

GIDDENS, ANTHONY. *Central Problems in Social Theory: Action, Structure and Contradiction in Social Analysis.* William A. Pearman   188

ISRAEL, JOACHIM. *The Language of Dialectics and the Dialectics of Language.* David L. Harvey   189

REINHARZ, SHULAMIT. *On Becoming a Social Scientist.* Henrika Kuklick   190

RIORDAN, JAMES. *Sport Under Communism.* James H. Frey   191

SLAWSON, JOHN. *Unequal Americans: Practices and Politics of Intergroup Relations.* Michael Fabricant   192

ECONOMICS

BERRY, R. ALBERT and WILLIAM R. CLINE. *Agrarian Structure and Productivity in Developing Countries.* Jay R. Mandle   193

GORDON, ROBERT J. and JACQUES PELKMANS. *Challenges to Interdependent Economies.* Russell Bellico   194

HITE, JAMES C. *Room and Situation: The Political Economy of Land-Use Policy.* Wallace F. Smith   195

LAKE, ROBERT W. *Real Estate Tax Delinquency: Private Disinvestment & Public Response.* Wallace F. Smith   195

KNAPP, JOSEPH G. *Edwin G. Nourse: Economist for the People.* F. B. Marbut   197

McGEE, LEO and ROBERT BOONE, eds. *The Black Rural Landowner-Endangered Species: Social, Political, and Economic Implication.* Frederick H. Schapsmeier   198

OWEN, JOHN D. *Working Hours: An Economic Analysis.* Roger Daniels   198

OZAWA, TERUTOMO. *Multinationalism, Japanese Style: The Political Economy of Outward Dependency.* R. Kent Lancaster   199

WRIGHT, ERIK OLIN. *Class Structure and Income Determination.* Dana D. Reynolds   200

The Crisis of the Professoriate

By PHILIP G. ALTBACH

ABSTRACT: The academic profession has been affected by substantial changes in the post-World War II period. The dramatic growth of universities in many nations in terms of enrollments and also of their societal role has placed the professoriate in a central social position. Challenges of expansion, pressures for reform and accountability, the student activism of the sixties, and other factors have endangered the traditional professorial role. Standard norms such as tenure and academic freedom have been questioned. Academic unions have appeared in many nations. This article focuses on a comparison of the major challenges to the academic profession. It discusses some of the ways in which the profession has been altered and analyzes how the professoriate has dealt with some of these difficult problems.

Philip G. Altbach is Professor and Chairman of the Department of Foundations of Education, and Professor of Higher Education at the State University of New York at Buffalo, where he also serves as Director of the Comparative Education Center. He is editor of the Comparative Education Review *and North American editor of* Higher Education. *He has taught at Harvard and the University of Wisconsin and has been visiting research professor at the University of Bombay, India. He edited* Comparative Perspectives on the Academic Profession *and coedited* The Academic Profession in India *among other publications.*

THE ACADEMIC profession has experienced much change and disruption in the last three decades.[1] Major changes resulted from the dramatic expansion of post-secondary education, from the student turmoil of the 1960s, from massive societal demands for curricular and other reforms in the universities, and most recently, from the decline in financial support and enrollments in many countries. These issues will be considered comparatively; a broad perspective may help to provide a more detailed understanding of national realities. While there are many differences among national university systems, there is much that can be learned from cross-national analysis. And as participants in a world intellectual community, academics and others concerned with higher education must consider the continuing systemic impact of unprecedented change on the profession from an international perspective.

Since World War II, the professoriate has most often been in a defensive position.[2] As intellectual workers dependent on the university, professors have basically reacted to external developments that produced alterations in the traditional university in most countries. It is, thus, necessary to speak to some of the more important changes in

higher education in order to provide a framework for this discussion.

The overwhelming reality of higher education in most countries has been expansion. Rapid growth was triggered by economic and political changes following the two world wars. Having fought a war to make the world safe for democracy and a war to end all wars, materially prosperous and highly industrialized "first world" countries had to address widespread popular expectations of a more egalitarian distribution of societal resources, both economic and political. The university was called on to participate in the creation of an egalitarian society as well as in advanced research and training. Higher education provided at one and the same time seemingly more equitable access to opportunity to win societal rewards and the well trained and disciplined labor force necessary for full industrialization and post-industrial technology. Many university systems doubled their student enrollments in little more than a decade in the period between 1950 and 1970. An expanded university served similar functions— although on a more limited scale— in second and third world nations eager to industrialize.

Expansion had wide ranging implications. The social class base of both the student population and the professoriate broadened and changed. Substantial segments of the student body were no longer recruited from elite and professional classes. This shift meant that members of the academic community were less and less likely to share a common understanding of the university and the way it traditionally related to the wider world. Sheer increase in numbers fragmented the academic

1. I am indebted to Sheila Slaughter, Thomas Eisemon, Robert O. Berdahl, E. Duryea, and Lionel Lewis for their comments on an earlier version of this paper. See Philip G. Altbach, ed., Comparative Perspectives on the Academic Profession, (New York: Praeger, 1977) for further analyses of this topic.
2. For general analyses of post-war higher education in comparative context, see Christopher Driver. The Exploding University, (Indianapolis, IN: Bobbs-Merrill, 1972) and Murray G. Ross, The University: Anatomy of Academe, (New York: McGraw-Hill, 1976).

profession and vitiated the base for shared action and perspectives.

The resource base for expanded post-secondary education also changed dramatically as it grew. In the United States private funds declined in importance as government funding for higher education greatly increased. Public expenditures dramatically increased in other countries as well. The use of public monies called for a corresponding growth in accountability. The work of the professoriate was more closely monitored and the academic career as well as academic institutions themselves became increasingly bureaucratized. Funds for research also increased and the orientation of higher education in the United States and other industrialized nations shifted in the direction of research. As funding agencies were interested in specific results, the conditions for the award of funds were made stringent, and academics were asked to provide careful accounting for expenditures. Cleavages between those academics with access to research and those without such funding grew, and general dissatisfaction increased.

As universities became more "central" institutions, they became arenas in which general societal demands and conflicts were worked out.[3] The public and government demanded accountability, students demanded relevance, minority groups demanded compensatory treatment, and the society attempted to use higher education as a means of solving social ills. These conflicts and other specific issues, such as the Vietnam war, became part of university politics, often part of the curriculum, and always part of the university's relation to the wider society.[4] As a corporate body, the professoriate seldom took stands on these matters and often attempted to ignore their implications. While the specific issues differed from country to country, similar developments took place internationally.

Many academic analysts and a significant part of the profession in many nations viewed the post-war crisis with considerable dismay and compared the contemporary situation to a somewhat mythic "Golden Age" when autonomy was entrenched, academic values respected, and the profession itself laden with prestige but somewhat removed from the societal mainstream. The historical referent for the Golden Age myth in the United States is the prewar elite, private Eastern graduate universities where small groups of scholars taught the sons and daughters of a political and economic elite, shared research and scholarly interests and, on the national scene, knew almost everyone who was working in their respective fields. They were part of an international academic system, familiar with their compeers in Britain, France, and Germany. Productive researchers, either tenured or confident of a good place in the academic system, they generally stayed away from oppositional politics, either to the right or left of center. It was this academic elite which benefited first from the massive research funds of the post-war period. When the academic system began to expand almost beyond recognition, the elite bemoaned the decline of the community of scholars.

3. See Robert Paul Wolff, *The Ideal of the University* (Boston: Beacon, 1969) for a discussion of different conceptions of the modern university.

4. See Edward Shils, "The Academic Ethos Under Strain," *Minerva* 13 (Spring 1975), pp. 1–37.

While the Golden Age recalled in such discussions was probably more revered myth than historical reality, at least it reflected the norms and values of a small but highly significant segment of the American academic system. Much of the current debate on the state of the academic profession is framed in terms of these values. Academics, particularly at prestigious institutions in the industrialized nations, look back to this tradition and compare the current situation to it.[5] This article will discuss some of the elements of the traditional view of the university and examine the current status of the academic profession in this context. When we consider the traditional norms and values of the profession, we do so with the understanding that these peceptions are at least in part a collective myth which has nevertheless shaped our image of academe. These traditional norms protect academic elites, but they have also shaped the collective historical consciousness of the university. It is questionable whether the traditional values are appropriate for mass higher educational systems, or, appropriate or not, whether the values can survive in the pressures of contemporary higher education. It is incumbent on the academic profession to think seriously about the meaning of these changes, and important for those concerned with the future of higher education to understand the rapidly changing academic scene.

We will discuss some of the key changes which have cross-national relevance, and which have most directly affected the academic profession. These reflections are necessarily quite general in nature and do not reflect the entire range of concerns. They indicate a composite of national conditions rather than a thoroughgoing analysis of a single country.

THE INTERNATIONAL ACADEMIC SYSTEM

In academic mythology knowledge is international. The only qualification for participating in a worldwide intellectual network is a commitment to the quest for truth. However, some universities and academic systems are more important than others. Since World War II, the speed of modern communications, the concentration of research efforts, and the mobility of students and staff has made an international academic hierarchy an important reality. The enormous influence of the central academic systems such as those in the United States, Britain, and France and the corresponding authority of the professoriate in these countries shapes the international knowledge structure. Most of the world's research is done by academics in the central university systems; the major publishers and journals are located in these countries.[6]

The primary languages of academic discourse are English and French. Increasingly, without access to publications in the major scholarly languages and without knowledge of these languages, it is impossible to follow current developments. Uni-

---

5. Among the most articulate defenders of traditional academe are Logan Wilson, *American Academics: Then and Now* (New York: Oxford University Press, 1979), and Robert Nisbet, *The Degradation of the Academic Dogma* (New York: Basic Books, 1971).

6. Philip G. Altbach, "The University as Center and Periphery," *Journal of Higher Education* (New Delhi) 4 (Autumn 1978), pp. 157–169 for an elaboration of these points.

versities throughout the world look to the major metropolitan institutions for leadership and often follow curricular and other practices of these universities. In the Third World especially, academics are often trained in the metropolitan institutions and carry back the ethos, orientations, and practices of the universities in which they have been trained. Further, the imbalance in academic power contributes to the brain drain as academics gravitate to the metropolitan nations and often remain there. But dependency is not simply a matter of a low level of economic development and poverty; even such countries as Canada, Kuwait, and the Netherlands are all, in different ways, dependent on major academic power centers.[7]

There has emerged in recent years a global academic stratification system with the major industrialized nations at the top of the system and with the prestigious research-oriented institutions within these countries at the pinnacle. The rest of the world occupies positions at lower reaches of the system, with the Third World nations at the bottom of the ladder. Currently, Third World countries are trying to change their position in the international system. In international forums—the press and the media—they are demanding a shift in the knowledge structure, especially technological knowledge, that would allow them to be producers rather than consumers of knowledge. Western academics and their governments have not yet shown themselves responsive to such demands. Central university systems presently constitute an international cartel of

technical knowledge, and world redistribution would significantly alter their material circumstances. While academics at the center deny knowledge is a commodity and speak of it as unfettered by national boundaries, in reality the international academic system links the academic profession in a web of inequality.

Academics and research

Traditionally, research and teaching have been viewed as mutually reinforcing, the two together constituting the scholarly orientation to which academics aspire. However, as advanced knowledge has become more central to modern industrial society, research is the function best rewarded. Indeed, the American graduate university, in its emphasis on the generation of new knowledge, has become a world model. While not all universities or colleges focus mainly on research, or use research criteria for academic advancement, the graduate-oriented model is the international standard of prestige. Institutions as well as individual scholars aspire to the high status roles of graduate teaching and research. While most academics have as their main responsibility the teaching of undergraduate students, the growing research emphasis has upset the balance of the profession and has disconcerted many academics.

In the past, researchers have always commanded greater prestige and generally higher salaries than academics who concentrated on teaching, especially at the undergraduate level. But all academics are increasingly encouraged to publish in scholarly journals and to write books. Merely teaching is no longer a choice at many universities. As competition for scarce tenured posi-

7. Edward Silva. "Cultural Autonomy and Ideas in Transit: Notes from the Canadian Case," *Comparative Education Review* 24 (February 1980), in press.

tions becomes more fierce, teaching and research are minimal requirements. However, there is no corresponding reduction in teaching load or increase in compensation. The situation is further complicated by the fact that most academics throughout the world publish very little. Thus, performance expectations are up while rewards remain the same or even decline due to worldwide inflation. Relatively few academic systems—the British, dominated by the ethos of Oxford and Cambridge are among the few exceptions—have withstood these pressures.

The point here is not that research, graduate training, and scholarly publication are detrimental. Indeed, these elements may be crucial to maintaining sufficient support for higher education and are intrinsically valuable. However, expecting research and publication from all faculty members in most universities and colleges does not fit either current reality or traditional norms, or perhaps even the needs of the modern mass higher education system.

DECLINE OF COMMUNITY

The traditional ideal of the community of scholars was, to a considerable extent, more folklore than reality. Nevertheless, shared concepts of the university, common academic practices, and similar aspects of academic life have lost much of their meaning in recent years. In many countries the profession has become increasingly divided by disciplinary specializations, orientations to scholarship, and even by politics, ethnic or class factors. The rise of trade unions among academics in the United States, Britain, France, India, and other countries is perhaps an indication of the decline of the sense of community. There are a number of complex factors which have contributed to this situation.

Size

Expansion has meant that universities commonly have student populations of 20,000 or more and academic staffs of more than 1,000. A sense of community among so large a group of individuals is very difficult.

Class and gender

As the academic profession has expanded numerically in many countries it has become less homogeneous. Traditionally, academics came from upper middle class or elite families and were predominantly male. While there are still relatively few professors from working class backgrounds, the profession has moved from its very narrow class base. Further, racial and ethnic minorities and women have moved increasingly into professional roles and while they constitute only a small minority in most countries, they are a new part of the academic equation.

Diversity of training

As the professoriate expanded, the monopoly of a few prestigious universities in the training of doctoral candidates has been weakened, and many newer and less prestigious universities now award doctoral degrees. The norms and values of traditional academe are often not as strongly entrenched in these newer universities, and thus the socialization of younger academics whom they graduate may not be as strong.

Generational anomoly

Because of the expansion of the past two decades, there is an unusually large number of relatively young academics now moving through the system. Because of stabilizing enrollments, there are relatively few new recruits entering the system. Thus, the profession will be dominated by the generation of professors of the 1960s for some time to come. Further, many of these younger academics participated in the student movements of the 1960s and have opinions concerning higher education, politics, and life style issues on which they may differ from their older colleagues. It is difficult to delineate the extent and the implications of these differences in a cross-national context, but it is clear that there are, at least potentially, substantial generational cleavages within the academic profession and also that the age structure of the profession in many countries will be skewed for a decade or more.

Bifurcation

As curricula have expanded and universities throughout the world have taken on new functions, the traditional core arts and sciences fields now constitute only a small part of the total university. Applied fields, from agriculture to business and engineering have little in common with the core disciplines. Faculty in these fields often have different values, orientations, and sometimes differing views of the university from professors in the traditional fields.

TENURE AND UNIONS

For many years, academics resisted the very notion of unionization despite the fact they were institutionally dependent intellectuals. Unionization was viewed as weakening professional status. But a trend toward unionism among professors is now evident in many countries. In the United States, Britain, and other countries, recent declines in enrollment and shifting foci of student interest have brought the issues of job security and retrenchment to the forefront. Academics are clearly worried about their professional status, their relatively prestigious positions in society, their roles and autonomy within universities, and in some instances their jobs. The traditional concept of tenure (which differs from country to country and is not clearly defined in most places) becomes less meaningful as the pressure on universities grows.

Unions have become an important part of the academic landscape in a number of countries, and this movement has had varying impacts. In Britain, where the Association of University Teachers has been active for several decades, the existence of a union which speaks informally for the academic profession has not diminished professional standing. In the United States, it has been argued by some that the union movement is deterimental to professionalism. In France, the rise of professorial unions has gone along with the radicalization of a segment of the profession and with the politicization of the sixties. The Indian academic union movement has reflected job insecurity and low salaries among many faculty members. The union movement has become increasingly widespread but it has different meanings in different nations. Without question, it reflects a growing insecurity among academics, and it also reflects increased political consciousness and perhaps a decline in professional orientation.

The issue of retrenchment has been a contentious one in many nations, and has affected the morale and status of the academic profession. It also relates to the meaning of tenure and academic freedom in the modern university. American universities have, in a sense, been among the least humane in their handling of the problems of declining enrollments and shifts in student interest. Some universities have been willing to fire faculty members regardless of commitment to tenure or continuing appointments. While there are no accurate statistics concerning the total numbers fired, the figure is not insignificant. Other university systems have been, in many cases, less willing to break with traditions or with commitments to permanent appointment. Britain, faced with declining enrollments in teacher training institutions, severe inflation, and general economic difficulties, nevertheless fired few education professors. Individuals were reassigned, were offered retirement, or other arrangements were generally made. Relatively few actually lost their jobs. In West Germany, academics have status as civil servants and are virtually immune from loss of their academic jobs. Even in India, a very poor country with an oversupply of academic staff, very few college or university teachers have been fired despite minimal procedural guarantees.

Academic systems have handled the problems of decline, job security, and the general stresses of the current "steady state" differently and it is fair to say that the American approach has been one of the most tension-producing for the profession.

The nature of tenure and job security, protection for academic freedom, and the general processes of academic advancement in a changing and deteriorating job market has major implications for the academic profession, for morale, and for a sense of professional commitment. The union movement, currently gaining strength in many nations, is one response to this crisis.

THE POLITICS OF PROFESSORS: THE ILLUSION OF CHANGE

It has been claimed that higher education has become infused with ideological politics in recent years and that the vaunted traditions of nonpartisan academic institutions have been shattered by the turmoil of the 1960s. This is only partly correct.[8] The student movements and associated commotions of the sixties stimulated political controversy in the universities; academics as individuals and occasionally as corporate groups have taken positions on a range of societal issues.

But it is an exaggeration to claim that professorial politics is a phenomenon of the sixties or that universities have been free from political pressures in earlier periods. Academics themselves have seldom protested against the societal status quo and, with the exception of strong dissident traditions in Latin America, universities have rarely been militant opponents of established political regimes. Indeed, university and state authorities have often moved against dissenting aca-

8. For arguments in this direction see Alan Montefiore, ed., *Neutrality and Impartiality: The University and Political Commitment* (Cambridge: England: Cambridge University Press, 1975) and "Report on the German Universities, *Minerva* 16 (Sring 1978), pp. 103–138.

demics or, as in Germany, barred academic positions to leftists for long periods. Even now, political criteria have been established by state authorities for appointments to academic positions in West Germany. In so far as universities are state institutions, they necessarily support mainstream politics. The neutrality of the university is equated with the political center.

However, professorial politics have become more visible and perhaps more widespread in recent years, due in considerable part to the partial 'radicalization' of the professoriate and to the increasing visibility and importance of universities. Academics in some countries have supported radical movements, and universities have become centers of political dissent. The largely accepted notion of institutional neutrality has been called into question during periods of intense political strife, and in some countries has been violated.

It is likely that the radicalism of the sixties was, in most countries, an aberration rather than a continuing academic trend, since the more recent period has seen a marked diminution of political consciousness and activism in the universities among both students and faculty. In a sense, the normal politics of the academic profession, which is by and large supportive of established institutions, has reasserted itself. But there are indications that a growing number of academics, in the industrialized nations at least, have moved in a leftward direction and the long term implications for the academic profession and for the universities of an articulate professoriate which holds dissenting views on many issues remains unclear.

Reform

The spectre of university reform is haunting the academic profession.[9] Despite the increasingly liberal opinions of academics on social issues, the profession has by and large oppposed efforts to change the university. The reasons for this opposition are complex and, as Edward Shils has pointed out, academics have opposed many proposals because the reform ideas have themselves been ill advised.[10] Academics are, in a sense, the conscience of the university, and tend to defend traditions whether or not these traditions serve the best long-term interests of the university. On the one hand, the conservatism of the professoriate may, in this way, protect the university from precipitous and ill-advised change. On the other hand, it may also insulate academic systems from desirable change. University reform is not always desirable, just as change for the sake of change may be unwise. But the role of the academic profession in the reform process has, almost without exception, been a negative one and it is worth examining some of the salient factors.

University reform in recent years has meant a diminution of the power of the professoriate. Prior to the 1960s, the academic profession gained in institutional power and societal prestige as a result of university growth and changes in higher education. More recent changes have negatively affected the professoriate,

9. For general essays on this topic, see Philip G. Altbach, ed., *University Reform: Comparative Perspectives for the Seventies* (Cambridge, MA: Schenkman, 1974).

10. Edward Shils, "Change and Reform," in "The Academic Ethos," pp. 15–27.

and particularly the influential senior faculty in the prestigious universities. Moves to expand participation in academic decisionmaking and, in some countries, to involve students might weaken the authority of the senior staff. *Dritteliparität* (student and staff voting on governance) in West Germany, expanded participation in France and Holland, and the U68 reforms in Sweden have all weakened professorial power and all have been opposed by the profession.[11] Most curricular reforms have been opposed by the faculty because they have tended to weaken the traditional orientation of the curriculum and the faculty's control over student educational experiences.

Very few reform proposals have emanated from the professoriate. Academics have, in general, tried to protect the status quo rather than attempting to change higher education. It has, in general, been in their interest to maintain established practices and patterns of governance. Reform proposals have come from students, administrators, government authorities, and official commissions. They have often been forced on a reluctant academic profession. Interestingly, one of the very few professorially inspired reform efforts are current American proposals to revive general education in the undergraduate curriculum. In a sense, general education reestablishes professorial control over the curriculum which, in America, has been put increasingly in the hands of the students through the elective system. The general education reform effort fits neatly into

the professorial orientation indicated in this discussion.

Professors have resisted reforms for a variety of reasons. They are reluctant to see changes that will diminish their power, prestige or authority. Academic institutions are typically run by committee structures, and these committees are often dominated by the senior staff. Governance by committee is cumbersome at best and proposals are often compromised by a multilevel governance structure. Thus, innate conservatism, self interest, and historical consciousness all have mitigated against successful internal reform.

In academic systems where reforms have been imposed from the outside, professors have often been able to successfully oppose their implementation. In West Germany, senior professors successfully prevented full implementation of the governance reforms through court action. In France, structural reforms have been less than fully successful, in part because of opposition from academics. Without the willing cooperation of the academics, successful university reform is almost impossible.

Autonomy and accountability

The academic profession has historically been protected within the universities by a complex set of legal and traditional mechanisms which permit considerable autonomy. Academics work within a large bureaucratic structure, the university, but at the same time they have many of the characteristics of the independent professions. They have considerable autonomy in controlling working conditions and time, and can collectively make key decisions concerning who is

11. Philip G. Altbach, "University Reform," in A. Knowles, ed., *International Encyclopedia of Higher Education*, (San Francisco: Jossey-Bass, 1977), pp. 4263–4274.

permitted to enter the profession, the curriculum, degree requirements and the like. This substantial degree of autonomy has, in recent years, been under considerable attack. Public authorities, who provide the bulk of increasing university budgets, demanded accountability for the expenditure of funds. Governments have also demanded that academic institutions be responsive to societal needs, that relevant curricula be offered, that socially useful research be conducted, and that universities generally provide services for the funds they receive.

In most countries, the academic profession has been ambivalent about the almost inevitable conflict between autonomy and accountability. Professors have generally accepted the increased funds which have accompanied expansion, and have been willing to perform research for governmental and other agencies. As they have become more orientated toward research, the undergraduate curriculum in many countries has been somewhat neglected. Yet academics have resented the increasing bureaucratization of universities and have particularly opposed demands for accountability with regard to their own work.

Opposition to accountability and bureaucracy expresses itself in many ways. The trade union movement among professors is one of the primary ways in which the profession has sought to protect its privileges. Many would argue, however, that unionism, which is growing not only in America, but also in India, Britain, France, Japan, and other countries, contributes to the declining professionalism of academic work.

Academics have also tried simply to ignore governmental and uni- versity authorities placed over them and have had surprisingly good luck with this tactic. Very few academics have been removed from their jobs for infractions of rules and the bureaucratic presence, while increasingly prevalent in higher education, has yet to fully dominate academic life. It is, nevertheless, clear that the highly complex issues involved with autonomy and accountability affect the academic profession and that, despite widespread opposition among the professoriate to increased bureaucracy, this is probably an inevitable current which will increasingly intrude on the lives of academics.

THE ACADEMIC STRATIFICATION SYSTEM AND ITS IMPACT

Having discussed some of the key issues affecting the academic profession in recent years, it is necessary to differentiate the profession, since there is not only international stratification but major divisions within national university systems. We have argued that the international academic system, made more visible through improved communications, is characterized by inequalities and by the domination of the central universities. In much the same way, national academic systems are similarly burdened by hierarchies and inequalities. Indeed, these differences have contributed to the sense of breakdown in the academic community. As higher education systems in most countries have expanded and have typically added new kinds of institutions, a class system of higher education has emerged. This system not only affects students but also has definite implications for the professoriate as well. In the United States, for example, the prestigious graduate oriented universities are clearly at the top of the system and dominate the norms and values of the rest of American higher education.

David Riesman identified this trend toward conformity in American higher education many years ago.[12] The functions of faculty members in the community colleges and four-year undergraduate institutions differ substantially from those in university centers. As Howard London points out, the community college teacher has considerable ambivalence concerning academic roles and the place of the community college at the bottom of the prestige hierarchy.[13] In addition, academics in the various segments of the system have somewhat different functions and are differentially remunerated. Not surprisingly, community college teachers are paid less and teach more than their compeers in four-year institutions. They are not generally expected to publish in scholarly journals, and seldom obtain research grants. Clearly, this academic hierarchy in the United States works against a unified community.

Other countries have also developed hierarchial systems in recent years as higher education has expanded and the traditional universities have been unable to absorb the increase. In some nations, there have been planned efforts to differentiate academic institutions by function. In others, previously non-university post-secondary institutions have simply been added to the university system. In West Germany, some *technische hochschulen* (technical higher schools) have been upgraded to university status. In many nations, new universities have been established which are significantly below established institutions in prestige. Even in Britain, where efforts have been made to equalize the quality of instruction, Oxford and Cambridge stand above the Redbrick institutions which in turn have higher prestige than the newer "Plateglass" universities. Similar situations exist in France, Japan, India, and much of Latin America.

There is now a national and international system of academic stratification which has divided the profession and created inequalities, tensions, and strains. Just as the metropolitan institutions in the industrialized nations dominate universities in the Third World, and their professorial staffs have high prestige and essentially control the flow of knowledge, the direction of research, and often the curriculum, so too the major universities in a particular nation dominate other institutions within their own milieu.[14] While these relationships of inequality may be inevitable, they nevertheless pose serious problems for the academic profession. They cannot be wished away by harking back to traditional values.

Within universities, there are also major divisions of power, status, roles, and prestige. Traditionally, the full professors completely dominated universities in Europe and

12. David Riesman, "The Academic Procession," in D. Riesman, *Constraint and Variety in American Education*, (Garden City, New York: Anchor Books, 1958), pp. 25–65.

13. Howard London, *The Culture of a Community College*, (New York: Praeger, 1978), pp. 29–60.

14. Michelle Patterson, "Governmental Policy and Equality in Higher Education: The Junior Collegization of the French University," *Social Problems* 26 (December 1976), pp. 173–183 and Raymond Boudon, "The French University Since 1968," *Comparative Politics* (October, 1977), pp. 89–119.

Japan, and had most power in North America.[15] While the reforms of the 1960s and recent expansion has weakened the senior professors, the academic hierarchy still exists although junior staff in general have more job security and often a greater role in decisionmaking. Nevertheless, the internal hierarchy remains important in determining the academic style of the university and in shaping the working conditions of the academic profession.

CONCLUSION

As student radicals used to say, "if you're not part of the solution, then you are part of the problem." The academic profession has found itself in the ambivalent situation of having benefitted from aspects of the post-war expansion in terms of increased salaries, greater prestige, and improved working conditions in most countries. But the profession has, by and large, been content to attempt, with decreasing success, to maintain the status quo. The professoriate has struggled for the ideal of the traditional university, and there is much in this ideal that is worth preserving. The crises of the current period are, however, immense and probably preclude a maintenance of the status quo.

The academic profession remains an important group in most societies. Despite accountability, bureaucracy, and in some nations political controls, the academic profession remains at the very heart of the university. If the teaching staff is unqualified or demoralized, the quality

of instruction at a university cannot be high. And if academics are not interested in research or are not rewarded for the creation of new knowledge, research productivity will inevitably be low and scientific and technological development slowed. The attitudes of academics also matter, not only because they provide instruction and sometimes role models for the next generation of society's leaders, but also because academics contribute to the national debate through their writing and occasionally through their participation in government.[16] The importance of the academic profession is unquestionable, but it is also unrecognized by many, including government officials and even some university administrators, in the current stress on accountability and the balancing of budgets. It is even more surprising that there has been very little research concerning the academic profession, either comparatively or in specific countries.

The professoriate has not done much to create solutions to the manifest problems of the universities. Professors were willing to accept the funds that were provided and did not worry much about the unanticipated consequences of this largesse or expansion generally. And when reforms were proposed, the academics by and large took a negative stance and offered few creative alternatives. The problem, therefore, is not simply one of external impact on higher education but it is in part a result of ostrich-like behavior by the profession.

This article has been an exercise in comparative consciousness rais-

15. Guido Martinotti and Alberto Giasanti, "The Robed Baron: The Academic Profession in the Italian University," in P. G. Altbach, ed., *Comparative Perspectives on the Academic Profession*, pp. 23–42.

16. For an example of the key role of academics in American politics, see Peter Steinfels, *The Neo-Conservatives*, (New York: Simon and Schuster, 1979).

ing. It has pointed out, in comparative context, some of the key elements of the crisis of the professoriate. While there are many differences among university systems, it is useful to reflect on the problems which face the academic profession. The crisis is worldwide, and because of the similar challenges—of expansion, fiscal constraints, public criticism, curricular malaise, and a declining sense of professionalism—it is certainly worthwhile to think in comparative terms about the problems of the professoriate in a period of crisis.

ANNALS, AAPSS, 448, March 1980

Dialectic Aspects of Recent Change in Academe

By LOGAN WILSON

ABSTRACT: Viewed in retrospect, recent changes in academe have not all been upward and onward. Divergent forces in a democratic society with a pluralistic culture generate conflicting pressures on the academic profession, as may be witnessed in the dialectic interplay of continuity and change, autonomy and heteronomy, meritocracy and egalitarianism. Internal accommodation to these dualities has necessarily entailed trade-offs, and losses as well as gains. Compromises intended to mollify adversaries during the turbulent 1960s and early 1970s have resulted in later difficulties for the profession, with the implication that to avoid future repetition of past mistakes, academe must calculate more realistically the probable outcomes of alternate courses of action and reaction.

From 1960–71, Logan Wilson headed the American Council on Education and since 1972 has been President Emeritus. He was President of The University of Texas at Austin, and later Chancellor of that system, from 1953–1961. After receiving his Ph.D. at Harvard, he held teaching and administrative posts in a variety of institutions. Author of a number of books, and numerous articles, most of them dealing with higher education, he is now retired and living in Austin, Texas, where he continues to do some writing.

HIGHER education's spectacular growth in the United States during recent decades has been widely noted. Just a few years ago, junior colleges were being established at a rate of about one a week, most four-year public institutions were metamorphosing into universities, and many universities were expanding their enrollments and multiplying their programs. Public demand for more teaching, research, and other services appeared to be unlimited. There was also a rapid rise in public support; between 1949 and 1975 the number of American colleges and universities almost doubled, reaching a total of more than 3,000, with doctorate-granting institutions growing in number from 90 to more than 400.

As members of the academic profession are acutely aware, the boom has ended. Higher education now finds itself in a steady state at best, with prospect of decline ahead. Unrealistic expectations followed by unrealized outcomes have resulted in public disenchantment, economic inflation coupled with recession has constricted finances, student enrollments have leveled off and are certain to dwindle further, so that academics now confront the tightest job market they have experienced in several decades.

Elsewhere I have delineated what might be termed a "still picture" of the state of affairs in the academic profession circa the year 1942. Another book of mine, published in 1979, gives a moving picture of continuity and change in the academic profession between the early 1940s and the late 1970s.[1] In evaluating the wide-ranging data brought together for my 1979 volume, I would have been pleased if all the evidence had pointed unmistakably to upward as well as onward movement. On the one hand, there was no question about the vast extension of advanced educational opportunity. American higher education had ceased being a predominantly elitist enterprise. High-level activity in scholarship and science was no longer confined to a few universities in just three geographic regions, but had become nationwide. Academics had steadily advanced knowledge, and their profession had attained a more important role in the larger society. In short, there were many indicators of progress.

On the other hand, one could perceive losses as well as gains. Benefits obviously entailed costs, with the implication that social change in academe, as elsewhere, seems at times to demonstrate Newton's third law to the effect that for every action there is an equal and opposite reaction. Many of the economic and social forces brought to bear on the academic profession have resulted in trade-offs among objectives, often without much weighing of losses alongside gains. Academic professionals are thus caught between contrary pressures to which they must somehow accommodate their actions. The purpose here will be to single out three aspects of this dialectic in recent developments. Granted, this approach does not encompass and explain every development of late in academe, but it may account for some current difficulties and suggest ways of minimizing future conflict or chaos.

1. See *The Academic Man: A Study in the Sociology of a Profession,* (New York: Oxford University Press, 1942) and *American Academics: Then and Now* (New York: Oxford University Press, 1979).

CONTINUITY AND CHANGE

To survive and endure, educational institutions like other social organisms must retain a distinctive identity lest they disappear or become transformed into something else. To maintain viability in altered environments, they also must avoid ossification and adapt themselves to change. Since continuity and change involve antipodal pressures on academe, however, historic development has from time to time been fraught with controversy and conflict, and particularly so in the recent period of rapid change.

With regard to continuity, one should begin by noting that the university as a social institution has shown remarkable longevity and that academics belong to one of the oldest professions. Some academic forms stem from the Middle Ages, and significant parts of the cultural heritage transmitted by academe go back even further. This persistence gives rise to the familiar criticism that academe is unduly tradition-bound. Traditionalists respond with the assertion that upholding continuity is an important function of the university, and that it not only accounts in part for institutional endurance but also performs a very useful societal service in eras of general uncertainty and instability.

A second thing to note about the university is that it evolved as a social enclave to insulate its members from outside intrusions that impair freedom of teaching and inquiry. Despite federal and other efforts to reshape the academic labor market, for example, academics get and hold or lose their jobs in ways significantly different from those of government, business, and industry. Professors do not hold office at the pleasure of voters, their individual securities and rewards are not tied to anything resembling the Neilson rating system used in commercial television, and they, rather than their employing agencies, still mainly determine the nature of their daily tasks. Few other workers in contemporary society have such latitude.

Regardless of its insulation, the academic profession is not isolated from the surrounding society. In our era it has become more and more affected by outside affairs. It no longer has as much control over its student clientele or its own membership. The higher learning itself has increasingly been thrust into a role of social engineering or reform as the public looks to institutions of higher education for solutions to vexing problems. Not only what will be taught to whom, but also the purposes and kinds of research to be pursued are being more heavily influenced by external pressures. Such perturbations are inevitably attended by some controversy and conflict. Advocates of continuity and of change become disputants and engage as adversaries pitted against one another regarding university purposes and the allocation of resources that are inherently limited. During the 1960s and early 1970s, the cleavages often led to disruption and sometimes even to violence.

A basic problem for many institutions has been the maintenance of a moving equilibrium. Some of them have erred by being overly responsive to pressures. New courses and programs have been added cumulatively, those already in place seldom dropped, with the consequence that educational resources have been thinly spread or dissipated. On some campuses during the 1960s and 1970s, a fetish was made of change for its own sake, and whatever was traditional became discredited. All across the country, the "university syndrome" spread and instead of attempting to better themselves to become first-rate colleges, many four-year institutions compromised the quality of their endeavor by opting to become what in effect were second- or even third-rate universities. The period witnessed various other trade-offs that later reflected deterioration rather than improvement.

By contrast, numerous institutions, particularly in the private sector, merged or disappeared because of failure to adjust to changed circumstances. Some were too small and could not cope because they fell below critical size factors required for efficient operations. Others became anachronisms serving outmoded purposes or catering to disappearing clienteles. Still others which could not be faulted for inherent defects of structure or function simply could not marshal the resources needed to meet mounting competition from their more heavily subsidized opposite numbers in the public sector.

The rates, no less than the dimensions of change imposed upon institutions of higher education by a shifting social order, entail complications. Impressive libraries and outstanding faculties are seldom if ever put quickly into place, and institutional newcomers to academe normally require a considerable period of time to reach high levels of performance. Unlike many commercial enterprises that quickly expand or contract operations to fit altered market conditions, small and large academic institutions confront more intricate adjustment problems. Campuses typically are rather costly and are permanent investments; they cannot be easily converted to other uses or easily relocated elsewhere. Many faculty members are tenured, and there are no assembly lines to shut down. Moreover, some academic programs are held to be intrinsically worthwhile, regardless of the number of takers at a given time or the short-run payoffs.

Even so, academics cannot escape their responsibility for seeing to it that necessary adjustments are made and adequately supported. They cannot continue, for example, to glut the educational job market with new doctorates for whom there are declining prospects of suitable employment, and they cannot continue to insist on upholding everybody's tenure in institutions where the need for academic employees is slumping. A stubborn unwillingness to make presently painful decisions can only result in greater future pains.

Autonomy and Heteronomy

Academics have always valued autonomy for their profession and for their institutions, and have consistently viewed it as a corollary for freedom of teaching and research. Despite the decline of autonomy and the rise of heteronomy, there is still a professorial nostalgia in most universities for what might be called a club-like scheme of governance. The conventional rhetoric of academe even refers to the president as being *primus inter pares*, and a good many professors regard nonacademic administrators as being either ancillaries or supernumeraries.

For more than three decades, however, academics have become progressively detached from direct involvement in the conduct of some institutional affairs. In 1942, there was an average of one administrative officer for every six teachers, in both small colleges and large universities. By 1977, there were in private institutions 35.7 administrators for every 100 faculty members, and in public institutions, 19 per 100.[2] It is thus obvious that insofar as internal conduct of the entire campus enterprise is concerned, the academic profession has experienced reduced autonomy.

University administration and governance, nonetheless, exhibit some rather curious anomalies and contradictions. Egalitarianism and elitism exist side by side; power moves up as well as down. Insisting upon independence of action for themselves as teachers and researchers, academics in general are reluctant to accord leeway to their administrative associates. Their willingness to hand over routine and onerous chores to staff specialists is frequently accompanied by an unwillingness to trade off much faculty authority. In some universities, the same professors who complain about the lack of strong top leadership may stoutly defend governance schemes which make such leadership difficult if not impossible. This tendency may help explain why between 1968 and 1972—a period of turbulent change in American higher education—the average term of office of the forty-eight presidents in the major universities belonging to the Association of American Universities dropped from six to three years.

Institutional unity and coherence have also been reduced in many places by departmental fiefdoms which, as Robert Hutchins once remarked, spawn overspecialization,

discourage faculty interest in broader university affairs, and are mindful mainly of their own expansion and prestige. Departments are likewise criticized for being the main instigators of an attenuated curriculum that spreads resources ever more sparsely.[3]

It would be reassuring if one could attribute the independence enjoyed historically by most American colleges and universities to a popular appreciation of institutional autonomy's virtues, but it should be acknowledged that this independence to some degree reflected a widespread public indifference to the inner workings of higher education.[4] At the turn of the century, for instance, when only four percent of the college age group went to college, not many Americans had much concern with what occurred inside academe. Campus independence in institutional decisionmaking was the rule.

Institutional proliferation in response to spreading public demand, institutional growth in size and complexity, and other circumstances have led to more outside pressures for accountability. John Millett has observed that academe's reputation for inefficient management and the long-standing tendency of professors to discuss problems of governance

2. In *The British Academics* (Cambridge, MA, Harvard University Press, 1971), A. H. Halsey and M. A. Trow have noted, by way of contrast, that British universities have relatively small administrative staffs, composed mostly of those who continue as parttime academics.

3. In *The Degradation of the Academic Dogma.* (New York: Basic Books, 1971), Robert Nisbet contends that the proliferation of bureaus, institutes, and other such entities has impeded the pursuit of knowledge for its own sake, and has eroded faculty control of the university's basic mission. Another sociologist and prominent intellectual, Edward Shils, has made similar observations about the influence on academic autonomy of federal involvements.

4. Logan Wilson, *Shaping American Higher Education* (Washington: American Council on Education, 1972), pp. 45–55.

to the exclusion of those pertaining to management (especially cost accounting aspects) may explain in part the growing cadre on many campuses of nonacademic, managerial types to fill gaps resulting from indifference or neglect on the part of the academic profession itself.

The recent evidence with regard to faculty control of university affairs, however, is mixed. In major institutions there is clearly less trustee and presidential authoritarianism, and internal decision-making is more broadly dispersed; in some of these same places, nonetheless, students and alumni now share in processes of governance that were formerly sole prerogatives of the faculty.

Concurrently, there has been a fairly steady shift in the loci of decision-making away from the campus to other agencies. Ever since World War II, statewide commissions or coordinating boards, comprised mostly of gubernatorially appointed lay persons assisted by their own staffs, have increased in number to the extent that almost all states now have them. These agencies have negative as well as positive reasons for existing. In some states a wasteful duplication of programs among public institutions, indifference to a sensible division of institutional labor, dysfunctional rivalries, and seemingly limitless ambitions to expand all pointed to the need for a central coordinating body. Positively viewed, there was also a desire to allocate public funds more equitably and effectively, and to insulate the legislature from the pressures of lobbying groups whose prime interests were not necessarily the best interests of the state as a whole. Whatever the pros and cons for these agencies, the effect has been to augment bureaucratic con-

trol from the state capital and to reduce the autonomy of local institutions and their academic staffs. Moreover, in a growing number of states public funds now assist the private sector of higher education and such aid is usually given with strings attached.

It is also important to consider the vastly enlarged role in the past three decades of federal government in the support, direction, and control of the nation's colleges and universities. In 1942, the federal role was very minor and indirect. By the late 1970s, the Congress was appropriating around ten billion dollars a year for higher education, with institutions involved in almost four hundred federal programs, and operating in conformity with rules, regulations, guidelines, and audit requirements emanating from several dozen congressional committees and approximately fifty executive agencies. Few such programs were intended directly to help support colleges and universities as such, but they all entailed involvements with central government.

Notwithstanding the numerous mutual benefits of these inter-relations, one cost has been reduced institutional autonomy and further politicization of the process of educational decisionmaking. By the mid 1970s, spokesmen for leading universities were beginning to complain loudly about what one of them called "outrageous federal intrusion" on academic self-governance. It is unrealistic, of course, to expect drastic deregulation and the withdrawal of bureaucratic surveillance as a response to academic protests; perhaps the most that can be anticipated is more reasonable modes of accountability for the expenditure of what are, after all, public funds.

In the United States and many other nations, the trend is one of increased governmental entwinement in both the finance and control of educational institutions. Although the recently authorized federal Department of Education is being heralded by many individuals in the public school sector as a prospect for increased funding of the nation's schools, numerous educators in colleges and universities foresee, in a tightened national economy, mainly the likelihood of more federal centralization and control.

MERITOCRACY AND EGALITARIANISM

Since Jeffersonian and Jacksonian concepts of American democracy are still not fully reconciled, there is a persisting conflict between merit and equality as social values. Most Americans are nominally in accord with a work ethic which appraises job performance and distributes rewards according to the merit principle of worth. This implies open competition. There is also, however, a strong belief that all individuals should be treated as equals—at the polls, in law courts, in access to educational opportunity, and so on.

As the political pendulum swings between conservatism and populism, the academic profession may be buffeted from opposite sides by the forces of meritocracy and of egalitarianism. Pursuit of higher learning has long been essentially meritocratic intellectually and, to some extent, elitist socially. For many years, to be sure, academics have been responsible for sifting and sorting a widening array of human talent, but more recently they have been pressured not only to enhance the qualifications of the more capable, but also to improve the life chances of many who were formerly excluded.

The momentum of such pressures is indicated by the fact that shortly after 1956 the proportion of high school graduates going on to college rose from 32 to 53 percent. Although these larger numbers included more bright students, they also included more at the other end of the ability spectrum. Between 1963 and 1977, CEEB verbal scores dropped from 478 to 429 and mathematical averages from 502 to 470. Some institutions were getting applicants who could read, write, and calculate at about an eighth grade level. Soon thereafter, campuses upholding former standards of selectivity came under fire as being "elitist," and the nationally standardized tests themselves were lambasted as being unfair to the economically and culturally deprived. Many egalitarians felt that the "qualifiable" as well as the "qualified" should be freely admitted almost everywhere and, if necessary, given remedial courses, intensive tutoring, and other special preferment to encourage equality of outcomes alongside equality of opportunity.

As evidenced by abandoning required courses, making the curriculum more "relevant" to student wishes, giving passing marks to virtually all students, and swelling the proportions of "honor graduates" each year, many institutions obviously relaxed their standards and relinquished certain sifting and sorting functions. Certification was increasingly bestowed by academic largesse rather than earned by students, and an egalitarian zeal for protecting the inept overrode concern for safeguarding against the damaging later consequences of ineptitude.

As might have been expected,

there has been a reaction. Graduate and professional schools became distrustful of the reliability of undergraduate grade records, and employers began to make outcries about being misled regarding individual capabilities. Many institutional offenders realized that their intent to further general uplift had inadvertently made them party to what was in outcome a benevolent fraud. Of late, colleges and universities, not to mention the public schools, are under growing pressures to move "back to the basics," require everybody to measure up in order to move ahead and, in general, to merit the various credentials handed out by educational institutions.

Within the academic profession itself, it is interesting to note the counter pressures of meritocracy and egalitarianism. Their institutions long enjoyed almost complete independence in their employment policies and practices, with academics determining criteria for membership in the profession. They recruited white males in the main, and of certain preferred scholarly and social backgrounds. Few of them gave thought to the scant numbers of women and blacks or other ethnic minorities in their midst, much less acknowledging that there might be a "problem" in this respect. Public advertising of job openings was unheard of and direct application for posts was *infra dig*.

Now, of course, much of this has changed. Some forms of discriminatory judgment once considered acceptable and proper have become unacceptable and even illegal. Even though the current supply of job seekers vastly exceeds the demand in academe, filling vacancies is in some ways a more complicated task than it once was. Colleges and universities are no longer permitted to search out and recruit "gentle-men as well scholars"; the demographic representativeness of recruits also must be taken into account.

In 1965 a federal executive order banned discrimination based on race, religion, color, or national origin, and a later executive order taking effect in 1968 barred sex discrimination—even more recently, age discrimination was forbidden. Various federal guidelines have been issued to let the academic profession know how its membership should be constituted, and many institutions have protested what some regard as "quotas" foisted upon them. The federal bureaucracy has insisted, nonetheless, that all of them must engage in "affirmative action" toward conformity with edicts. As a consequence, lawsuits having to do with discrimination and "reverse discrimination" have multiplied, with judges and federal officials rather than professors and administrators deciding outcomes.

Inside academe, a further instance of collision between ideologies of merit and of equality is evidenced by increased numbers of academic employees forgoing individualistic professionalism and opting for trade unionism and collective bargaining. Following union successes in organizing public school teachers for more aggressive bargaining, unionism began to spread more rapidly on the higher education level, particularly in some metropolitan areas of the northern and eastern part of the country. By May 31, 1977, there were bargaining agents on 544 campuses. Although press coverage might have left the impression that unionization was a tidal wave, the fact of the matter is that only 17.8 percent of the nation's 3,055 institutions were unionized, and with junior colleges excluded from the count, only 10.8 percent.

It is significant also that few of the faculties of major universities had chosen collective bargaining, and none of those in the Association of American Universities had made that choice.

Whether unionization will grow, level off, or recede in the years immediately ahead is as yet uncertain. Whatever the outcome, on many campuses it has already had effects on the academic's status as an employee, as a professional, and as a longtime partner in collegial governance. In the ever more intensified scramble of organized self-interest groups for larger pieces of the total "pie," it is understandable why many academics may feel that they face a Hobson's choice. Many others among them, nonetheless, are unwilling to barter away what they deem to be their intellectual birthright as professionals for a mess of pottage as trade unionists.

Despite the ascendancy of egalitarianism, society still places a high premium on many kinds of excellence in individual accomplishment. Outstanding academics may not get very much popular acclaim, but inside the realm of scholarship and science the merit principle largely determines the distribution of recognition and reward, with the most prestigious kudos going to the highest achievers. Commenting on the matter of election to membership in the National Academy of Sciences, for example, its president had this to say in a recent annual report:

The external world views us with a cocked eyebrow. Egalitarianism and populism are in the flood. There are those who would urge upon us public nomination of candidates for membership in the Academy. . . . There are . . . those who would have the membership of the Academy reflect the proportion of various groups within the population; by states, by sex, by ethnic groups. And there are those who consider the Academy to be an elitist relic of the past.

Perhaps so. . . . But the hallmark of the Academy must continue to be excellence in all things and we must, above all else, retain our single criterion for election.

Movement of the academic marketplace into a steady state undoubtedly implies a reduced demand for persons of mediocre or lesser capability, but not by the same token in my judgment a declining need for those exceptional individuals who contribute substantially to the advancement of knowledge. In a time of adversity there is likely to be, on the contrary, a greater need than in a time of prosperity for creativity in the intellectual sphere. With a lessened need to allocate major resources to plant and staff expansion, moreover, academe now has an opportunity to renew its emphasis on excellence.

CONCLUSION

As John B. Bury and other historians have pointed out, progress is an important idea but one that is not always demonstrable in the whole course of human events. Benefits usually entail costs, and forces moving in one direction may be offset by counter forces moving in another. Some objectives are achieved only at the expense of trading off others. In complicated situations there may be no consensus about priorities for organized effort, and the means to attain agreed-upon ends are more often than not scarce and hence not commensurate with all the ends sought.

Although academe was traditionally guided mostly by internal consensus, the profession's membership has become more heterogeneous and its values more divergent. Outside influences are also more varied and some of them more potent than in the past. Since there is no single yardstick for measuring overall social progress, whether recent changes represent a desirable democratization or an undesirable subversion of the higher learning is at least in part an ideological issue.

However disturbing current incertitudes may be to some academics, others will doubtless conclude that the pivotal role of their profession for intellectual leadship can become more rather than less important as society gropes for answers to very difficult questions. Indeed, this may be one reason that most academics find many satisfactions in their occupation, and may account for the fact that, if starting anew, the majority of them would again choose the academic profession and their same fields of specialization.

Careers for Academics and the Future Production of Knowledge

By ROBERT T. BLACKBURN

ABSTRACT: The paradox of the current knowledge explosion and a predicted generation gap of new scholars is analyzed with regard to its consequences, the evidence relating to the essential conditions for knowledge production, the realities of opportunities for young Ph.D.s, their need in the growth of disciplines, and the possible courses of action for dealing with a serious problem. The historical record was not found to be especially helpful. Analysis of studies on the personal and organizational characteristics related to scholarly productivity identified critical variables. The gloomy forecasts for academic openings were acknowledged, although contradictions in the reported data call for more careful examination. Two of the proposed solutions hold some promise for mitigating a future hiatus in the growth of knowledge and in the solution of critical social problems.

Robert Blackburn studied at the University of Wisconsin, at Harvard University, and at The University of Chicago. His S.B., S.M., and Ph.D. degrees are from Chicago. His principal teaching positions have been on the faculty of Natural Sciences in The College at The University of Chicago, as an Assistant and Associate Professor of Physical Science at San Francisco State College, and as Member of the Faculty and Dean of Faculty at Shimer College. In 1966 he joined the faculty at the Center for the Study of Higher Education at The University of Michigan as Professor of Higher Education. His research focuses on careers of academics.

TODAY an interesting paradox challenges higher education. On the one hand there has been, is, and will continue to be a knowledge explosion. In the field of language and literature alone, disciplines which are expanding at a slower rate than are the sciences, the number of journals has escalated from some 54 to 215 within the last ten years. A teacher facing a graduate class in the study of Alexander Pope, for example, can list a selected bibliography of 915 books and articles about the writings of that poet, and they are continuing to appear at the rate of 50 per year. Furthermore, even with a constant or slightly diminished number of academics over the next two decades, the volume output is rightfully predicted to accelerate. Publishing faculty increase, not decrease, their productivity rate with age.[1] In addition, it will be the productive faculty who will acquire and maintain college and university positions in an increasingly competitive job market. Furthermore, new entrants can be expected to produce at accelerated rates in their efforts to secure their future in the organization, effects already seen in the 1977 Ladd and Lipset survey.

On the other hand, there is little room for new scholars in academe, despite increased knowledge production. While there would seem to be no cause for alarm about the future production of knowledge, some harbor fears about the 1980s and 1990s, and for good reasons. That is what produces the paradox. Those who have expressed concerns are not questioning the quantity of current work nor are they denigrating its quality. Rather they worry about other matters, most of which have to do with the inability of new scholars—recently graduated Ph.D.s—to acquire faculty positions.

For example, the Carnegie Council believes that if there were to be a double decade of almost no new appointments, that is, a loss of a generation of potentially able faculty, then higher education's vitality would suffer appreciably. Raising the retirement age to 70 in 1982 has some observers worried that colleges and universities will become geriatric wards, knowledge production will stop, and teaching will become a travesty—contrary to existing evidence. The Carnegie Council also expresses concern about the nation's prestige should the influx of new faculty be halted.[2] This parochial concern carries little weight once it is recognized that the academic labor market is in a similarly depressed state in other developed countries. Even if it were not, the problems needing solution—peace, health, and energy, to name but three—no more have national boundaries than does knowledge.

The position taken here is not unconcerned with institutional vitality, prestige, and the careers of

1. See Fritz Machlup, *The Production and Distribution of Knowledge in the United States* (Princeton, NJ: Princeton University Press, 1962); Philip Handler, "Basic Research in the United States." *Science* (May 1979), pp. 474–479; Paul D. Allison and John A. Stewart, "Productivity Differences Among Scientists: Evidence for Accumulative Advantage," *American Sociological Review* (August 1974), pp. 596–606; Robert T. Blackburn, Charles E. Behymer, and David E. Hall, "Research Note: Correlates of Faculty Publications," *Sociology of Education* (April 1978), pp. 132–141.

2. Roy Radner and Charlotte V. Kuh, *Preserving a Lost Generation: Policies to Assure a Steady Flow of Young Scholars Until the Year 2000* (Berkeley: Carnegie Council on Policy Studies in Higher Education, 1978), pp. 1 and 13.

young scholars. There are good reasons for their need. For example, were there an appreciable hiatus in the "normal" inflow of young professors into colleges and universities, leadership crises could arise a generation from now. An even more, or at least equally, serious consequence of a lack of new talent would be the erosion and dismantling of many extraordinarily fine scholarly units. Graduate departments are the training place and proving grounds for new scholars. For these units to function effectively, they must be preparing Ph.D. students. A first-rate productive department is a combination of talented students and faculty. When a unit is closed down, it cannot be created again over night—say 20 years from now when the need for faculty will rapidly accelerate as the current chairholders retire in mass numbers. Maintaining units is a critical offshoot of the need for new scholars as knowledge producers.[3]

In addition to these important concerns, there is the danger to all mankind if the production of new knowledge is seriously interrupted. That potential hiatus is the principal argument for new scholars adduced here. Speaking as director of the National Science Foundation (NSF), Richard Atkinson addressed this issue when he referred to the "new, young professors who must, of course, pick up the torch if we are to maintain a strong basic research capability in our universities."[4] De

Solla Price believes growth has already stopped, and not just because his own department is being phased out at Yale. When speaking of the monies needed for research as an investment, he saw the urgency: "the only chance we have to train people in new knowledge and techniques, at present unforeseen, but needed in the future, to increase and even to preserve our quality of life."[5] A distinguished panel of the National Research Committee has just released its report and states that "our analysis of the process by which first-class research is produced in universities leads us to conclude that an interruption in the flow of new faculty hires over a period of years may seriously impair the vigor and effectiveness of the academic-research enterprise. Given the key role of the university as a producer of basic research for the entire U.S. research-and-development system, we conclude that federal action to offset the threat to academic research effectiveness is warranted."[6]

THE GROWTH OF KNOWLEDGE: THE HISTORICAL RECORD

When asking the question about how knowledge has grown, one naturally turns to the historians. An answer is not found there, however. Those who study knowledge raise questions about its validity— as philosophers do; or about its structure and organization—as sociologists do; but not about its crea-

3. See Robert T. Blackburn, "Part-Time Faculty and the Production of Knowledge," in David W. Leslie, ed., *Employing Part-Time Faculty, New Directions for Institutional Research* (1978), pp. 99–111.
4. Richard C. Atkinson, "The Threat to Scientific Research," *The Chronicle of Higher Education* (March 1977), p. 40.

5. As quoted by John Walsh, "Historian of Science States Case for Catching up on Basic Research," *Science* (March 1978), pp. 1188–1190.
6. Jack Magarrell, "Panel Says Government Should Help Universities Hire Young Scientists," *Chronicle of Higher Education*, vol. 19, no. 9, (29 October, 1979), pp. 1 and 10.

tion. As an economist, Machlup examined costs and benefits of knowledge production. A few have chronicled the growth of a discipline. However, the evidence sought—what are the necessary conditions for the healthy development of a discipline?—has not been assembled as yet by anyone.[7]

Nonetheless, some observations are helpful. The first professional associations formed for the specific purpose of advancement of knowledge (The Royal Society in London in 1662, for example, and even earlier in Naples in 1560) brought together amateurs, not professionals, frequently people of means, but not college professors. It was not until the 19th century and the development of the German university that research and scholarship became a significant academic function. It was at the newly founded Johns Hopkins University, the University of Chicago, and a scattering of other places—Michigan and later at Harvard—that faculty in this country were hired to produce knowledge. Disciplines formed sub-parts—specialties—and splits occurred leading to new disciplines, new journals, new associations, and new knowledge.

At the turn of the century, universities in the U.S. changed from being largely transmitters of knowledge, a teaching role, to a knowledge producing role. Some people and places made more salient contributions than others. For example, Deutch, Platt, and Senghaas have shown that the major discoveries in the social sciences have occurred in

a relatively few places in the world. The findings suggest that a profitable way to proceed is to analyze the personal and organization variables related to significant knowledge production.[8]

THE NECESSARY CONDITIONS FOR CREATIVE PRODUCTION

Pelz and Andrews provide a model for treating the essential ingredients for solving problems. In particular, Pelz combines personal and organizational variables into a construct he calls "creative tension," an amalgam of psychological and organizational attributes needed for the production of new knowledge.[9]

Personal dimensions

Personal attributes include innate talent and acquired skills. There is no shortage or problem here. There is a sufficient supply of bright people desiring an academic career and good places in which they can learn. There are, however, a couple of debatable points which affect the argument. One of these is the relationship between age and creative productivity; the other has to do with psychological characteristics—drive, competitiveness, challenge.

As for the latter, while the evidence is not conclusive, it does

7. Fritz Machlup, *The Production of Knowledge*; Mary O. Furner, *Advocacy and Objectivity, A Crisis in the Professionalization of American Social Science, 1865–1905* (Lexington: University of Kentucky Press, 1975).

8. Karl W. Deutsch, John Platt and Dieter Senghaas, "Conditions Favoring Major Advances in Social Science," *Science* (February 1971), pp. 450–459. Their paper was debated in the Letters section of *Science*. Perhaps some breakthroughs are on the horizon. A new scholarly quarterly, *Knowledge: Creation, Diffusion, Utilization*, began publication in September 1979.

9. Donald C. Pelz and Frank M. Andrews, *Scientists in Organizations* (New York: Wiley (revised) 1976); Donald C. Pelz, "Creative Tensions in the Research and Development Climate," *Science* (July 1967), pp. 160–165.

appear that curiosity and desire to succeed are positively related to scholarly productivity, but just how has not been established. As for age, productivity rates vary over time, most frequently in a saddle shape curve; that is, an early rise, a fall, another rise, and then a fall, although there is variation from discipline to discipline. When the issue is a scholar's most significant rather than total contribution—that is, how old he was when he made his most important discovery—the evidence is less clear and the debate more intense. There are disciplinary differences. For example, mathematicians tend to be younger than historians when their most noted work is accomplished. In general, though, by itself an aging professoriate is not critical to the development of a discipline, a point which is elaborated below.

Other personal attributes which correlate with both the rate of production and total career production include the faculty member's preference for a higher research/ teaching balance than less productive colleagues have, the frequency of communication with colleagues at other colleges and universities, the number of journals subscriptions held, and the degree to which scholarship is highly valued. These characteristics and practices seem to persist over a period of time. Even though interest in research wanes a bit in later years, productivity only falls slightly.[10]

Structural/organization dimensions

Despite the unquestioned individualistic nature of a new insight, knowledge production is very much a social phenomenon. An idea needs to be critiqued by competent peers before its truth and usefulness can be ascertained. According to Storer, there is no new knowledge until the social act of presentation and response has taken place.[11]

The social dimension in knowledge production is more than validation or verification. Organizational factors have demonstrated relationships to the generation of ideas. The importance of an informal network of scholars, mentors at early career stages, homogeneity and homology of interests, leadership and structure, competition, a critical mass of experts, and support— for example, research sabbaticals— among other variables, all correlate with productivity. Also, tenure, that is, work security so as to allow risk taking, and membership in a democratically run, autonomous unit correlate with scholarly productivity, as does the importance one's institution gives to research. As Lightfield and Long demonstrate, place of work, that is, the social conditions for scholarship, is the single best predictor of scholarly output.[12]

Two critical, and unresolved, social issues remain, however. One of these has to do with the way knowledge grows and how revolutionary concepts emerge and affect the development of a field of knowledge. The other has to do with the role of disciples in the development of a discipline.

10. Blackburn, Behymer, and Hall, "Research Note."

11. Norman W. Storer, The Social System of Science (New York: Holt, Rinehart and Winston, 1966).

12. Blackburn, Behymer and Hall, "Research Note"; E. Timothy Lightfield, "Output and Recognition of Sociologists," American Sociologist (May 1971), pp. 128–133; J. Scott Long, "Productivity and Academic Position in the Scientific Career," American Sociological Review (December 1978), pp. 889–908.

The first is frequently labeled the Ortega hypothesis. A body of knowledge builds like an edifice, brick by brick, from the bottom up, and each stone is essential even if unimportant and relatively insignificant by itself. When enough sound information has been accumulated, then and only then can someone create the synthesizing conceptual framework, generate a new theory, even a new paradigm, which then rapidly spawns new knowledge. This cumulative view is aptly expressed by Ziman:

The invention of a mechanism for the systematic publication of fragments of scientific work may well be the key event in the history of modern science. . . . A typical scientific paper has never pretended to be more than another little piece in a larger jigsaw—not significant in itself but as an element in a grander scheme. This technique, of soliciting many modest contributions to the store of human knowledge, has been the secret of Western science since the seventeenth century, for it achieves a corporate, collective power that is far greater than any one individual can exert.[13]

This cumulative view of scientific growth was expressed by Newton in his acknowledgment to his predecessors; he saw farther "because he had stood on the shoulders of giants." This view of knowledge production calls for a continuous influx of new scholars if new structures are to be erected.

The truth value of this hypothesis on how knowledge grows has been disputed by Glueck and Jauch and by Cole and Cole. Their studies find that the growth of knowledge is essentially discontinuous. Key discoveries derive from a small number of selected contributions. Advances in knowledge are more like quantum jumps than they are the regular and orderly accumulation of brick and mortar. Knowledge is to be likened to a ladder, not a pyramid.[14] Rungs are separated by gaps, not a continuous surfaced incline.

Turning to the role of disciples, a regular influx of new Ph.D.s is needed for a second and important reason, irrespective of the truth value of Ortega's hypothesis. Following Mannheim's theory of generations, Buss has argued that a steady supply of new recruits is essential for the sustenance of a productive unit. The middle-to-advanced-age researcher's breakthrough discovery must be developed, tested, modified, and amplified. Such a researcher's peers are not likely candidates for these critical activities; they are already committed to other frameworks, and perhaps less open to an alternative theory. As Hull, Tessmer, and Diamond have shown with regard to the acceptance of Planck's Principle, the death of his contemporaries was what mattered most. Colleague converts were few.[15] Hence, for a new insight to attain recognition and bear fruit, disciples are needed. Disciples are in part

13. J. M. Zinman, "Information, Communication, Knowledge," Nature (1969), pp. 318–324.

14. William F. Glueck and Lawrence R. Jauch, "Sources of Research Ideas Among Productive Scholars: Implications for Administrators," Journal of Higher Education (January/February 1975), pp. 103–114; Jonathan R. Cole, "Patterns of Intellectual Influence in Scientific Research," Sociology of Education (Fall 1970), pp. 377–403; Jonathan R. Cole and Stephen Cole, "The Ortega Hypothesis," Science (October 1972), pp. 368–375.

15. Allan R. Buss, "Psychology's Future Development as Predicted from Generation Theory," Human Development (1974), pp. 453–459; David L. Hull, Peter D. Tessner, and Arthur M. Diamond, "Planck's Principle," Science (November 1978), pp. 717–723.

drawn from advanced graduate students, but mostly they are the new, young faculty members of a department who can be provided a supportive and secure place to work and to grow.

In other words, without a regular supply of new talent into an organization, stagnation can occur in the production of knowledge. A disruption in disciplinary evolution can take place even in a stable unit if new scholars are not brought into it. The data Ben-David and Collins display on the origin and growth of the discipline of psychology provide an excellent illustration of the relation between the originator, forerunner, and the disciples, founders and followers who developed branches of psychology. Tracing the students of Wilhelm Wundt in Germany, France, England and the United States, Ben-David and Collins show clearly the sequence of generations that developed between Wundt, his founders, and their followers, who built the specialties of psychology. Had there been a hiatus in the opportunity to mine and enrich early discoveries, psychology's development would have been aborted.[16]

ACADEMIC OPPORTUNITIES FOR NEW PH.D.s

While the figures on academic opportunities vary appreciably from one source to another—for example, NSF predicts a 7.7 percent surplus of life-science Ph.D.s in 1985 for all labor markets, not just in colleges and universities, while the Bureau of Labor Statistics forecasts a 46.9 percent surplus—the studies are alike in their dismal prognoses.[17] Current projections of the predicted number of Ph.D.'s who will be graduated over the rest of the century forecast about 30,000 per year. However, these estimates do not take labor force dynamics into account and must be treated with caution. There is greater certainty about how many new doctorate hires there will be from now until the year 2000. While different assumptions regarding retirements, student enrollments, faculty to student ratios, will raise or lower the estimates, the predictions are for a peak of about 10,000 new hires in 1980 declining to 5,500 in 1985–86, rising to 10,000 in 1989 only to fall again to an almost 50 year low of 3,500 in 1992. From then on there is a steep rise to nearly 16,000 in the year 2000.[18]

Many variables enter the predictive equations, most of which are both uncertain and subject to change. Future Ph.D. production, percent of 18 year olds who will go on to college, changes in faculty retirement practices with the introduction of new plans and incentives for early retirement and the counter effect of the raised mandatory retirement age after 1982, inflation, and optional or compulsory continuing education for some professions are but a few of the unpredictables which can affect the number of available positions for new Ph.D.s. Furthermore, employment opportunities will vary from discipline

16. Joseph Ben-David and Randall Collins, "Social Factors in the Origins of a New Science: The Case of Psychology," *American Sociological Review* (August 1966), pp. 451–465.

17. See Gina B. Kolata, "Projecting the Ph.D. Labor Market: NSF and BLS Disagree," *Science* (January 1976), pp. 363–365.

18. Robert E. Klitgaard, *The Decline of the Best? An Analysis of the Relationships Between Declining Enrollments, Ph.D. Production, and Research* (Cambridge: Howard University, J. F. Kennedy School of Government, Discussion Paper Series, May 1979), table 2, p. 18.

to discipline and by institutional type as today's steady state situation in higher education passes into retrenchment and decline for the better part of this century. Thus far the data remain unaggregated. They need to be broken down by fields.[19]

Even with all of the hazards of prediction recognized, the evidence is nonetheless overwhelming that there will be fewer opportunities tomorrow than there are today, including absolutely none at all in some fields. A few figures are advanced to document this vital point. Then the consequences and possible courses of action for dealing with future knowledge production can be discussed.

The seminal report was Cartter's 1965 ACE study which culminated in his 1976 work for the Carnegie Council. The Council has supported a number of studies on Ph.D. production and on projected institutional faculty needs. Their 1975–76 faculty survey provides much of the data— on age distribution for example. Some cautions are in order, however. Their 1968 and 1972 national faculty surveys—they were then the Carnegie Commission—have age data which do not mesh with what they and others now say. For example, in 1968 median faculty age was 41, increasing to 43.4 in 1972, as expected from the forecasts made then with respect to a tighter market. But their 1976 report shows a median

age of 41.7. The 1977 Ladd and Lipset survey has a median of 42.3. Furthermore, the Ladd and Lipset 1977 data have 33 percent of the faculty under 36 years of age and 11 percent over 55 in contrast to the 1972 figures of 23 percent and 11 percent respectively. These figures indicate a trend opposite to that predicted and asserted to be the case. At the same time, a 1979 release by the American Council on Education reports that the percent of science and engineering faculty who have had Ph.D's seven or less years has dropped from 43 to 24 percent in the decade from 1968 to 1978.[20]

Others have built upon the Carnegie data or launched complimentary studies. Fernandez has constructed models which show the general ineffectiveness of early retirement in creating new positions and how the percent of faculty over 50 will increase from about 25 percent in 1975 to 57–58 percent by 1995. Atelsek and Gomberg have reported the rapid decrease in younger faculty in science fields since 1968. Ochsner and Solomon have shown the drop in new history Ph.D.s in colleges and universities from 92 percent in 1967 to 60 percent in 1977. The corresponding figures in psychology were 81 percent and 36 percent respectively. In Breneman's 1975 survey, nearly half of the about-to-be English Ph.D.s saw no possibility of academic employment. In another study he predicts hiring will be as

19. Allan M. Cartter, "A New Look at the Supply of College Teachers," *Educational Record* (Summer 1965), pp. 259–266; Allan M. Cartter, *Ph.D.'s and the Academic Labor Market* (New York: McGraw-Hill, 1976); Dael Wolfe and Charles V. Kidd, "The Future Market for Ph.D.'s," *Science* (August 1971), pp. 784–793; Charles V. Kidd, "Shifts in Doctorate Output: History and Output," *Science* (February 1973), pp. 538–543.

20. Reexamination of fundamental base line data is called for. See Everett C. Ladd, Jr., and Seymour M. Lipset, *Technical Report: 1977 Survey of the American Professoriate* (Storrs: University of Connecticut, 1978); Carnegie Council National Survey, 1975–1976, *Faculty Marginals* (Berkeley: Carnegie Council on Policy Studies in Higher Education, 1978).

low as 10 percent in some areas in the 1980s.[21] In short, unless new strategies are developed, the influx of new scholars is going to be extremely low, even nonexistent.

SOME POSSIBLE COURSES OF ACTION

Several strategies are available, most of which are not novel except in the emphasis they would receive. In addition, the recommended courses of action are not panaceas. Nothing can change the root cause of the problem, that is, the age maldistribution of Ph.D.'s.

Extra-university organizations

Orlans has chronicled the origin, operation, and growth of Research and Development centers, research institutes, and similar organizations which are in the problem-solving and knowledge production business.[22] They continue to grow in size and number. On the one hand, the questionable ones have been labeled "empty entrepreneurship" by Wolfe for most often they do not have the material and human resources that a research university has. They can be expected to have a short half-life span. On the other hand, there are now a number of well established, highly reputable centers and institutes who hire young scholars and produce sound research. Indeed, they are direct competitors for the same research dollars higher education needs in order to maintain its units and to prepare new talent. Therein lies the flaw in this solution; it is a competitive rather than supportive situation. The possible discontinuity at the university training site is jeopardized rather than strengthened by the proliferation of extramural organizations.

Dispersion of the research task

About 10 percent of U.S. academics publish about 90 percent of the journal articles, a figure Wilson reported some time ago and a proportion which seems to have held despite the growth of the number of professors then until now, an increase of 500–700 percent.[23] Yet theoretically, all professors were prepared to be scholars. Furthermore, the majority of the producers, most of the 10 percent, are housed in a few universities. Even many doc-

21. Luis Fernandez, *U.S. Faculty After the Boom: Demographic Projections to 2000* (Berkeley: Carnegie Council on Policy Studies in Higher Education, 1978); Frank J. Atelsek and Irene L. Gomberg, *Young Doctoral Faculty in Science and Engineering: Trends in Composition and Research Activity* (Washington, DC: American Council on Education, 1979); Nancy L. Ochsner and Lewis C. Solmon, "Forecasting the Labor Market for Highly Educated Workers," *Review of Higher Education* (Winter 1979), pp. 34–46; David W. Breneman, *Graduate School Adjustments to the "New Depression" in Higher Education* (Washington, DC: National Board on Graduate Education, 1975); David W. Breneman, "Predicting the Response of Graduate Education to No Growth," in *Assessing Academic Progress Without Growth*, Allan M. Cartter, ed. (San Francisco: Jossey-Bass, 1975). There are real hazards in predictions, as witness the earlier records. See also Richard B. Freeman and David W. Breneman, *Forecasting the Ph.D. Labor Market: Pitfalls for Policy* (Washington, DC: April 1974).

22. Harold Orlans, *The Nonprofit Research Institute: Its Origin, Operation, Problems, and Prospects* (New York: McGraw-Hill, 1972).

23. Logan Wilson, *The Academic Man* (London: Oxford University Press, 1942). Ladd uses the figure of 25 percent as the proportion of faculty who are producers. See Everett C. Ladd, Jr., "The Work Experience of American College Professors: Some Data and an Argument," in *Current Issues in Higher Education* (Washington, DC: 1979), pp. 3–12.

toral granting institutions have a faculty with low publication rates, although they are linked through mentorship to professors at research universities.

Why should not other colleges and universities expand their production of knowledge. Theoretically they could. Realistically, however, supportive environments and key people cannot be easily or quickly developed where research has been infrequent and irregularly timed. Long-standing behavior patterns are not easily altered, despite good intentions. In many ways it is easier to build a completely new research facility than it is to convert a non-scholarly college or university into a productive one.

Part-time, one-time arrangements

In their concern for the interruption of the flow of new scholars into university research environments the Carnegie Council has recommended a "Junior Scholars Program."[24] It calls for 1,000 or more research professorships and post-doctoral fellowships over five-year periods into the 1990's, funded by the government, positions which eventually would be converted into full-time academic appointments. A National Research Council committee has recommended that the National Science Foundation grant 250 awards a year to outstanding faculty to pay a part of their salary for five years thereby freeing institutional funds to hire new faculty. The 20 year program would cost $381,000,000.[25] This plan is similar to that proposed in the *Report of the Committee on MIT Research Structure* where inter-

disciplinary research units linked to teaching departments were proposed.

Blackburn had recommended filling vacancies with two one-half time academics, the other one-half to be administrative, operational or whatever, to increase the inflow by creating a kind of permanent parttime faculty.[26] His plan, however, is not free from undesired consequences. The recent growth of part-time faculty positions, now over 50% of the total faculty in two-year colleges, the nontenured track appointments, and the one year only (OYO) contracts has been phenomenal. This institutional practice, justified on the basis of enrollment and economic uncertainties, has already created a new breed of academic nomads, a distinct group of second class citizens whose scholarly and academic careers are not only aborted but more likely destroyed. They will not become knowledge producers. They are never in one place long enough to establish a research program.[27] Presumably well designed part-time programs could avoid such undesirable consequences.

Business and industry relationships

Another constructive solution would be for business and industry to utilize universities for solving their problems, in addition to, or in place of their own research and development branch. Were industry to supply research grants to universities, more Ph.D.s could be hired, more knowledge produced, and the feared generation gap would never materialize. Some courting will be

24. Radner and Kuh, *Preserving a Lost Generation.*
25. Margarrell, "Panel Says . . ."

26. Blackburn, *Part-Time Faculty.*
27. Robert E. Roemer and James E. Schnitz, "The Day Laborer of Academia: Nontenure Track Positions in Higher Education," paper presented at AERA National Meeting (April 1979).

needed in this strategy for business has rarely expressed a fondness for educational organizations. Nonetheless, this solution could have a significant impact on the hiring rate. It does not call for new organizations to be formed or converted. Universities have research capacities most businesses cannot possess or afford to build. Solutions are more likely to be found in academic settings. This strategy minimizes costs and maximizes benefits.

CONCLUSIONS

The problem of knowledge production and disciplinary development is a real one, a serious one, and a debatable one. While some matters are known regarding the production of knowledge and the growth of disciplines, ignorance and uncertainties remain. The field is in need of systematic investigation.

Even with the acknowledged limitations of the various predictive models of new Ph.D. hires into colleges and universities, one im-portant inference is warranted. For the remainder of this century there will be more new Ph.D.s being produced and seeking typical academic positions than there will be openings. Most of the proposed remedies build their cases on the need for knowledge production, a premise which itself is open to question. The long term disruption in knowledge production is easier to argue for. Furthermore, many of the proposed remedies are expensive and call for federal dollars. Consequently they must be considered as plans with little likelihood of implementation given today's political realities. The plans which explore the establishment of university based research and development centers for business and industry, or plans which develop a corps of integrated part-time faculty with academic status, therefore, become worthy of serious attention. The maintenance of productive units and the orderly development of disciplines could take place under either or both of these arrangements.

ANNALS, AAPSS, 448, March 1980

Teaching, Research, and Role Theory

By MICHAEL A. FAIA

ABSTRACT: The issue of publish-or-perish is essentially a matter of the complementarity (or lack thereof) of teaching and research roles. Role complementarity is a traditional concern of social psychology, and theories of role complementarity are applicable to the teaching-research relationship. While available evidence shows little objective incompatibility of teaching and research roles, it is possible that misperceptions of incompatibility may act as a self-fulfilling prophecy. Those concerned about incompatibility of teaching and research should find ways of heading off this process. Some ways are suggested.

Michael A. Faia is professor of sociology at the College of William and Mary, Williamsburg, Virginia. He has written extensively on the academic profession in such journals as Sociology of Education, Research in Higher Education, College English, and the Pacific Sociological Review.

DESPITE the fact that social interaction is an inherent part of the teaching-learning dialectic, anybody delving into the copious research literature on education soon discovers that the more closely a study focuses on teaching and learning, the more likely it is that the investigator will be a psychologist. While sociologists develop an impressive expertise on such topics as status attainment—the ways in which people end up in certain schools, jobs, or income categories—psychologists are likely to be studying the process of intellectual and artistic creativity. However, psychologists who measure and map cognitive and affective differences among individuals tend to ignore questions about social interaction, the social structure of scholarly organizations such as universities, the ways in which individuals are rewarded for academic work, and so forth. While a book like Harriet Zuckerman's *Scientific Elite* might ask whether Guillemin and Schally's spiteful competition against one another stimulated their inexorable pursuit of a Nobel prize, it would rarely raise questions about the relation of work setting or organizational constraints and rewards to the process of spectacular cognition or accidental discovery, although these are fundamental to scientific creativity. Accordingly, this paper takes a body of sociological theory—specifically, role theory—and applies it to the teaching-learning process in which faculty participate to see if academic roles might be structured to enhance their contributions to teaching and discovery.

ROLE BEHAVIOR: CONCEPTUAL DISTINCTIONS

First, a few elementary definitions. *Social roles* may be defined as the beliefs, attitudes, and behaviors typically exhibited by persons occupying given statuses in society. Beliefs, attitudes, and behaviors are produced and maintained by *normative regulation*—the processes whereby members of society exercise social control over one another's role playing activities. *Role expectations* are subjectively held notions as to how one *should* play a given role, but actual role playing may diverge sharply from such ideals. *Role fulfillment* is measured by whatever convergence may exist between role expectations and the actual beliefs, attitudes, and behaviors of those active in a given role.

In any society, but particularly in modern societies with their elaborate division of labor, any given individual is likely to occupy a number of statuses, and therefore is expected to play a number of social roles. Thus, a person who has a status-role in each of several realms of social behavior—the kinship realm, the educational realm, the political realm, and so forth—may find himself making frequent transitions among such roles, and perhaps even trying to play some roles simultaneously. If, for instance, during a given week one occupies the status-roles of father, husband, business executive, school-board member, political-party activist, Army reserve officer, and consumer, one has a total of seven major roles, and no doubt a very active life.

Whenever a given combination of roles occurs frequently among members of society, it is possible to speak of *complementarity* versus *incompatibility* of these roles. In the above example, we could ask about the complementarity, or incompatibility, of the father-husband combination, the father-business executive combination, the church member-reserve

officer combination, the party acti-
vist-consumer combination, and so
forth. If a given individual occupies
a total of seven major status-roles,
then for that individual we could
specify $7(7 - 1)/2 = 21$ instances in
which the issue of incompatibility
could be raised.

Little agreement exists among
social scientists on how to assess
role complementarity. Perhaps the
most common technique is merely
to take measures of role fulfillment for a pair of social roles,
and then to determine whether high
fulfillment on one role tends to go
with high fulfillment on the other.
If the relationship turns out to be
inverse, we conclude that the roles
are probably incompatible. The
major shortcoming of this approach,
however, is that it focuses only on
those role combinations that already
exist and for which reliable and
valid measures of fulfillment are
available.

Among academicians, the belief
that political activism interferes
with good professorial performance
can hardly be tested if we are to
believe Lipset and Ladd's claim that
few professors have high levels of
political activism. Furthermore, a
given instance of role incompatibility is likely to have many exceptions, and it is arguable that our
major task should be that of explaining how such exceptions arise.

Incompatible roles and the conflict created by them are the stuff
of which fine literature is made.
Emma Bovary, Richard III, and
Humbert Humbert differ in many
ways, but what they have in common
is a desperate attempt to reconcile
incompatible roles. More recently,
the fascinating case of the Catholic
priest accused by seven witnesses
of being a "gentleman bandit" has
stimulated tremendous curiosity,
and for those interested in the drama

of incompatible roles it was a keen
disappointment when the real bandit
decided to reveal himself. During
the era of Senator Joseph McCarthy,
many American professors found
themselves in a situation where the
role of social critic had become
incompatible with the role of loyal
citizen.

ROLE STRAIN AND THE DYNAMICS
OF MISPERCEPTION

According to Secord and Backman, ". . . structural features of
systems that reduce role strain are
differences in the power of various
role partners to exert sanctions, restrictions on multiple position occu-
pancy [e.g., anti-nepotism and con-
flict-of-interest rules] and spatial
and temporal separation of situations
involving conflicting role expectations."[1] Among academicians expected to play the roles of teacher
and researcher among others, each of
these structural features may be observed to some extent. One's teaching constituency and research constituency often have different degrees of power, not merely in the
obvious sense that students typically
cannot countervail against the demands of publish-or-perish, but in
terms of subtle social arrangements
such as the practice found at many
universities of denying junior faculty
—teachers not yet proven as researchers—any significant role in
peer evaluation. In addition, restrictions occasionally are placed
on simultaneous access to teaching
and research roles; one extreme advocate of such restriciton has recommended "segregating excellent researchers."[2] Finally, academicians

1. P. F. Secord and C. W. Backman,
Social Psychology (New York: McGraw-Hill,
1964), p. 496ff.
2. M. Kline, Why the Professor Can't Teach
(New York: St. Martin's Press, 1977), p. 252.

who do research only after hours or during the summer, if at all, illustrate the third method of reducing incompatibility.

Along with Secord and Backman's "structural features," the practice of "audience segregation" is another way of reconciling incompatible roles, and it has been argued that such roles are often reconciled by the simple expedient of merging them into a single role. The first option seems to be favored in academe, where teaching and research are often performed before different audiences. In summary, insofar as we succeed in reducing role strain, we do so largely by manipulating audiences—either segregating them or playing down the demands of a constituency—or by manipulating the roles themselves —segregating them, separating them in space and time, or merging them into a single integrated role. In any instance where such devices are invoked on a large scale, we are probably in the presence of perceived role incompatibility.

At an intuitive level, however, one cannot help but feel that teaching and research roles are inherently more complementary than, say, the roles of priest and "gentleman bandit." Great literature will never be written about professors in the throes of trying to meet demands of both teaching and research; little potential exists here for high moral drama. Yet, there is a substantial body of opinion in academe which, contrary to the orthodox views of the presidents of major universities, holds that basic incompatibilities exist between the two paramount academic roles. In the main, this literature argues that what is given to one role must be taken from the other, that role fulfillment in the realm of teaching is inherently less amenable to measurement than role fulfillment in research, and that teaching must therefore receive short shrift, and so forth.

The remainder of this paper challenges the notion that strong incompatibility exists between the teaching and research endeavors. Furthermore, and contrary to recent inflammatory works premised on the incompatibility doctrine,[3] it is argued that the surest way to eliminate whatever incompatibilities do exist between the two roles is to merge them into a single role by means of the "teaching-and-research subculture" outlined below. Such a merger, in the Madison Avenue buzz word, could well turn out to be "synergistic."

If insurmountable incompatibilities existed between teaching and research, one would expect that among several empirical studies of teaching-research interaction a substantial proportion would have turned up inverse relationships between measures of role fulfillment. Table 1 demonstrates that such inverse relationships have never appeared in recent studies, and that studies in this area typically show either no relationship between teaching and research performance or a slight positive relationship.[4] This result is highly encouraging to those who never have had much enthusiasm for the incompatibility doctrine as championed by countless student protesters during the sixties and, in its most extreme form, in works such as Kline's *Why the Professor Can't Teach*. Our major burden, then, would seem to be that of identifying circumstances under which institutions fail to take advantage of potential complementarities of teaching

3. *Ibid.*
4. A summary of earlier studies is found in M. A. Faia, "Teaching and research: rapport or messalliance?", *Research in Higher Education* 4 (1976):235–46.

TABLE 1
RECENT EMPIRICAL STUDIES OF TEACHING-RESEARCH COMPLEMENTARITY

Author(s)	Date	Unit of Analysis	Sample Size	Measure of Teaching Proficiency	Measure of Research Productivity	Major Findings
Hayes[1]	1971	Individual instructors, Carnegie-Mellon University	N = 355	Student evaluations and evaluations by administrators	Publications (last 5 years, standardized by career age); colleague ratings of research ability	Positive association (administrators' evaluation of teaching) No relationship (student evaluation of teaching)
Cope et al.[2]	1972	Academic departments, University of Washington	N = 17	Student evaluations	A.C.E. departmental rankings	No relationship, except for a slight positive association for social science
Aleamoni and Yimer[3]	1973	Individual instructors	N = 362 (faculty evaluations) N = 28 (CEQ) N = 360 (instructor evaluation)	Faculty evaluations; student evaluation questionnaire (CEQ) and overall evaluation of instructor	Publications (unweighted sum, 1966 through 1969)	No relationship.
Hicks[4]	1974	Individual instructors, San Jose State Univ.	N = 459	Student evaluations	Publications	Positive association
Hoyt[5]	1974	Individual instructors, Kansas State Univ.	N = 222	Student academic progress	Publications (yearly average since 1952)	No relationship
Linsky and Straus[6]	1975	Individual instructors, 16 colleges and universities	N = 1,422	Student evaluations	Publications (20-year period); citation scores (10-year period); Cartter rating of instructors' graduate schools	No relationship

McCollagh and Roy	1975	Individual instructors, Appalachian State Univ.	N = 52	Student evaluations	Publications (recent); time spent per week in preparing work for publication	No relationship
Rothman and Preshaw[8]	1975	Individual instructors, health sciences education center	N = 25	Student evaluations	Science Citation Index recent references	Positive association (fourth-yr. students) No relationship (third yr. students)
Dent and Lewis*[9]	1976	Individual instructors	N = 90	Student evaluations	SCI recent references; publications	No relationship
Faia[10]	1976	Individual instructors	N = 53034 (weighted sample)	Receipt of teaching award	Publications (recent)	Weak positive association
Hoyt and Spangler*[11]	1976	Individual instructors, natural-mathematical and social-behavioral sciences, Kansas State Univ.	N = 183	Student evaluations	"Time commitment and accomplishment"	Positive association, esp. for natural science instructors

* Based on summary, College Student Personnel Abstracts.

[1] J. R. Hayes, "Research, teaching, and faculty fate," Science 1972 (1971):227–30.

[2] R. G. Cope, J. G. McMillin, and J. M. Richardson, A study of the relationship between quality instruction as perceived by students and research productivity in academic departments. U.S. Office of Education, 1972.

[3] L. M. Aleamoni and Makonnen Yimer, "An investigation of the relationship between colleague rating, student rating, research productivity, and academic rank in rating instructional effectiveness," Journal of Educational Psychology 64 (1976):3–16.

[4] R. A. Hicks, "The relationship between publishing and teaching effectiveness," Calif. Journal of Ed. Research 25 (1974):140–46.

[5] P. Hoyt, "Interrelationships among instructional effectiveness, publication record, and monetary reward," Research in Higher Education 2 (1974):81–88.

[6] A. S. Linsky and M. A. Straus, "Student evaluations, research productivity and eminence of college faculty," Journal of Higher Education 46 (1975):89–102.

[7] R. D. McCollagh and M. R. Roy, "The contribution of non-instructional activities to college classroom teacher effectiveness," Journal of Experimental Education 44 (1975):61–70.

[8] A. I. Rothman and R. Preshaw, "Is scientific achievement a correlate of effective teaching performance?" Research in Higher Education 3 (1975):29–34.

[9] P. L. Dent and D. J. Lewis, "The relationship between teaching effectiveness and measures of research quality," Ed. Research Quarterly 1 (1976):3–16.

[10] M. A. Faia, "Teaching and research: rapport or mesalliance?" Research in Higher Education 4 (1976):235–46.

[11] D. P. Hoyt and R. K. Spangler, "Faculty research involvement and instructional outcomes," Research in Higher Education 4 (1976):113–22.

and research, circumstances under which "structural features" intended as a means of adapting to incompatibility—for example, segregation of research and teaching audiences— have become a major cause of incompatibility, or, more properly, reduced complementarity.

Such a reverse causal pattern is highly plausible. A very perceptive paper by Hammond *et al.*, assuming, perhaps wrongly, that "knowledge either of a professor's teaching quality or of the quality of his research does not help in knowing the other," tries to explain "misperceptions" of the relationship as resulting from precisely those structural features identified by Secord and Backman.[5] Audience segregation, for instance, creates "differing visibility," with faculty colleagues and administrators knowing far more than students about a professor's research, and with students knowing far more than faculty members or administrators about a professor's classroom performance. Because teaching effectiveness is rather normally distributed while research productivity is likely to be narrowly distributed, there is an inescapable segregation of roles. The various audience and role sectors "have only segmental contact with each other, thus rendering a campus-wide culture very unlikely. Consensus is thus also unlikely, leaving each person to form opinions largely from the perspective of his own structural position." In other words, structural features may create misperceptions of role incompatibility, despite the apparent lack of incompatibility as objectively assessed. It is entirely possible, of course, that such misperceptions could act as a self-fulfilling prophecy, precluding or reducing complementarity in instances where it potentially exists.

MISPERCEPTION AND THE SELF-FULFILLING PROPHECY

To understand how this self-fulfilling prophecy may operate, we return for a moment to Secord and Backman's discussion of adaptations to perceived role incompatibility. Since Secord and Backman provide no empirical evidence that adaptive mechanisms do in fact reduce objectively measured incompatibility, it is reasonable to suppose that such mechanisms may have as much impact on perceived incompatibility as on its objective counterpart. If, moreover, the argument of Hammond et al. has any validity, it is entirely possible that adaptive mechanisms of the sort described by Secord and Backman, acting as self-fulfilling prophecies, would tend to increase objective incompatibility rather than reduce it. We end up with all the incompatibility we expect to have. The "structural features that reduce strain," as described by Secord and Backman, have their counterparts in the behavior of individuals: "The individual is . . . very active in attempts to reduce role strain to which he is subjected. He may . . . establish his own hierarchy of values; he may use rationalization, displacement, or wish-fulfilling fantasy; or he may leave the system."[6] In addition, individuals allocate time and energy to various roles according to ". . . norm commitment, estimate of reward and punishment by role partners, and estimate of reactions of a

5. P. E. Hammond, J. W. Meyer, and D. Miller, "Teaching versus research: sources of misperceptions," *Journal of Higher Education* 40 (1969):682-90.

6. Secord and Backman, *Social Psychology* pp. 519-20.

third party or an audience."[7] Any one of these individual adaptations could tend to reduce role complementarity.

Using data from the 1973 American Council on Education faculty survey,[8] a preliminary test was made of the notion that individual adaptations to role strain, such as large disparities in the amount of time allocated to each role (a condition approaching role segregation), tend to reduce whatever complementarity may exist between teaching and research performance. At universities with a "strong research emphasis,"[9] role complementarity appears to be somewhat stronger among those faculty members who maintain a rough balance in their time commitments to teaching and research. Among such professors, those who have published in recent years have a probability of .19 of ever having received an award for teaching, compared to .12 for non-publishers. Among those who currently allocate relatively little time to teaching, the corresponding probabilities are .12 and .08; among those who spend an unusually large amount of time on teaching, .18 and .16. The strongest nexus between publication and good teaching, then, appears to occur among those professors who maintain a balanced pattern of time allocation, although

any inference of causation between balance and complementarity is not yet warranted.

Making prophecy fail

If the objective complementarity of teaching and research is reduced by personal and structural adaptations to perceived incompatibility, then any effort to ameliorate this effect must begin by limiting the impact of such adaptations. When Linsky and Straus, finding little apparent complementarity between teaching and research, suggest that ". . . there would seem to be some value in developing more independent reward systems for teaching and for research than currently exist . . .,"[10] they are merely invoking another "structural feature" that, in all likelihood, would operate as a self-fulfilling prophecy creating incompatibility. The glaring irony of the Linsky-Straus proposal, of course, is that it has already been implemented on a large scale.

Most institutions, in setting faculty salaries and other rewards, such as tenure or promotions in rank, tend to derive separate "scores" for teaching and research performance and to add these scores together; this procedure, at least by statistical definition, involves "independent" reward systems.

If we wish to encourage complementarity between teaching and research, we need to include a "multiplicative" term in our implicit salary formulas. Imagine, for instance, two professors, each with a score for teaching and research performance adding up to, say, six units, but distributed as follows:

7. T. R. Sarbin and V. L. Allen, "Role Theory" in Gardner Lindzey and Elliot Aronson, *The Handbook of Social Psychology*, V. I. (Reading, MA: Addision-Wesley, 1968), p. 539.

8. The 1972-73 faculty data were collected by the American Council on Education's former Office of Research under a grant from the RANN Division of the National Science Foundation. A summary of survey results is found in A. E. Bayer, *Teaching Faculty in Academe: 1972–73* (Office of Research: American Council on Education, 1973).

9. Faia, "Teaching and Research," p. 244.

10. A. S. Linsky and M. A. Straus, "Student evaluations, research productivity and eminence of college faculty," *Journal of Higher Education* 46(1975):89–102.

Professor A: $S = a + 1(T) + 5(R)$

Professor B: $S = a + 3(T) + 3(R)$

If "a", the base salary, were about $12,000, and each unit of merit were worth $1000, then each professor, allowing for "errors" arising from our usual unwillingness to apply formulas rigidly, would receive about $18,000. Clearly these salaries are not influenced by the relative involvement of the two professors in teaching and research. If, however, we wished to confer an additional reward on Professor B for having a more balanced approach to teaching and research than his colleague, we might use the following formula with a multiplicative term:

Professor A: $S = a + 1(T) + 5(R)$

$\qquad + (1 \times 5) = \$23,000$

Professor B: $S = a + 3(T) + 3(R)$

$\qquad + (3 \times 3) = \$27,000$

This formula gives each professor a tidy raise, and has the additional virtue of encouraging professors to cultivate both teaching and research (insofar as such behavior can be encouraged by anticipated financial rewards) and, presumably, the complementarity thereof. If, in fact, complementarity has a large impact, we could reasonably expect Professor B, who cultivates both roles, to achieve an unusually high overall merit score, perhaps as follows:

Professor B: $S = a + 4(T) + 4(R)$

$\qquad + (4 \times 4) = \$36,000.$

The assumption that balance would enable Professor B to improve his overall merit score, as compared with Professor A, is critical. It asserts that despite the fact that both pro-fessors may be working the 60–65 hours per week typically claimed by faculty members in time-utilization surveys, Professor B, by virtue of role complementarity, is relatively more productive. He provides an instance of David Riesman's paradigm "the more . . . , the more . . . ," a direct challenge to the "scarcity" theory of role behavior. A recent paper on role theory argues that a strong, balanced commitment to a multiplicity of roles, rather than having the enervating impact assumed by the scarcity approach to human endeavor, has a strong energizing impact.[11] From Freud to Goode[12] to Lewis and Rose Coser[13], scarcity theorists have assumed that what is given to one role must be taken from other roles; yet, according to Marks, ". . . while considerable empirical evidence is offered that multiple-role players tend to run out of time and energy, there is also evidence of a minority . . . who do *not* seem to be experiencing the effects of scarce personal resources."[14] Identifying and expanding this minority would appear to be a task of first priority.

It is suggested, first, that all aspects of audience and role segregation be removed so that undergraduates no longer live in not-so-blissful ignorance of the research enterprise and so that faculty colleagues become involved in one another's teaching in the same ways they now become involved in one

11. S. R. Marks, "Multiple roles and role strain: some notes on human energy, time and commitment," *American Sociological Review* 42 (1977):921–36.

12. W. J. Goode, "A theory of role strain," *American Sociological Review* 25 (1960):483–96.

13. L. and R. Coser, *Greedy Institutions* (New York: Free Press, 1974).

14. Marks, "Multiple roles," p. 925.

another's research.[15] Second, reward processes need to be redesigned so that, in addition to rewarding both teaching and research performance equally, ways are found to encourage scholars to cultivate whatever complementarities may be latent in this critical interrole relationship; regarding balance as a dimension of merit would not be inappropriate. Third, an effort should be made to develop teaching-and-research sub-

15. Whenever one proposes that faculty members get involved in one another's teaching, one soon hears cries about threats to academic freedom. Threats to academic freedom are no more severe in the teaching realm than in the research realm, and yet I've rarely heard research scholars accuse their harshest and most strident critics of assaulting academic freedom. I suspect that the insularity of teaching from peer review is a way of buttressing the notion that teaching is inherently more difficult to assess than research, a notion championed among those who consider teaching and research to be incompatible.

cultures comparable to the research subcultures that often exist at major universities, or the teaching subcultures that seem to exist at a number of smaller colleges.

The former produces exchanges of research papers and critical commentaries on one another's work; daily brownbag luncheons and assorted late-afternoon symposia in which scholars test ideas on peers; countless informal gatherings in which, inevitably, the discussion turns to research; boundless enthusiasm among graduate students involved at all levels of the research enterprise. If the concerns of teaching could be made part of the research subculture, and vice versa, the prospects of complementarity —indeed, the prospects of a merger of teaching and research roles— would be greatly enhanced, and we would perhaps thrust ourselves into a far more energetic and productive pursuit of our academic goals.

ANNALS, AAPSS, **448**, March 1980

The Danger Zone: Academic Freedom and Civil Liberties

By SHEILA SLAUGHTER

ABSTRACT: This paper examines the way "corresponding rights and duties" surrounding academic freedom were negotiated between professional associations and organizations of university managers and trustees. The subject is approached through an analysis of the American Association of University Professors' (AAUP) major documents on academic freedom. In general terms it is argued that American academics, as intellectuals dependent on their employing institutions, have consistently sacrificed individuals and substantive principles in order to gain compliance for procedural safeguards from university officials for the profession as a whole. Restitution or reinstatement were not serious issues: the goal of the AAUP was a uniform personnel policy recognizing tenure. Even this goal was difficult to achieve. To win its acceptance, professors effectively traded civil liberties for job security.

Sheila Slaughter is an Assistant Professor of Education at Virginia Polytechnic and State University. She is the co-editor of volumes on higher education and publishing, and the author of articles on student protest, departmental decision-making, the historical structure of the American publishing industry, and ideology formation among social scientists.

A S MEMBERS of the university community, we too often see academic freedom as a tangible right, the privilege of our profession that distinguishes us from other intellectual workers. We know theoretically every right entails corresponding duties and responsibilities, but rarely is there inquiry as to their nature or consequence for our practice. Our unthinking acceptance of academic freedom suits the dominant ideology of the liberal university: questions about the limits of knowledge in a materialist society remain comfortably unexamined. However, the assumption of rights without an examination of responsibilities leaves us unprepared, bewildered, and defenseless before periodic and vicious societal assaults on academic freedom.

The purpose of this paper is to look at the way "corresponding rights and duties" surrounding academic freedom were negotiated and to explore the degree of freedom this leaves us in our profession. Concepts of professionalization are illuminated by exchange theory:[1] it is assumed that those who control resources are concerned that institutions they fund or support maintain an ideological hegemony beneficial to them; that academic rights are not god-given nor even freely granted but won through organization and agitation; that once acknowledged these rights are not secure but must be constantly defended; that notions of profession as a "monopoly of knowledge" conferred by the "community-at-large" can be given concrete,

1. For a more detailed account of the relation of professionalization and exchange theory see Edward T. Silva and Sheila Slaughter, "Prometheus Bound: The Ideological Limits of Social Science Professionalization in the Progressive Period, 1900–1917," forthcoming, *Theory and Society*, 1980.

situational definition; that examination of the changing nature of this contract between profession and society reveals the degree to which we are able to exercise academic freedom.

The American Association of University Professors (AAUP) appropriated the profession's definition of academic freedom in 1915 and has been responsible for enforcing it at least through the 1960s, when unions and individual litigants began to offer competing means of protection. Although the AAUP is no longer the exclusive custodian of academic freedom, the precedents and procedures it established continue to inform other organizations as well as the courts. Thus, the responsibilities and duties accepted by the profession in return for academic freedom are approached through the AAUP's formal definitions and interpretations. Since the Association is composed of eminent professors in many academic disciplines, an analysis of its major documents on academic freedom—produced in 1915, 1925, 1940, 1956, 1958 and 1970— should provide a reasonable idea of what the profession, in its collective wisdom, accepts as necessary limits on freedom of inquiry and expression. Because even limited rights are meaningless if not exercised and protected, AAUP definitions are also considered in light of known violations of academic freedom to see how successful the profession has been in guarding its changing privileges.

In general terms it is argued that American academics, as intellectuals dependent on their employing institutions, have consistently sacrificed individuals and substantive principles in order to gain compliance for procedural safeguards from university officials for the profession as a whole. Restitution or reinstatement were not serious issues: the goal of the AAUP was a uniform personnel policy recognizing tenure. Even this goal was difficult to achieve. To win its acceptance, professors effectively traded civil liberties for limited job security.

The 1915 Declaration

In an organization claiming to represent professional custom by policy statements interpreted through case procedure, the 1915 "Declaration of Principles" remains critical to our understanding of academic freedom.[2] It is an exact statement of the reciprocal rights and responsibilities the academic profession and the community-at-large owe to each other. Later documents continue to be viewed by the Association as confirmation and elaboration of this initial setting-out of the contractual obligations between the profession and the public.

The 1915 Declaration was the outcome of a convergence of two separate movements on the part of the American professoriate. First, professors concerned with working conditions—including salaries, pensions, the growth of administrative controls, and the encroachment of philanthropic foundations—began to discuss the creation of an association that would speak to problems common to professors across disciplines.[3] They were responding to the recent and rapid transformation of a collection of small, errati-

cally staffed, regionally based colleges into a national network of universities comprised of faculties holding Ph.D.s. As academic careers were routinized, these professors organized to represent their own interests.

Second and simultaneously, professors in the social sciences, alarmed by a new outbreak of academic freedom cases, the first since the celebrated cases of the 1880s and 1890s, formed a Joint Committee on Academic Freedom and Tenure in 1913. This Committee represented the American Economic Association, the American Political Science Association and the American Sociology Society, three disciplines especially vulnerable to violations of academic freedom.[4]

Social scientists had reason to look to the defense of their disciplines. In the Progressive era, many of the leading figures in their associations had achieved positions of prominence, sometimes of considerable power, as advisors to leaders of state, as experts consulting with the rapidly growing federal bureaucracy, as implementors of government policy, all while retaining academic posts.[5] When the Progressive era was unable to fulfill its promise in the years immediately preceding the first World War, economic depression and mounting social unrest made these scientific activists targets for reprisals. If they were to preserve their ability to participate in social policy formation, they had to act.

The Joint Committee made a pre-

2. Ralph S. Brown, Jr. and Matthew W. Finkin, "The Usefulness of AAUP Policy Statements," *Academe* 64 (March 1978):5–11; see also W. Todd Furniss, "The Status of AAUP Policy," *Educational Record* 59 (Winter 1978):9.

3. Walter P. Metzger, "On the Origins of the Association: An Anniversary Address," *Bulletin of the American Association of University Professors*, 5 (June 1965): 236.

4. "Preliminary Report of the Joint Committee on Academic Freedom and Tenure," *American Economic Review*, 5 (Supplement March 1915):316–323.

5. Sheila Slaughter McVey, "Social Control of Social Research: the Development of the Social Scientist as Expert, 1875–1916" (Ph.D. diss., University of Wisconsin, 1975) 443ff.

liminary report in December, 1914 and planned to put forward a final report the next year. However, storm signals—like the investigation of professors working for and with the state in Wisconsin—made the climate of repression so ominous that the Joint Committee sought wider support. Its Chairman attended the AAUP's organizational meeting; on his motion, an AAUP committee was created and merged with the Joint Committee.[6]

The Declaration offered at the end of 1915 was an effort of the social science associations and the AAUP; the working committee was "Committee A," staffed by seven social science representatives and six AAUP members from a variety of disciplines. At the AAUP's inception, it was only one of many proposed committees, indeed, not even among the more widely discussed. However, in the words of its closest and only historian, ". . . the AAUP was 'Committee A' to all practical purposes."[7]

This fusion of occupation interests, initially represented by the AAUP, with issues of academic freedom, represented by the social scientists' Joint Committee, was the critical juncture where the American academic profession tied job security (tenure) to academic freedom, foreclosing the possibility of separate institutional treatment of the two issues. The decision to join these issues was probably no more than the reflex action of a new profession defending its tenuous claims to

autonomy from societal encroachment. Yet its consequences for the academic community were enduring.

Analytically, the Declaration can be divided into three parts: formulation of claims to academic freedom; an assessment of the political and economic restraints posed by vested interests; presentation of the concessions the profession was prepared to make in return for job security. Before making any claims, however, the profession had to undercut the proprietary rights held by American university trustees. As suitable in a document written largely by social scientists, the Declaration borrowed from economic theory; specialized knowledge was assumed to be a "natural" monopoly and, like public utilities, whether privately or publicly held, subject to regulation in the public interest. Thus, Trustees had "no moral right to bind the reason or conscience of any professor." The real responsibility of the professor is "primarily to the public itself and the judgement of his own profession." The professor is not a "mere employee" because the university does not fall under the jurisdiction of private sector contractual arrangements.[8]

The profession grounded its justification of academic freedom on society's need for specialized, objective knowledge. As the drafting of social science professors from "almost every one of our higher institutions of learning . . . into more or less unofficial participation in public service" indicated, the "complexities of economic, social and political life" in a modern democracy were such that it was no longer possible to solve problems

6. See "Preliminary Report of the Joint Committee," 316–323; and "Meeting for the Organization of the Association," *Science* (January 1916): 16–17.

7. Walter P. Metzger, "On the Origins of the Association," An Anniversary Address *AAUPB* 5(June 1965):236. Metzger continues to be the Associations only historian because the AAUP has refused to open its archives to any other scholar.

8. "Report of the Committee on Academic Freedom and Tenure," *AAUP* (December 1915):9, 12.

without "technical knowledge." As important as technical skill was the quality of expert advice. "Prolonged and specialized technical training" guaranteed knowledge characterized by "disinterestedness and impartiality"—a commodity difficult to come by in a society rife with special interests. As expert technicians certified by graduate training to be beyond bias of class, party or creed, academics used objective knowledge to resolve and defuse widespread social conflict. Despite the importance of their social function, the "magnitude of economic rewards" was not great. Thus, freedom of conscience and security of position were necessary to attract qualified and dedicated men. This freedom also enabled professors to better perform their other functions —research and teaching.[9]

Although staking broad claims to academic freedom, professors realized these would be difficult to enforce. As members of the middle and professional classes, they lacked resources to produce technical knowledge independently.[10] They needed the university, thus their bargaining position was weak, not even reenforced by a societal tradition of professional autonomy. Their assessment of the political economy of American higher education revealed an acute awareness of the problems they faced. Social scientists in particular were in the "danger zone." Their subject matter, by definition, always touched "private or class interests." If housed in "privately

endowed institutions" where boards of trustees are "naturally made up of men who through their standing and ability are personally interested in great private enterprises, the points of conflict are numberless." Moreover, the student population of such universities is drawn from "the more prosperous and therefore usually . . . more conservative classes." As a result, "pressure from vested interests" may be used to curtail academic freedom. Conversely, in state institutions, strong popular opinion may result "in the repression of opinions deemed ultra-conservative rather than ultra-radical."[11]

Rather than opposing vested interests in the name of science or seeking support from popularly based groups, the Declaration denied the revolutionary potential of knowledge. The profession voluntarily undertook the conservative management of new knowledge in return for a commitment to limited job security on the part of university managers. Thus, the university was defined as "likely always to exercise a certain form of conservative influence," indeed the university:

. . . is committed to the principle that knowledge should precede action, to the

9. *Ibid.*, All quotes this paragraph taken from pp. 11–16.
10. For the social class background of social scientists active in framing the Declaration see E. T. Silva and Sheila Slaughter, "Substantive Differentiation and Internal Confirmation of the Expert Role, 1904," unpublished manuscript.

11. "Report of the Committee on Academic Freedom and Tenure," 19. Although the AAUP may have anticipated state universities suppressing professors who were political conservatives, there is only one well-known instance in the period, that of Kansas State University, where Populists gained control, fired conservatives, and introduced radicals. Within several years, this policy was reversed. See Mary O. Furner, "Advocacy and Objectivity: the Professionalization of Social Science 1865–1905" (Ph.D. diss., Northwestern University, 1972), pp. 214–215. All the cases the AAUP investigated at state universities prior to the First War involved professors who were dismissed for their liberal views. Thus, professors in state as well as private universities had to contend with conservative, local elites.

caution (by no means synonomous with intellectual timidity) which is an essential part of the scientific method, to the practice of taking long views into the future, and to a reasonable regard for the teaching of experience.

The Declaration also offered to use the emerging rhetoric of the profession to manage "the hasty and unconsidered impulses of popular feeling." As trained experts representing objective science, their verdict on social and technical issues commanded respect. However, this respect was contingent on the public's belief that the university was organized "in such a way as to make impossible the exercise of pressure on professional opinions." If this were the case, then "the public may respect and be influenced by, the counsels of prudence and moderation which are given by men of science." Open commitment to academic freedom by university managers would convince the public of the impartiality of science and allow professors to mold moderate popular sentiment on potentially explosive social issues.[12]

These guarantees that science would not go too far or too fast, nor sway the public to any extreme course was a tacit admission that the exchange of disinterested knowledge for academic freedom would not be regarded as fair value by university managers. When it came to dissemination of knowledge that touched on vested interests, some surety for the content of that knowledge had to be given. Although professional rhetoric claimed academics were responsible to the public and their peers, the institutional reality of elite dominance of higher edu-

cation was explicitly accomodated. Professors agreed to blunt the cutting edge of knowledge potentially able to slice through class privilege and power, and thus conceded any absolute right to academic freedom.

The Declaration was an appeal to university managers and the public to endorse the principle of academic freedom by recognizing that professors needed job security to perform functions necessary to society's well-being. Yet the Association, did not have the strength to demand that universities make formal provision for tenure. Indeed, professors' employment rights were still so ill-defined that all the AAUP's energies were concentrated on bringing universities to the point where they would adopt written personnel policies stating terms of appointment, providing notice of non-renewal, and involving senior faculty in decisions to terminate long standing positions. Using the techniques of Progressive reformers—investigation and publicity—the AAUP tried to limit unilateral decision making by university managers.

However, brief examination of the seven institutions investigated between 1915 and U.S. entry into the European conflict illustrates some of the problems resulting from resting the defense of academic freedom on university adoption of written personnel policy. The AAUP reprimanded the University of Utah after two faculty members were discharged for lack of loyalty to its President. But the professors were not reinstated, nor was the plight of the 17 professors who resigned in protest over the firings addressed. After Scott Nearing was fired by the University of Pennsylvania for his outspoken crusade for laws prohibiting child-labor, the Association claimed he was arbitrarily dismissed.

12. "Report of the Committee on Academic Freedom and Tenure," all quotes this paragraph pages 17–19.

Yet in the same report it praised Pennsylvania for ex post facto adoption of a personnel policy that included faculty in decisionmaking.

When James Brewster was fired by the University of Colorado for acting as counsel for the Western Federation of Miners during the Colorado Coal Wars, the university was not faulted. As a temporary appointee, Brewster, although previously a full professor of law at Michigan, did not have the same claims as permanent faculty; thus personnel procedure had not been violated. Similarly, the University of Washington followed the rules when dismissing union activist J. K. Hart, and was absolved of any wrong-doing. At Winona College, the University of Montana and Alleghany College, the pattern was repeated. All told, 29 persons lost their jobs; none were reinstated and only 4 institutions publically censured.[13]

The Association, then, placed development of bureaucratic procedures above the merits of individual cases. As Max Weber pointed out, bureaucratic apparatus often presents obstacles to the suitable discharge of the individual case and disregards substantive justice for formalism, all while serving the interests of a plutocracy.[14] Yet reliance on procedure allowed the AAUP to begin reducing arbitrary personnel decisions without directly challenging the beliefs, values and ideologies of university managers and trustees. And even though individual careers were lost through technicalities, reinstatement never attained, and treatment of substantive issues avoided, the Association made some inroads with regard to the special conditions of academic employment.

Then, World War I confronted the AAUP with a nationwide challenge to academic freedom. The Association as a whole responded by vigorously supporting the war effort and abandoning its commitment to freedom of inquiry and expression.[15] It issued the "Report of the Committee on Academic Freedom in Wartime" which not unexpectedly denied professors the privilege of academic freedom if they disobeyed any statute or executive order relating to the war. However, the AAUP demanded more from professors than the law. Institutions were encouraged to dismiss professors engaged in any propaganda that *might* cause others to resist the war or who tried to dissuade others from rendering voluntary service to the government. And a special requirement was extracted from professors of German or Austro-Hungarian birth or parentage. They must refrain from public discussion of the war, and avoid any hostile comment toward the United States in their private intercourse with neighbors, colleagues and students.[16] Professors opposing the war on grounds of science or conscience had no claim to academic freedom.

13. Compiled from BAAUP, 1-4 (1915-1918). At this point the AAUP does not use the term "censure" or have a "censured" list, but it does pass positive or negative judgements on the institutions investigated. The case of Willard Fisher at Wesleyan is omitted since this occurred prior to the AAUP's organization.

14. H. H. Gerth and C. Wright Mills, eds., *Max Weber: Essays in Sociology*, (NY: Oxford University Press, 1958):215, 221, 230.

15. For Association support of the war effort see "Committee U, Patriotic Service," BAAUP 3 (October 1917):14-16; "General Announcements: Annual Meeting," BAAUP 4 (January 1918): 6-8; and J. M. Coulter, "President's Address to the Members," BAAUP 4 (January 1918): 3.

16. "Report of the Committee on Academic Freedom and Wartime," BAAUP 4 (February March 1918):29-47.

While most professors wholeheartedly supported the war, some
openly stood forth against it, exercising their political rights as citizens. And some were dismissed on
suspicion of opposition rather than
proof positive. Among the well
known cases are William A. Schaper,
Minnesota; James McKeen Cattell
and Henry W. L. Dana at Columbia
—dismissals which prompted Charles
Beard to resign from the AAUP and
abandon academe altogether; Scott
Nearing, then at the University of
Toledo; his mentor, Simon N. Patten,
at the University of Pennsylvania.
Emily Balch of Wellsley took a leave
of absence to spare her department
the embarrassment of her opposition
to intervention. At least 17 additional
professors all located at major state
universities lost. their jobs. While
these cases involved professors at
substantial universities where events
are chronicled there is some suggestion that history has lost sight
of many others.[17]

In sum, the AAUP refused to use
its offices to protect professors opposed to the war or under suspicion
of opposition. At least adherence to
personnel procedures would have
allowed those professors falsely accused to try to prove their innocence.
In failing to meet a nationwide
crisis that imperiled academic freedom, the AAUP established a pattern
it followed subsequently. As with
the wartime firings, massive violations occurred when professors
tried to exercise their political rights

in periods of social unrest. Again the
Association exchanged civil liberties
to protect the profession.

The 1925 Conference Statement

The AAUP was not the only educational organization concerned with
academic freedom. Associations of
managers—like the Association of
American Colleges—were equally
interested in definitions of academic
freedom, especially as these im-
pinged on personnel policy. Their
interest is obvious; they had to
develop procedures that took the
profession's demand for academic
freedom into account while still preserving managerial prerogatives and
safeguarding the resource base of
their institutions from being jeopardized by professors who took positions
openly at odds with trustees. Almost
from the AAUP's inception, these
associations had offered competing
and more limited definitions of
academic freedom.

The 1925 Conference Statement,
made by the AAUP and the American Association of Colleges under
the sponsorship of the American
Council of Education, was essentially an accommodation between
professors and university management. As an association of university professors, the AAUP did not
extend membership to university
staff whose duties were wholly or
mainly administrative; too many
conflicts of interest might arise.
However, as an elite body of eminent
professors, many of its members
were drawn into higher education
administration. By 1925, there were
70 honorary members, the organizational niche reserved for professors
turned managers, and 22 of these
were university presidents.[18] The

17. Carol S. Gruber, *Mars and Minerva:
World War I and the Uses of the Higher
Learning in America* (Baton Rouge: Louisiana
State University Press, 1975):174–175. For
a more detailed account of the Columbia
dismissals see William Summerscales, who
treats Beard's reaction in *Affirmation and
Dissent: Columbia's Response to the Crisis of
World War I* (New York: Teachers College
Press, Columbia University, 1970):94–95.

18. "Members of the Association," *BAAUP*
11 (January 1925):54–56.

distinction between managers and professors, while formally preserved, was blurred outside the Association. As the ranks of university administrators were permeated with AAUP honorary members, the definitions of academic freedom and personnel policy held by managerial groups came closer and closer to those of the AAUP. Committee A noted this congruence in 1924, and took the position that "by ourselves we can only investigate cases and point out wherein principles which we believe to be fundamental have been violated . . . [this] is not nearly so effective as would be an enunciation of principles made not only by professors but by professors and bodies authorized to speak for the institutions themselves."[19]

The 1925 Conference Statement was more or less a manual of operating procedures augmenting the 1915 Declaration by making the code of conduct governing freedom of expression more explicit. The university teacher in the classroom was enjoined to confine himself to his field of expertise, to present all sides of controversial questions, and to show special restraint when instructing immature students. When speaking outside the university in his area of specialization, he had full "freedom of exposition in his own subject," as well as the same political rights as any other citizen.

Although some universities had instituted tenure, the Association did not yet insist that it be uniformly incorporated into personnel policy. However, if academics observed the rules of classroom conduct, the only grounds for termination of a permanent or long term appointment were "gross immorality

or treason, when the facts are admitted." The Statement, then, recognized tenure where it existed and offered some protection to senior faculty, the most likely to hold long term appointments at institutions without tenure. The treason clause, which never appears again, was probably an attempt to guard against making another emergency statement like that issued in World War I. If opposition to war was not construed as a political right, but a crime against the state, political activity could be permitted without caveat.

The AAUP, one other professional organization, and seven major associations of higher education managers endorsed the Statement.[20] Although endorsement did not guarantee the good conduct of member institutions, the AAUP's cautious definition of academic freedom and the corresponding need to show cause for terminating a long standing or permanent appointment began to be recognized as a condition of academic employment with which managers would have to deal.

The 1925 Conference Statement was formulated under conditions of "normalcy" and did not withstand the onslaught of the depression. Systemic economic crisis produced intense ideological conflict. In many instances, political and economic elites reponsible for the governance of universities refused to tolerate their faculties' outspoken participation in activities overly critical of capitalism. The number of academic freedom cases on the AAUP docket piled up rapidly. The point at which professors most often alleged violations of academic freedom was in exercise of their civil

19. "Committee Reports: Report of Committee A," BAAUP 10 (February 1925):12.

20. "American Council on Education: Conference on Academic Freedom and Tenure," BAAUP 11 (February 1925):99–102.

liberties. The Association had approved almost without reservation academics' right to engage in political activity and was now asked to offer protection.

However, the AAUP was sometimes unwilling and often unable to intervene effectively. When radical groups demanded protection of professors' right to dissent and engaged in litigation as well as active protest to win reinstatement for ousted colleagues, they acted on the revolutionary potential of social knowledge and went further and faster than stipulated in the gentlemen's agreement established by the 1915 Declaration. And the AAUP was reluctant to move beyond its narrow definition of academic freedom.

Thus, when both the AAUP and the American Federation of Teachers (AFT) investigated the celebrated Jerome Davis case, they came to different conclusions. Davis, an associate professor employed for many years by the Yale Divinity School, was long on radical activity and short on publications. When he wrote an open letter to President Roosevelt in 1936 criticizing reform capitalism, he was dismissed. The AFT found Yale guilty of violating academic freedom, and demanded that Davis be reinstated while the AAUP found him professionally inadequate but tempered this judgment with a recommendation of a year's severance pay.[21]

Bound by its 1915 commitment to conservative management of knowledge and the molding of a moderate public opinion, the AAUP sidestepped the radical thrust of the 1930s. The 1925 accommodation with management further limited

its scope for vigorous, independent action. While managers might support freedom of inquiry within the university, they could not condone radical political activism without endangering material and political support for their institutions in a time of great economic uncertainty.

Throughout the 1930s the AAUP more often than not interpreted alleged violations of academic freedom as administrative quarrels or personality clashes, even though 21 states had legislated loyalty oaths aimed at eliminating radical educators and professors from public educational systems by 1935.[22] As a result of the AAUP's reluctance to take a militant stand, many professors turned to more aggressive organizations, such as the AFT or the American Civil Liberties Union (ACLU). These organizations were not concerned with personnel policy as a safeguard for academic freedom, but with substantive protection of civil liberties. The AFT, for example, mounted crusades to attract attention to the plights of W. G. Bergman, dismissed from Detroit Teachers College on charges of sedition based on his opposition to military training; J. C. Granbury, Texas Tech, dismissed for economic liberalism and pacifism; Leo Gallagher, Los Angeles law professor dismissed for defending political minorities; G. McLean, an economics professor in Memphis, who lost his job for serving as an advisory member of the Unemployed Citizens League; and Hugh De Lacy, a Washington English professor and AFT delegate to

21. Robert Iverson. *The Communists and the Schools* (New York: Harcourt Brace, 1959):166–169.

22. James Allan Belasco. "The AAUP: A Private Dispute Settlement Agency," *BAAUP*. For another view of the nature of academic dismissals see "Restrictions on Professors," in *The Gag on Teaching* (American Civil Liberties Union Pamphlet, April 1936): 34–37.

the Seattle Central Labor Union who was dismissed when he ran for political office.[23]

The AAUP had recognized the inadequacy of the 1925 Conference statement in the early 1930s, and started working with managerial groups on a more comprehensive agreement. The need for a new document became more urgent as the 1930s drew to a close and firings increased. Moreover, AAUP membership held steady while other organizations were growing rapidly.[24] If the AAUP were to continue to speak for the profession as a whole without abandoning its commitment to defense of academic freedom through uniform personnel policy, it would have to offer professors something tangible in the way of job security.

The 1940 Statement of Principles

The 1940 Statement drawn up conjointly with the Association of American Colleges is of critical importance since it still stands, subject to 1970 interpretations, as the AAUP's basic formulation of academic freedom and tenure. The 1940 statement in essence exchanges professors' civil liberties for tenure. And the profession, faced with organized repression in the form of the Ives Laws, the MacNaboe, Dies and Rapp-Courdet Investigating Committees, accepted the bargain.

With regard to "extra-mural utterances" made in the course of exercising the political rights of a citizen,

the professor no longer has the same latitude as other men and women. "His special position in the community imposes special obligations." While the professor should be "free from institutional censorship or discipline," he should nonetheless always keep in mind "that the public may judge his profession and his institution by his utterances. Hence he should at all times be accurate, should exercise appropriate restraint, should show respect for the opinions of others, and should make every effort to indicate that he is not an institutional spokesman."

In return, precise definition is given for the first time to the tenure process. After a probationary period of a maximum of seven years, professors, after review, should have permanent or continuous tenure of office that can be terminated only by "adequate cause." What adequate cause might be is not addressed, but the interpretation appended to the 1940 document specifically states that the exercise of professor's political rights as a citizen might legitimately be considered sufficient.[25]

Exactly how a professor may fail to meet his "special obligations" is not treated; indeed, it still remains subject to a variety of interpretations both inside and outside the Association. However, in 1940, the AAUP was no longer obligated to insist that professors be accorded the same rights as all citizens in a time of widespread social unrest. As a president of the AAUP, William Van Alstyne, has pointed out:

. . . the trade-off that the AAUP appeared to have accepted with the Association of American Colleges in 1940 (namely, to cultivate public con-

23. Compiled from the *American Teacher*, 1930–1940.

24. Jeanette A. Lester, "The American Federation of Teachers in Higher Education: A History of Union Organization of Faculty Members in Colleges and Universities" (Ph.D. diss., University of Toledo, 1968), Figure 1, Membership in AFT College Locals and the AAUP, 25.

25. "The 1940 Statement of Principles on Academic Freedom and Tenure," in *Academic Freedom and Tenure: A Handbook of the AAUP*, 33–39.

fidence in the profession by laying down a professionally taxing standard of institutional accountability for *all* utterances of a public character made by a member of the profession) is substantially more inhibiting of a faculty member's civil freedom of speech than any standard that govenment is constitutionally privileged to impose in respect to the personal political or social utterances of other kinds of public employees.[26]

Essentially, political activity was left to the discretion of individual professors. The AAUP did nothing to discourage it, indeed even worked to make a special exception for professors under the Hatch Act. However, the AAUP no longer had an obligation to defend professors engaged in such activity. The Association was relieved of the dilemma of antagonizing professorial factions on the one hand or university managers, trustees, and other representatives of vested interests controlling higher education's funding on the other. For example, when the Rapp-Courdet Committee began hearings in New York City in 1941 to investigate Communism in the schools, the AAUP was not forced to take a definitive position even though 69 faculty members in the City College system were called before the tribunal.[27]

The profession, then, traded its civil liberties for tenure. Academic freedom was permitted in the classroom, within the confines of the scholarly community, and in seemly extra-mural utterance in one's field of expertise, but did not extend to intercourse with the general public in the political arena. The commitment to manage knowledge conservatively was honored by protecting the majority of professors, those displaying conventional behavior and acceptable ideologies, while placing political deviants and activists in jeopardy.

Academic freedom and the quest for national security (1956)

During World War II, the AAUP made a deliberate effort not to let history repeat itself and was justly proud of the fact no emergency measures were taken. Indeed, only two cases involving conscientious objectors were brought to the formal attention of Committee A during the war years.[28] Communists and fellow-travelers did not present the problems they had in the 1930s, regardless of the Smith Act, so long as the U.S.S.R. remained an ally. The AAUP's confrontation with the conflicting claims of academic freedom and national security was delayed until after the war. Then the very success of science in the dramatic end to hostilities in the Pacific theater turned governmental and public attention to the university.

As World War II gave way to the Cold War, instances like the Lattimore and Oppenheimer cases made the university, as the home of scientists and intellectuals, a target for national security. The Un-American Activities Committee (HUAC) was made a permanent Committee of the House in 1945; Truman instituted the Federal Loyalty Program by executive order in 1947; the National Security Act was passed in 1950; numerous states began to con-

26. William Van Alstyne, "The Specific Theory of Academic Freedom and the General Issue of Civil Liberty," in *The Concept of Academic Freedom*, ed. Edmund L. Pincoffs (Austin: University of Texas Press, 1975), 81–82.

27. Iverson, *The Communists and the Schools*:215–216.

28. Edward C. Kirkland, "Academic Freedom and Tenure: Report of Committee A for 1945," *BAAUP* 32 (Spring 1946):6.

duct their own investigations into professors' pasts. Education became one of the major battlefields in the post-war struggle for control of domestic policy.[29] Professors who throughout World War II had planned for a new peace in a more democratic social order were among the first to fall in this ideological struggle that stifled even liberal critiques of capitalism. The AAUP, having traded civil liberties for tenure, had nothing left to give and was unable to protect the profession from persecution on grounds of political activity.

According to the AAUP's own calculations, there were at least 77 dismissals between 1949 and 1955. Ironically, tenure offered little security since its protection did not extend to the professor in his role as citizen outside the university. And almost all firings were the result of professors alleged participation in politics. Thus, in 1949, three tenured professors at the University of Washington were dismissed without severance pay, two for membership in the Communist party, one for refusal to testify; in 1950, at the University of California, 32 faculty members, more than half of them tenured, were dismissed for their refusal to take a Regent-imposed disclaimer oath in regard to past or present Party membership; in the New York City Municipal Colleges, 14 were dismissed in 1953 after refusing to testify at Congressional hearings, four more in 1954 and 1955 under the Feinberg Law. In addition to these 53 mass dismissals another 24 individuals were dismissed from an additional 20 institutions, in most cases for refusal to testify before a university, state or federal investigating committee.[30]

These dismissals are only a rough index of the degree to which academic freedom was curtailed. When professors were falsely accused, as was the case with Melvin Rader at the University of Washington, or mistakenly identified, as in another instance, and forced to spend thousands of dollars in legal fees as well as endless hours in proving perjury on the part of a witness or correcting a bureaucratic mistake, all professors felt themselves vulnerable.[31] As Lazarsfeld and Thielens have pointed out, the climate of repression significantly affected academics' willingness to treat controversial issues even in their own fields of expertise.[32]

In 1956, prodded by membership pressure and encouraged by recent judicial decisions, the Association issued a position paper. Presented as a reappraisal of the question of national security, this statement is a massive and pathetic equivocation. Basically, the document argues that a professor cannot be dismissed for past or present Communist Party membership, as long as it is demonstrated that these do not affect fitness to teach. Nor can he be compelled to testify. However, participation in educational subversion is evidence of unfitness, refusal to testify may be a strong indication of

29. Richard M. Freeland, *The Truman Doctrine and the Origins of McCarthyism: Foreign Policy, Domestic Politics and Internal Security, 1946–1948* (New York: Schocken).

30. Compiled from "Academic Freedom and Tenure in the Quest for National Security: Report of a Special Committee of the AAUP," in *The American Concept of Academic Freedom in Formation*, ed. W. P. Metzger (New York: Arno, 1977) irregular pagination:61–107.

31. Melvin Rader gives his account and others in *False Witness* (Seattle: University of Washington Press, 1979 edition).

32. See Paul L. Lazarsfeld and Wagner Thielens, Jr., *The Academic Mind: Social Scientists in Times of Crisis* (Glencoe: the Free Press, 1958).

such subversive activity and, if questioned by institutional authorities, the professor has a duty to disclose, even though this means loss of Fifth Amendment protection in inquiries outside the university.[33] Confined by the 1940 Statement, the AAUP had little scope for argument; what was needed was full protection of civil liberties, and this the Association could not give without abrogating its earlier document.

The courts moved faster than the AAUP. When they upheld the legality of the Fifth Amendment, Committee A had to issue a supplement to its 1956 document. The Association, however, was not as liberal as the courts. Its 1958 Supplement still insisted the institution had a right to information touching on a faculty member's fitness. As a strategy it was suggested that professors under institutional investigation offer off-the-record testimony to officials, and if this candid gesture was rejected, then the professor had fulfilled his obligation to his employer, and the institution was open to possible censure by the AAUP.[34]

In summary, the Association continued to put its faith in personnel policy that accommodated university managers and trustees while professors were forced publicly to recant ideological sins committed a decade or more before. However, uniform promotion and tenure policy protected those faculty members who stayed away from politics, and this was the lesson learned by the

profession. The vast majority of the professoriate kept their jobs and held their tongues.

1970 Interpretative Comments

The safeguards offered by the courts in the mid-1950s may have been a turning point in terms of the AAUP's role in defining and protecting academic freedom and tenure. The AAUP's failure to redefine academic freedom so as to include civil liberties marks the time when professors consistently began to use litigation to protect their employment while exercising their constitutional right to free speech.

The 1970 Interpretative Comments did little to reassert the Association's claim to speak for the profession as a whole. Although the Comments were formulated during the campus upheavals of the 1960s, and substantive revision of the 1940 Statement was expected, little was changed. Professors still have a "particular obligation" as representatives of the academy outside the university.[35] Even in the 1970s professors claims to civil liberties are not firm.

However, the AAUP still wields considerable force when it comes to defining tenure. The Courts recognize the Association as the custodian of "professional custom" and often turn to its precedents when ruling. Many colleges and universities have adopted the 1940 Statement as their personnel policy; thus the document becomes part of the formal contract between professors and university, governing litigation as well as day-to-day procedures. Unions too are

33. "Academic Freedom and Tenure in the Quest for National Security: [1956] report of a Special Committee," in Joughlin, ed., *Academic Freedom and Tenure: A Handbook:* 47–56.

34. "A [1958] Statement of the Committee on Academic Freedom and Tenure Supplementary to the 1956 Report," in Joughlin: 56–63.

35. "Academic Freedom and Tenure. 1940 Statement of Principles and [1970] Interpretative Comments," *AAUP Policy Documents and Reports* (Washington, D.C.: AAUP, 1977 edition):1–4.

informed by the AAUP definition of tenure, and offer no greater substantive protection of academic freedom than the Association.

The problem with all these definitions remains the same as in 1915. Tenure does not necessarily insure academic freedom, let alone the exercise of civil liberties. Although tenure does offer job security to senior faculty, even this is limited. Tenured professors can still be fired for incompetence, financial exigency, or failing to act in a manner that fulfills their "particular obligation" as faculty members. While the courts offer some protection, they have not established binding definitions of academic freedom. Since the concept has no constitutional status, professors must defend their civil liberties under the First Amendment, and tenure as property right under the Fourteenth. Despite the AAUP's long struggle, academic freedom is not a condition of employment in higher education.

Although we tell ourselves the day is past when wholesale attacks on academic freedom are possible, evidence argues the contrary. In the years 1965–1975, professors were fired on overtly political grounds at a rate unmatched since the height of the McCarthy era. As always, professors in the danger zone were political activists, often using their academic expertise to challenge dominant ideologies.

Among the more well know cases were George Murray, English instructor at San Francisco State and Black Panther "Minister of Education," suspended for allegedly advocating that minority students arm themselves for self-protection; Staughton Lynd, historian who travelled to North Vietnam in defiance of State Department orders in 1966, denied employment by the Board of

Governors of the State Colleges and Universities in Illinois because his journey went "beyond mere dissent;" Angela Davis, U.C.L.A. philosopher fired for her Communist Party membership; Michael Parenti, anti-war political science professor at the University of Vermont, denied renewal despite unanimous recommendations by department, dean, and university administration, on grounds of unbecoming "professional conduct" detrimental to the image of the university; Peter Bohmer, radical economics professor at San Francisco State, fired on charges of discriminating in his grading practices against conservative students even after being cleared of the charges in three separate investigations; Morris Starsky, activist philosophy professor at Arizona State, fired in connection with his anti-war stance despite support from two faculty committees and the university president.[36]

When professors combine intellectual work with outspoken political activism they are vulnerable. At that point trustees exercise their legal authority, often reversing the decisions of the collective faculty and university administrators by asserting their own definition of ideological orthodoxy and the limits of professors' civil liberties.

Dismissals on political grounds are, of course, the exception; they occur only in the relatively few instances when professors regularly and vehemently challenge the established order in a public arena. However, such dismissals are an index of societal concern about the beliefs, values, and ideologies of academics.

36. Robert Justin Goldstein, *Political Repression in Modern America, 1870 to the Present* (Cambridge, MA: Schenkman, 1978), 522–523.

These concerns are widely shared by the majority of the faculty and by university administrators who often use what power they have to screen out potentially troublesome colleagues through devices such as the tenure review process and budget cuts.

Indeed, the tenure review process, governed by senior faculty who have already proved to be responsible, respectful, and conscious of their particular obligations, is probably the major mechanism for insuring the continued conservative management of knowledge. Ideologically suspect and politically active young faculty are often denied permanent positions on grounds of professional inadequacy. In the late 1960s and early 1970s, the campus climate was such that these charges could not be lightly made. Junior faculty who thought their tenure decisions turned on their politics often asked for and received public hearings, as was the case with Frank Bataglia, Elaine Reuben and Joan Roberts at the University of Wisconsin. But as tenure slots become scarce and students apathetic, activist and junior faculty are more easily let go, often internalizing their senior colleagues verdict of professional inadequacy without serious question.

Current economic conditions also allow administrators wider scope in removing ideological deviants, activists and "difficult" faculty. The dissolution of the radical activist School of Criminal Justice at Berkeley on grounds of financial exigency is a case in point. At a time when economic uncertainty is increasing and administrators are routinely asked to turn in retrenchment plans, the importance of holding our jobs makes us less likely to speak out and identify ourselves as targets for budget cuts. These internal controls on academic freedom—tenure review and the budget—are pervasive, subtle, and not easily fought.

While tenure may not protect academic freedom, nor even guarantee job security, given the vulnerability of men and women prepared to voice or act on ideas at odds with the dominant culture, it may be necessary, if only to make dismissals more difficult. However, it is perhaps time to raise the question of how the profession can better protect academic freedom that guarantees civil liberties. Our inability to safeguard the rights we claim is painfully apparent. When economic instability is compounded by ideological conflict—as was the case in the Progressive era, the 1930s, and the period following World War Two—academic freedom has no real meaning. With academe in a steady state and the economy in an unsteady condition, we should remember our collective past and use our insight to guard against the future.

In Between: The Community College Teacher

By HOWARD B. LONDON

ABSTRACT: Viewing community college teachers as a distinct subculture of the larger professoriate, this article analyzes the consequences for these teachers of the extraordinarily rapid growth of two year institutions during the past two decades. Lines are drawn between the community colleges' status, the special mission of the community college, and the teachers' conceptions of their school, their work, and themselves. A large proportion of two year college teachers are seen as demoralized and uncomfortably isolated from the larger academic culture.

Howard B. London received his undergraduate degree from Bowdoin College and his M.A. and Ph.D. in sociology from Boston College. He teaches in the Department of Sociology, Tulane University, New Orleans, Louisiana. He has recently published The Culture of a Community College, *an ethnography based on one year of participant observation. In addition to his community college research, he is beginning a social history of the New Orleans schools from 1865 to 1975.*

OTHER THAN a conscript army, it is difficult to think of a work institution in our society with tens of thousands of frontline employees who have both aspired and trained to work elsewhere. The community college, however, is such an institution, as most of its full-time teachers have come from high school faculties, from graduate schools where they were preparing to become four year college or university professors or, to a lesser extent, from the professoriate itself.[1]

This unusual circumstance is in part a consequence of the extraordinary growth of community colleges. Between 1960 and 1977 the number of public community colleges more than tripled from 315 to 920,[2] enrollments increased more than ninefold from 392,000 to 3,901,000,[3] and the number of teachers quintupled from 40,000 to 200,000,[4] so that students in these schools now account for over one third of all undergraduates and their teachers for over one third of the academic profession. Yet, as community colleges grew, those who came to teach in them were often faced with unexpected problems concerning their work, roles, and self-conceptions. These difficulties, as they will be discussed here, include the career alteration indicated above, the teaching of poorly prepared students, and academic isolation. While not limited to community colleges, these problems are more pronounced in them, a matter of degree if not always of kind, and they help give community college teaching its flavor.

This is not to imply that all community college teachers confront the same problems in identical ways; there is always some variety and divergence in these matters. At a

1. Leland Medsker and Dale Tillery, *Breaking the Access Barriers: A Profile of the American Junior College* (New York: McGraw-Hill, 1971), p. 89. For more recent studies of faculty backgrounds in individual states see Doris Weddington, "Faculty Attitudes in Two Year Colleges," unpublished manuscript (Los Angeles, CA: Center for the Study of Community Colleges, 1976), p. 39–40.

2. Center for Educational Statistics, *Digest of Educational Statistics, 1979* (Washington, DC: USGPO, 1979), p. 101.

3. Department of Health, Education and Welfare, *Digest of Educational Statistics, 1975–76* (Washington, DC: USGPO, 1977), p. 86 and *Digest of Educational Statistics, 1979*, p. 88. The causes of community college expansion vary with one's view of society. Some sociologists see it as an inevitable response to new technologies channeling more people into occupations requiring increasingly complex skills. See, for example, Burton Clark, *Educating the Expert Society* (San Francisco: Chandler Publishing Company, 1962). Other sociologists claim that schools do not teach skills so much as they socialize people into status cultures, and the rising enrollments are a consequence of higher status groups raising educational requirements to protect their status cultures and the privileged positions that go with

them; to improve their own position in the social hierarchy in the face of this primarily social (and only secondarily technological) escalation, groups of lower socioeconomic status then demand increased access to more education, contributing further to the educational spiral. For a full statement of this view see Randall Collins, "Functional and Conflict Theories of Educational Stratification," *American Sociological Review* 36 (December 1971): 1002–1019. Neo-Marxists, to cite a third view, claim that the increasing number of new students is a result of an attempt by elite planning groups to train people for new blue and white collar proletarian positions commensurate with their social origins, thus insidiously helping to maintain an unjust status quo through the illusion of educational opportunity. This argument is advanced in Jerome Karabel, "Community Colleges and Social Stratification," *Harvard Educational Review* 42 (November 1972):521–562.

4. Arthur M. Cohen and Florence B. Brawer, *The Two Year College Instructor Today* (New York: Praeger Publishers, 1977), p. xi.

higher level of abstraction, however, widely shared problems of individual teachers become problems for the profession, and the common solutions a part of the profession's culture. This analysis, then, views community college teachers as a professional segment, that is, as a subculture of the professoriate whose members are confronted by distinct contingencies and who, therefore, share values, interests, and a sense of belonging together.[5] Because community colleges first appeared in the early part of this century it is not fully correct to say that this segment is newly born, but its recent growth spurt has been a gangling, awkward, adolescent one, complete with problems of self consciousness and identity.

RECRUITMENT AND THE STATUS OF THE COMMUNITY COLLEGE

Discovering who community college teachers are and from where they were recruited is difficult, for the career path is as yet uninstitutionalized. Although there are approximately 100 preparatory and in-service graduate programs expressly for community college instructors—most offering a masters degree, a few the still experimental Doctor of Arts—their enrollments are small, and it is doubtful that they have graduated more than five percent of all two year college faculty.[6] As of 1975,

only seven states required professional credentials, and their requirements are loose; in California, for example, a *"pro forma* credential is granted upon request to those with a master's degree (or equivalent) who are free of tuberculosis and Communism, and who can pay the $20.00 fee."[7]

Despite the lack of a formalized or bureaucratic course to be run, there are regularities in the career path. Various studies report that by the early 1970s, 65 to 80 percent of community college teachers had a masters as their professional degree, 14 to 27 percent had a bachelors as their highest degree, and only 3 to 10 percent had a doctorate.[8] Approximately 33 percent come directly from high school faculties versus one third of that—11 percent—from four year college faculties; about 25 percent come to the community college directly from graduate studies which, as discussed below, they may not have completed, compared with 5 percent who begin teaching after college graduation; the remaining 25 percent come from the trades, industry, business, and government administration.[9]

It is, of course, no accident that community colleges have recruited most from the educational layers between which they are sandwiched. Since their inception they have occupied, as David Riesman calls it, a twilight status between high schools on the one side and colleges and universities on the other. Drawing from each side helps

---

5. The concept of professional segment is from Rue Bucher and Anselm Strauss, "Professions in Process," *American Journal of Sociology* vol. 66 (January 1961):325–334.

6. Terry O'Banion, "Alternate Forms of Graduate Education for Community College Staff: A Descriptive Review," in *Graduate Education and Community Colleges: Cooperative Approaches to Community College Staff Development,* edited by S. V. Martorana, et al. (Washington, DC: National Board on Graduate Education, 1975), p. 48.

7. Charles C. Collins and Chester H. Case, "On Site, Programmatic Approach to Staff Development," in Martorana, "Graduate Education," p. 64.

8. Weddington, "Faculty Attitudes," pp. 39–41 and Cohen, "Two Year College Instructor," p. x.

9. Weddington, *ibid.*

solidify the historical and philosophic claim that community colleges are of, by, and for the local community at the same time that they are part of the larger world of higher learning.

This in-between status is also reflected in the traditional attempt of the community college to provide, or come close to providing, something for almost everyone. Indeed, the contemporary public two year college offers curricula in the liberal arts and several vocations, as well as programs in adult, continuing, remedial, general, and sometimes pre-professional education. Yet this hybrid quality makes it difficult for community college teachers to define their institution and their own roles.

TEACHERS' AMBIVALENCE AND THE MISSION OF THE COMMUNITY COLLEGE

There is considerable evidence that community college teachers are ambivalent about their setting and their work,[10] with perhaps none more significant than that about half of all instructors report that while satisfied with their current positions they would rather teach in a four year college or university.[11] Yet to conclude that community college teachers are frustrated college professors and that their ambivalence comes solely or even primarily from unmet career aspirations is, in many cases, too facile and even when true tells us nothing about how their

disappointments may be expressed or managed in the work culture. Such a conclusion also ignores the socialization of once reluctant teachers into the community college ethos and mission. Indeed, that so many have an eye on the four year college, whether as a far off wish or an immediate next step, is in part related to what has increasingly become the special province of community colleges—the teaching and counseling of "marginal" students.

Most of these "new students to higher education," as they are called by K. Patricia Cross, are white, urban, and working class.[12] More recently there has been an increase in the proportion of minority group students and of older students in search of new careers, occupational updating, cultural enrichment, hobbies, or in some cases, simple entertainment. Indeed, by 1977 the average age of community college students was 28.[13] Yet what distinguishes community college students more than any other measurable variable—including race, socioeconomic status and age—are low test scores: they typically score in the lowest third on conventional tests of academic ability.[14] Test results, of course, are not sacrosanct and there are community colleges, most notably those in California, which have long been closely integrated with the state's college and university system, where the academic abilities of students are high. There is also a small but growing number of students who already have baccalaureates from liberal

10. Arthur M. Cohen and Florence B. Brawer, *Confronting Identity: The Community College Instructor* (Englewood-Cliffs, NJ: Prentice Hall, 1972), p. 12.

11. Cohen and Brawer, *The Two Year College Instructor Today*, p. xi, pp. 80–82. A figure of 44 percent is reported in Leland Medsker and Dale Tilley, "Breaking the Barriers," p. 11.

12. K. Patricia Cross, *Beyond the Open Door: New Students to Higher Education* (San Francisco: Jossey-Bass, 1971), pp. 13–16.

13. *Digest of Educational Statistics, 1979*, p. 108.

14. Cross, "Beyond the Open Door," pp. 12–13.

arts colleges but have been unable to land a job and now seek vocational training. Although there may be a broad range of talent in every community college, the empirical and impressionistic literature is replete with accounts of two year college students for whom education has thus far failed, students whose performance in the three R's is still on an elementary level.[15]

While every school has students who are unsure of themselves in these or other ways; most community colleges now claim a special expertise in and commitment to helping them in large numbers, and it is this contribution more than any other which helps distinguish community college teachers from the larger professoriate. In the past two decades there has been a prodigious increase in the number of new programs, pedagogies, and instructional technologies for high risk and other special problem students. Because of this emphasis on teaching, community college instructors spend one and a half to two times as many hours in the classroom as their contemporaries in four year institutions;[16]

they also bring counseling into the classroom more frequently in the form of credit granting "self-awareness workshops," "educational development seminars" or other such courses designed to help motivate students and assist them in making educational, occupational, social, and personal decisions.[17]

The ways in which this mission and the work that goes with it are associated with teachers' ambivalence or frustration are complex, and it is difficult to be exact about them. It is possible, however, to point to at least three general connections. First, despite the relatively unique mission and a growing body of knowledge to carry it out, two year faculty do not have the larger voice in determining academic or public policy with respect to their services. The increased but still not overwhelming influence of the professoriate, has not yet reached the same proportions in the community college.[18] Thus, among community college teachers there is a deep concern about their professionalism and relative powerlessness; as Roger Garrison reported, "They are being asked to implement a policy [they] had no part in formulating: namely, the 'open-door' or 'after - high - school - education - for - everyone - who - wants - it' policy."[19] This is especially the case for beginning teachers who withdraw from graduate school for family, financial

---

15. Howard B. London, *The Culture of a Community College* (New York: Praeger, 1978). O'Banion claims that 70–75 percent of all students in two year institutions may be categorized as having special needs, and have been or should be assigned to some type of remedial or developmental program. See Terry O'Banion, *Teachers for Tomorrow: Staff Development in the Community-Junior College* (Tuscon, Arizona, University of Arizona Press, 1972), p. 93. Gleazer reports that "Of nearly 300,000 people who took one or more courses in North Carolina community colleges and technical institutions in 1970, 47.5 percent enrolled in work at the elementary or secondary level." See E. Gleazer, *Project Focus: A Forecast Study of Community Colleges*, (New York: McGraw-Hill, 1973), p. 14.

16. A. E. Bayer, "Teaching Faculty in Academe: 1972–73" *ACE Research Reports*, No. 8, (Washington, DC: American Council on Education), p. 26.

17. Descriptions of such counseling courses are detailed in London, *Culture of a Community College*, pp. 130–135 and in Steven Zwerling, *Second Best: The Crisis of the Community College* (New York: McGraw Hill, 1976), pp. 186–194.

18. Christopher Jencks and David Riesman, *The Academic Revolution* (Garden City, NY: Doubleday, 1968).

19. Roger Garrison, *Junior College Faculty —Issues and Problems: A Preliminary National Appraisal* (Washington, DC: American Association of Junior Colleges, 1967), p. 15.

or academic reasons and, instead of the anticipated four year college or university position, unexpectedly and rather quickly find themselves in the community college having little if any familiarity with its ethos or reality.[20]

Second, many faculty question the open-door philosophy and all that they are asked to do in its name. David Bushnell, for example, reports that an "analysis of faculty support for selected goals of the two year colleges . . . demonstrates that many faculty members do not fully endorse the concept of the open-door."[21] Despite new teaching techniques, especially individualized learning, he believes their position is understandable "when one realizes that the responsibility for educating a mixture of low-achieving or under-achieving students and more able students falls squarely on the shoulders of the faculty."[22] Indeed, individualized learning itself has been found to threaten teachers' roles as they come to see themselves as, in the parlance of the trade, "managers of a learning environment rather than as directors of learning."[23] It is not surprising, then, that while attitude surveys show widespread belief in individualized education as one of the best ways to meet the challenges of the open-door, there are repeated observational findings that instructors resist this pedagogy, sometimes to the extent of sabotaging their own materials.[24]

Third, even faculty who in practice accept the open-door policy have difficulty with its day to day exigencies. Special types of students, be they exceptionally bright or otherwise, have lasting effects on teachers, and the consequences for those who teach "marginal," "low ability," "unmotivated" or other similarly labeled students have recently been much investigated.

Cohen and Brawer, for example, report that instructors of remedial or low ability classes often feel isolated and, unable to maintain their identification with higher education, come to resent their students, the school, and sometimes themselves.[25] Similarly, Roueche and Kirk found that the "negative feelings of instructors were quickly communicated to [low ability] students to the extent that 'high risk' students prematurely left the college in great numbers."[26] So too, William Moore points to the seeming paradox that in the very institution which claims a special interest in the marginal student, "few teachers can, or want to, teach him at the college level, even fewer understand him; many reject him academically and socially. . . ."[27] Finally, David Riesman suggests that "a certain amount of poor communication and distorted feedback may be necessary if faculty are to maintain their morale in the face of an enervating environment of mediocrity."[28]

20. London, *Culture of a Community College,* pp. 29–59.

21. David S. Bushnell, *Organizing For Change: New Priorities for Community Colleges* (New York: McGraw Hill, 1973), p. 39.

22. *Ibid.*

23. Weddington, "Faculty Attitudes," p. 29.

24. R. O. Carlson, *Adoption of Educational Innovations* (Eugene, OR: The Center for the

Advanced Study of Educational Administration, 1965), p. 78.

25. Cohen and Brawer, *Confronting Identity,* p. 113.

26. John Roueche and Wade R. Kirk, *Catching Up: Remedial Education,* (San Francisco: Jossey-Bass, 1973), p. 23.

27. William Moore, Jr. *Against the Odds: The High Risk Student in the Community College,* (San Francisco: Jossey-Bass, 1970), p. 84.

28. In Alden E. Dunham, *Colleges of the*

As damning as these observations may appear when taken out of context, none are simply accusations of elitism. In each case the authors attempt to explain the fundamentally human efforts by teachers to cushion themselves against the fears of self-doubt in situations for which, in the face of rapid educational expansion, they were unprepared. Put differently, one of the general findings of the sociology of occupations is that people define themselves in large measure through their work; academics usually do this through notions of the league their institutions play in as well as through evaluations of their students. This is not to say that there is no snobbery in the ranks of community college teachers: in the community college about two-thirds of those who graduate do so with a vocational degree, and the literature does contain complaints by and about teachers who look askance at this "merely" vocational preparation of students for work with low occupational ceilings.[29] The Marxian critique, itself not always devoid of condescension but of a radical kind, attacks vocational education from a different direction, claiming that the preparation of working class students for working class occupations buttresses an unfair social order.

There is something of the self-fullfilling prophecy in all of this. Throughout their education students' intelligence is evaluated on the basis of criteria other than native ability. With striking regularity researchers have found that spurious statements about prior and expected academic performance, as well as assessments of social characteristics, physical characteristics, styles of language, and tastes in clothing all contribute to teachers' labeling of students which in turn influences the students' self-conceptions.[30] Thus, to a considerable degree teachers unintentionally help students become the kinds of people they find so difficult, thereby reinforcing the alleged validity of the initial categorizations even though these may have had little or nothing to do with the capacity to learn. It is ironic that having bureaucratized education ostensibly to make it more rational and efficient, schools also facilitate the conditions which produce failure.

In regard to labeling, community college teachers are like teachers elsewhere: if they feel negatively about working with poorly prepared students, they make judgements about the causes of their academic deficiencies. Community college instructors generally use one of three sets of judgements or perspectives —the conservative, liberal or radical.[31] Each perspective provides the faculty member both with an explanation for student performance, and a general guide as to how students should be approached.

The conservative perspective, for

Forgotten Americans, (New York: McGraw Hill, 1969), p. 172.

29. See Moore, Against the Odds, pp. 63–84 for a vivid example of a president's bemoaning the elitism of many teachers. For a summary statement of the relationship between a school's "league" and faculty self-appraisals, see Everett C. Hughes, "Non-Economic Aspects of Academic Morale," in Seymour E. Harris, ed., Higher Education in the United States, (Cambridge, MA: Harvard University Press, 1960), pp. 118–121.

30. An excellent summary of this research is Ray Rist, "On Understanding the Processes of Schooling: The Contributions of Labeling Theory," in Jerome Karabel and A. H. Halsey, eds., Power and Ideology in Education (New York: Oxford University Press, 1977), pp. 292–305.

31. London, Culture of a Community College, pp. 119–139.

example, is that students' academic problems are mostly attributable to weaknesses in character or mind, and that social background and other contextual factors are of little importance. From this perspective, individuals are held solely responsible for their fates, and the mass of students are to rise or fall on their virtue and merit—by which is meant diligence, self-discipline, and intelligence—without any extraordinary teacher intervention. Conservative teachers, then, tend to concentrate more on their successful students which, though it violates the ideology of focusing on the untalented and disadvantaged, provides these faculty with their chief source of professional satisfaction. It remains to be seen whether conservative teachers can effectively maintain this strategy in the face of an increased emphasis on retention and a diminished growth rate in community college enrollments.

The liberal perspective is that the student problem is in actuality a social problem; citing poor inner-city high schools, the lower value placed on education, and the absence of a college tradition in working class families, liberal teachers claim that the community college has the power and duty to intervene in the lives of students to compensate for social injustices. Specifically, this is done by creative pedagogies, innovative curricula, extensive counseling, and lessening the difficulty of course work while simultaneously inflating grades. The rationale for these last measures is that without at least a temporary period of moderation during which students might gain confidence in themselves, the school is less likely to help them cope or succeed within the present social order. While these teachers, like their conservative col-

leagues, receive a sense of professional identity and pride from cultivating promising students, they also report that working with less able students and seeing them progress, even slightly, provides different but still important rewards.

Like the liberal teachers, radical faculty also locate the source of students' difficulties in the social system, and they too lower course requirements and inflate grades. They wish to do more, however, than aid society's "victims;" in addition to the liberal psychological and individualistic approaches, they attempt to sensitize students to the causes and effects of various social and political problems. By politicizing students they hope to emancipate them so that they might become new agents of social change.

While only empirically verified in one case study, the occupational ambivalence and frustration seem for many teachers to stem from the inability of whichever strategy they adopt to resolve or minimize sufficiently the difficulties of community college teaching.[32] For example, a conservative teacher admitted that her hard line approach returned too few dividends:

I suppose that in an ideal situation I would prefer being in an environment where it was more intellectually exciting. I don't get the feeling I must reach toward them [the students]. . . . I enjoy the good students, but I can't tell you I get great satisfaction from either. There aren't very many . . . good students. . . . To that extent, yes, everyday when I come in here I have to close my eyes a bit.[33]

Among the liberal teachers were some who doubted that the school could effectively intervene in the lives of students, and consequently

32. *Ibid.*, pp. 140–145.
33. *Ibid.*, p. 140.

they found it difficult to infuse their work with meaning. Reported one such teacher:

One perceives even within the community college itself that there's not as much of a premium placed on developing a student's intellectual capacity . . . so that he *really does grow.* . . . There are times when I've been very unhappy about it. I can't talk about this with my colleagues because I think they're more committed to the community college than I can be. I have spoken about this to the president because I have had thoughts about leaving.[34]

Finally, those of the radical teachers who were disenchanted doubted both the possibility and the morality of converting their students into agents of social change. Commented one:

In fact, what I'm doing could be more harmful than anything else. I made certain political assumptions about what would be the best living situations for all of us in terms of society changing, and those assumptions are very alien to my students. . . . I can't tell you how much [this bothers her] when I think I'm not accomplishing what I want to accomplish, or if I think that I'm banging my head against a stone wall, or if I think I'm sick of not getting any gratification from this.[35]

For all three kinds of teachers, then, successes with students — whether successes be conservatively, liberally, or radically defined — can be sufficiently insubstantial that continued hard effort only brings them further past the point of diminishing returns. In such cases, as the teachers themselves make evident, there is a sense of futility and demoralization.

Most prone to this dilemma are new liberal arts faculty who expected to become college or uni-

versity professors but had to withdraw from their doctoral studies due to personal, academic, family or economic circumstances. Their career switch is troubling because most have internalized the university values of disinterested inquiry, scholarship, research, and the worth and efficacy of working with ideas. With the exception of the last, these activities are not institutionalized in the community college, often creating gaps between these teachers' anticipated work, their realized work and their self-conceptions. Despite this, some are successfully socialized into the community college ethos and make the necessary revisions of what they can do and want to do. Others quite clearly do not make the transition, especially if there is too great a fracture between expectations and reality in regard to the level of intellectual inquiry they experience in the community college.[36]

The least demoralized are the vocational instructors who prepare students to enter the occupations in which they themselves once worked. The most difficult aspects of their career change are the strains in changing work settings and breaking relations with old colleagues while establishing relations with new ones; but the new distance from their previous work is subjectively viewed as upward mobility. Furthermore, vocational teachers are more likely to report an affinity for their students as a result of the similarity in their socioeconomic backgrounds.[37]

Some words of caution are necessary to put these findings into con-

34. *Ibid.*, p. 142.
35. *Ibid.*, pp. 144–145.

36. *Ibid.*, pp. 38–46 and p. 175. See also Cohen and Brawer, *Confronting Identity*, p. 113.
37. London, *Culture of a Community College*, pp. 145–149.

text. Not all community college instructors teach "marginal," "high risk," or "special problem" students, but most do have students—frequently a majority of them—who cannot meet or will not stand for demands for great effort. Yet, there are teachers who demand and get high quality work because of their special talents and willingness to work imaginatively with students. Others carry on in rather unremarkable ways but find the successes of teaching, however large or small deeply satisfying. It is always difficult to say precisely what proportion of teachers these are at any level of education or at what point, if ever, their satisfactions may be superceded by frustrations. But the question of morale is important not only for reasons of school administration or the education of students, but also because in this new and changing profession of community college teaching it is a barometer of the faculty's acceptance of their purpose; and the appearance of "new students" is recent enough that while some teachers are committed to them, others are still troubled and uncertain about what to make of their schools, their work, and themselves.

THE DILEMMA OF ACADEMIC ISOLATION

While the mission of the community college helps define the profession, it has also removed individual teachers from the mainstreams of their academic disciplines. Community college teachers are, for example, less likely to publish than their counterparts in four year institutions; an American Council on Education survey in 1972–1973 found that only 13 percent of the former published in the previous two years compared to 43 percent

of the latter.[38] Furthermore, when two year college faculty do publish it is more likely to be in either a journal devoted primarily to problems of community college teaching, for example, *Community College Social Science Quarterly*, or in "trade" publications which specialize in reporting on innovative programs or the opinions of teachers and administrators on professional or institutional rather than scholarly matters.

Community college teachers are also less likely than four year professors to read scholarly journals and to attend meetings of discipline related associations.[39] Distance from their discipline is further increased by a continued reluctance to hire new Ph.D.'s, especially if they are seen as products of sterile, straightjacketing graduate departments who are more interested in esoteric research than in teaching high risk students. Hiring the best teacher regardless of degree is, therefore, preferred by most department chairpersons, and while this of course admits some Ph.D.'s, their higher salary ranges contributes further to limiting their number to the current approximately 10 percent.[40]

Academic isolation, particularly in the smaller schools, is also caused by faculty having to teach two or three subject areas or, if teaching in only one area, having no colleagues in the same discipline; in either case there is a tendency to lose contact with one's original field of study. Never having the opportunity to teach courses beyond the freshmen and sophomore levels also makes keeping up in one's field

38. A. E. Bayer, *Teaching Faculty in Academe*, p. 26.
39. Cohen and Brawer, *The Two Year College Instructor*, pp. 109–118.
40. *Ibid.*, pp. 75, 137.

less urgent. Furthermore, in many community colleges the liberal arts faculty teach their subjects to vocational students—for example, teaching a social science course to medical technology majors—and while important in its own right, it does not call for familiarity with advanced or new knowledge, and in fact may be so elementary it will in time have an enervating effect.[41]

Community college teachers are also frequently snubbed by academic associations: in the field of sociology, for example, community college teachers who attend regional and national meetings perenially complain that they are treated as inferiors or, even worse, that they are ignored. While this state of affairs is changing, most major professional associations cannot be accused of attending to the needs of their members who teach in two year colleges.

The isolation of the community college segment also reflects the higher cultural value placed on the production of new knowledge than on the diffusion of what is already known. The former always carries with it a higher status—be it the creation of new knowledge in the physical or social sciences, law or theology—because it helps define the nature of nature, of human nature, or of supernature. The closer a profession is to this defining function the greater its control over services and clients and the greater its prestige.[42] The further an academic segment is separated from this function the more likely its members can be made to feel removed from higher education, however important their teaching may be for their students. Community college teachers, too, are susceptible to seeing themselves as "less than" rather than the "different than" that the profession's ideology puts forth.

The most unfortunate aspect of this is what David Riesman calls a new provincialism, where unionization or students' evaluations are sometimes used by faculty "to protect themselves from the need for scholarly visibility." The new provincialism, then, is one "of captivity by one's student disciples, charismatically courted as the road not only to retention but to feelings of worth."[43] Riesman's comment is on the four year college and university, but as Cohen and Brawer comment in the conclusion of their survey of humanities teachers in two year colleges, if this phenomenon has been seen in the university

where there has been a tradition of scholarship and cosmopolitanism, think how much more it is accentuated in the two year college whose roots are in the local community, where academic disciplinary affiliation has always been weak.[44]

While all professions have an internal division of labor between the more theoretical and the more practical, the community college segment has so far been less than ingenious in protecting itself from charges, often from within, of failing to be sufficiently academic. In part this is a result of a realistic appraisal by community college teachers and

41. London, *Culture of a Community College*, pp. 115–119. For a classic statement on what the title makes evident, see Willard, Waller, "What Teaching Does To Teachers," in *The Sociology of Teaching* (New York: John Wiley 1932), pp. 375–409.

42. Everett Hughes, "Professions," *Daedalus*, vol. 92, no. 4 (Fall 1963):656–657.

43. David Riesman, "Thoughts on the Graduate Experience," *Change* (April 1976): 12.

44. Cohen and Brawer, *The Two Year College Instructor*, p. 102.

administrators that its clientele would not respond well to an excessively academic approach. In this regard, there have been many ingenious programs and individual strategies incorporating the academic with the vocational, or which preserve or sometimes bring alive the academic without sacrificing content. However, to the extent that there is no commonly agreed upon formula on how and to what degree to mix the special purposes of community colleges with the world of higher learning, many of those who teach in two year institutions will continue to feel uncomfortably alone and in-between. At this period in higher education, such feelings seem to come with the territory.

Faculty Unionism: The First Ten Years

By JOSEPH W. GARBARINO

ABSTRACT: The record of faculty collective bargaining in four year colleges and universities for the past decade shows that about one-eighth of all institutions have been organized. The proportion rises to about 30 percent in public institutions. Unionism is highly concentrated in public institutions, in the 22 jurisdictions where state bargaining laws have been in effect for a substantial period—only about 27 institutions remain unorganized in these states. Growth has been slowing in recent years and there is little to indicate a significant increase in the future unless the public employee bargaining movement resumes its growth and additional states enact supportive laws. While the number of elections has been declining, the percentage of rejections of unionism has been rising in public institutions and falling in private institutions in recent years. Faculty unionism appears to have increased centralization in decisionmaking, bureaucratization of administration at all levels, led to more open personnel processes, and introduced some elements of an appeal system while having inconclusive effects on compensation.

Joseph W. Garbarino is Professor of Business Administration and Director of the Institute of Business and Economic Research at the University of California, Berkeley. He has been director of the Faculty Unionism Project, supported by the Carnegie Foundation and the Carnegie Commission on Higher Education. He is the author of Faculty Bargaining, Change and Conflict, *and a contributor to several books on unionism in higher education.*

Research assistance in data collection was provided by John Lawler and, in earlier years, Bill Aussicker and Nancy O'Connell. The Carnegie Foundation provided financial support.

A S THE FIRST decade of faculty collective bargaining in the nation's four year colleges and universities draws to a close, the movement has lost some of the momentum built up in the first half of the 1970s. Although the United States Merchant Marine Academy was organized in 1966 and a number of smaller institutions also elected bargaining representatives in 1969, it was the formal organization of the City University of New York (CUNY) in late 1969 that brought faculty unionism to national attention and marked the effective beginning of the movement. The CUNY elections dominated the early phase because they produced what eventually became a single bargaining unit of 15,000–16,000 faculty and staff, located in the nation's largest city and the center of the public sector unionism movement. In addition, the publicity accorded the contract brought CUNY's salary scale to general attention and, rightly or wrongly, the then lofty maximum salary of $31,275 was associated with the fact of unionization.

Since 1969 about 200 additional four year institutions of higher education have chosen bargaining representatives and at the end of 1979 almost 86,000 faculty or staff were represented by these unions. In this paper the record of this decade of growth will be reviewed and an attempt will be made to assess the current status and future prospects of faculty unionism.[1]

PATTERNS OF ORGANIZATION

As Table 1 indicates, the rate of growth of organization has slowed in the past three years at least as measured by the numbers of represented faculty added to the total. The number of institutions choosing agents held up in 1978, but in none of the past three years has the number of organized faculty been as large as it was in seven of the eight previous years.

The most obvious point made by Table 1 is that faculty unionism is concentrated in public institutions. Almost 12 percent of all four year institutions were organized in 1979, but among public institutions 29 percent were organized while the figure for private institutions was about 5 percent. Put differently, although private institutions outnumber public institutions three to one, private institutions make up only about one in four of the organized. If the number of faculty and staff represented is compared, private institutions account for just over one in every ten persons. The declining trend in organization noted in the last three years can be observed in both sectors, but is somewhat more precipitous among public institutions.

Because the difference in the prevalence of organization is so striking, the two sectors will be analyzed separately with most attention devoted to the public sector.

Public institutions

The record clearly demonstrates that the most important single predictor of the level and location of organization in the public sector is the existence of a state law that supports the right of faculty to organize. Table 2 presents the pattern of organization by state. It includes all states with any union organization if this is defined as the formal recognition of an organization as the exclusive bargaining agent for most of the faculty of the institution.

1. Data in this paper supersede earlier data published at various times by the Faculty Union Project.

TABLE 1

UNIONIZED FOUR-YEAR INSTITUTIONS, 1966–1979[a]

	TOTAL		PUBLIC		PRIVATE	
YEAR	INSTITUTIONS	PERSONS	INSTITUTIONS	PERSONS	INSTITUTIONS	PERSONS
1966	1	200	1	200	0	0
1967	1	90	0	0	1	90
1968	0	0	0	0	0	0
1969	24	18369	23	18299	1	70
1970	15	5626	12	4686	3	940
1971	45	19994	41	18694	4	1300
1972	16	7895	11	6689	5	1206
1973	20	4794	7	2895	13	1899
1974	11	3328	4	2380	7	948
1975	29	6670	15	4602	14	2068
1976	27	12860	23	12414	4[b]	446[b]
1977	10	1197	6	810	4	387
1978	21	4138	17	3515	4[b]	623[b]
1979[a]	3	398	0	0	3	398
Totals	223	85559	160	75184	63	10375

[a] To 9/30/79.
[b] Net of one decertification each year.
An "institution" is essentially a campus with a president or chancellor or the equivalent as its chief executive officer. This is equivalent to the definition used in *Education Directory, Colleges and Universities*, 1977–78, National Center for Education Statistics, USG PO, 1978, except that system headquarters are not included.
Data on "persons" represented are collected by questionnaire, from newspaper reports, and election reports. Community colleges in comprehensive systems have been excluded.
Six unionized law schools and one medical school in institutions in which no other faculty are organized were excluded.

TABLE 2

BARGAINING STATUS OF PUBLIC INSTITUTIONS, 1979[a]

	INSTITUTIONS	
	ORGANIZED	UNORGANIZED
States with Laws and 100% Organization		
Connecticut (5), Delaware (2), Florida (9), Hawaii (2), Maine (7), Massachusetts (15), New Jersey (13), New York (37), Rhode Island (2), South Dakota (7), D.C. (3)	102	0
States with Laws: Less than 100% Organization		
Alaska (0–2), California (0–29), Iowa (1–2), Kansas (1–5), Michigan (9–3), Minnesota (7–1), Montana (4–1), Nebraska (4–3), New Hampshire (1–2), Oregon (3–5), Pennsylvania (16–2), Vermont (3–1)	49	56
Excluding California	(49)	(27)
States without Laws with Organization		
Ohio (3–9), Illinois (5–7), Maryland (1–9)	9	25

SOURCES: Number of institutions from *Education Directory* op. cit. Four "state related" institutions in Pennsylvania are classified as public institutions. The legislation status of each state is taken from Doris Ross, *Cuebook: State Education Bargaining Laws*, (Denver, Colorado: Education Commission of the States, 1978). Some laws differ in the degree of support for organization provided and a few require only "meet and confer" sessions but all are included.
[a] As of 9/30/79.

TABLE 3

ELECTIONS AND REJECTIONS[a] BY CONTROL

	TOTAL	1966–70	1971	1972	1973	1974	1975	1976	1977	1978	1979[b]
All Elections	198	18	14	23	29	19	36	26	15	15	3
Rejections[a]	70	0	5	8	11	8	13	13	7	5	0
Public	22	0	1	1	1	2	3	7	5	2	0
Private	48	0	4	7	10	6	10	6	2	3	0
Percent Re-jections											
Total	35	0	36	35	38	42	36	50	57	33	0
Public	26	0	17	10	17	33	25	47	56	29	0
Private	42	0	50	54	45	46	42	55	33	38	0

[a] Rejections include a small number of cases in which the vote was against collective bargaining per se and two decertifications.

"Percent rejections" means the percentage of all elections in that category in which unionism was rejected. Elections in which an existing agent was retained are excluded.

[b] As of 9/30/79.

As of 1970, 22 states and the District of Columbia had bargaining laws concerning four year faculty. In one of these states, California, the law became effective only on July 1, 1979. There are therefore 22 jurisdictions that have had a law in effect long enough for organization to develop. Except for California, no state has passed a law covering four year faculty since 1975.

The importance of the legal environment as shown by Table 2 is remarkable. In the 23 jurisdictions with laws 85 percent of all public institutions are organized. In 11 of the 23, all public institutions are organized. In Vermont, where the University of Vermont is the only unorganized institution, it appears that it is specifically excluded from coverage while the state colleges are included. Perhaps the greatest significance of this situation is that it means that, excluding California which has 29 public institutions subject to its new law, there are only 27 public institutions in the states with applicable legislation that were not organized as of 1979. The high degree of organization is certainly one reason for the falling off in the rate of organization in recent years.

The lower section of Table 2 shows the status of bargaining in the 29 states without a supportive law. The only states without laws in which a significant amount of organization has occurred are Ohio and Illinois where 3 and 5 institutions have been unionized respectively. In Maryland one state college has been organized; only in these three states has organization occurred in the absence of a law.

It can be argued that the close correspondence between legislation and organization is artificial in that it is created by the definition of unionization that has been adopted. The key element in this definition is the formal recognition of an exclusive agent. Yet it is true that a good deal of bargaining goes on between administrations and one or more faculty organizations that do not have exclusive bargaining status. Such relationships undoubtedly exist in many institutions, but it would be impossible to devise a technique to identify at what point, if any, such an institution would be said to be unionized. In many institutions, committees of the academic senates regularly meet with administrators and discuss salary policy, but neither party to the discussions would regard the institution as unionized. Certainly a form of bargaining existed in CUNY when the Legislative Conference met with administrators in the years before 1969 and at Rutgers when the local American Association of University Professors (AAUP) salary committees met with the administration prior to 1970, but all parties would undoubtedly agree that a dramatic qualitative change occurred when the organizations acquired formal status as exclusive bargaining agents under the law.

The low level of formal recognition and organization in nonlaw states suggests that while it is possible for a determined organization to secure explicit bargaining status without the imposition of a legal requirement for the administration to bargain, it is difficult and unlikely to spread rapidly.

Further large scale organizing activity appears to depend on the passage of supportive legislation in states currently without laws. However, faculty members have usually played a minor part in the general upsurge in public employee bargaining during the last two decades. There are a few states with laws supporting bargaining for public employees in general that exclude faculty in four year institutions from coverage. The extension of coverage to faculty has been an issue for years in at least Wisconsin and Washington, and it is possible that new territory may be opened by new legislation. While the passage of a national law that gave all state and local government employees the right to organize would open the possibility of new and large scale organizing in unorganized four year institutions, the chance for such a law has faded as general support for public employee bargaining has apparently declined. In view of the lack of organization in states without laws, any substantial expansion of bargaining in the public sector depends on a revival of growth in public employee unionism in general.

Who organizes?

Because of the high degree of organization in the 23 jurisdictions with collective bargaining laws covering faculty, and the dearth of organization in the states without laws, it might seem to be of limited value to raise the questions of whether institutions with certain characteristics are more likely to organize than others. However, if the likelihood of organization is interpreted to mean which institutions within states with supportive legislation are likely to organize first, then a clear cut pattern can be detected on which there is a general consensus among researchers. The emerging universities—which typically means former teacher's colleges converted to liberal arts colleges or university status —usually are the first to unionize and push for collective bargaining.

The pattern of organization has varied. A single institution may take the lead as at Central Michigan or Southeastern Massachusetts Universities. The catalyst typically is a conflict between a president and his faculty. When the colleges are organized into a single system, the issues are likely to be less personal and more bureaucratic, relating to changes in the structure and function of the institutions and their impact on the faculties. In the states with comprehensive systems including all levels of higher education, the issues are similar to those in the systems of state colleges, since the principal support for organization has come from the second tier colleges. Single units of major universities are the least likely to organize.[2]

Who are the unorganized?

A great deal of analysis of the organized sector has been carried out so that it may be fruitful to concentrate on the 27 institutions that have remained unorganized in the 23 jurisdictions that have bargaining laws.

If the concept of a traditional state university is loosely defined as a long established public institution which has offered a wide range of degree programs for most of the post-World War II period (Iowa, Iowa State, Michigan, Michigan State), then 18 of the 27 unorganized institutions are traditional universities. Two more are health centers that are now classed as separate institutions but were formerly part of the traditional university in their respective states. Only 7 of the 27 unorganized institutions are state colleges, all of them single unit institutions.

Among the ten states in which all the traditional universities are organized, in 6 of the 10 the traditional universities were organized as part of a large multiinstitutional bargaining unit.[3] The only instances in which traditional state universities voted for unionization as single units are the universities in Con-

necticut, Rhode Island, Delaware and New Jersey (Rutgers).[4] As would be expected, all 9 of the public institutions that have been organized in the states without a bargaining law are state colleges, with the possible exception of the University of Cincinnati.

In short, the institutions remaining unorganized in those states where some organization has occurred, are the more prestigious, well established universities plus a small number of the newer state colleges.

This discussion leads to a consideration of the relation between institutional quality and organization. There has been considerable published material suggesting that there is an inverse relationship between some measure of quality and union organization.[5] Quality is an amorphous concept that is difficult to quantify over any significant range of institutions, although the extremes of the range can be distinguished quite readily.

For example, the Association of American Universities (AAU) is a group of some 50 institutions which are often described as major research universities. Although the inclusion or exclusion of particular institutions could be questioned, there is no doubt but that these represent a large majority of the quality universities in some sense.[6]

---

2. For some empirical analysis of this topic, see J. W. Garbarino, *Faculty Bargaining, Change and Conflict* (New York: McGraw Hill, 1975), Chapt. 3.

3. Massachusetts could be considered an exception; there are only two institutions in the University of Massachusetts' bargaining unit.

4. At the time of unionization, Rutgers was classed as a single multicampus institution. It, however, now is a multi-institutional system.

5. See Garbarino, *Faculty Bargaining*, pp. 73–78; E. C. Ladd and S. M. Lipset, *Professors, Unions and American Higher Education* (Berkeley: Carnegie Commission on Higher Education, 1973), pp. 48–57.

6. But note that by definition this excludes the whole set of prestigious colleges that probably provide some of the highest quality undergraduate education in the U.S.

Twenty-four of the members of the AAU are public universities. None of these are unionized, although ten of them are located in states with bargaining laws. Representation elections have been held at seven of the universities and all have resulted in rejections.[7] Elections have been held at only two of the 24 private AAU universities (New York University and Syracuse) and both resulted in rejections.

Rather than discuss this pattern in terms of putative quality of institution, it is more informative to focus on the facts that in their respective states, faculties of what have been called the traditional universities typically enjoy higher salaries, lower teaching loads, better conditions of employment in terms of office facilities, leaves, travel budgets, and student and clerical assistance. They also usually have a greater influence in university governance and well established traditions and customs of administrative relationships. These factors are likely to be negatively related to the propensity to organize (they are undoubtedly also positively related to quality) and are a more useful way of approaching the question of the propensity to organize. In any event, a breakthrough at one of the prestigious universities would do a good deal for the morale of the faculty union movement and it is hard to believe that sooner or later one will not occur.

Private institutions

As noted, just under five percent of all private institutions are unionized. This is true in spite of the fact that all private institutions are

7. The seven are Colorado, Michigan State (two rejections), Minnesota, Nebraska, Oregon, Penn State, and Pittsburgh.

covered by the National Labor Relations Act (NLRA) nationwide. The trend of organization has been similar to that of the public institutions with the years of largest growth in the first half of the decade. Because of the low level of organization, there has been relatively little study of unionism in private institutions. An impressionistic view of the reasons for the low level of organization might include the following.

Although the NLRA has been applicable to private college faculty since 1970, the institutions are isolated from the private sector labor movement. There has been no wave of organization in the private sector of the economy to serve as a stimulus to faculty organization comparable to the upsurge of public employee unionism. Although there has been some organization of nonacademic employees in private colleges, the atmosphere of competitive unionism that has characterized much public employee bargaining has been lacking. In the public sector, the employee interest groups compete in the budgetary process in a more open and visible way than is the case in the private sector and this encourages defensive organization.

Private institutions are smaller in size, less bureaucratic in operation, and have experienced no upheavals similar to the massive expansions and reorganizations of the public sector institutions. Few private universities are multi-institutional systems or even multi-campus institutions. Relations with administrators and governing boards are more direct and personal than in public systems.

Partly because of the smaller size and more informal relationships, faculty members may be more reluctant to engage in organizing activity due to the fear of possible subtle or not so subtle reprisals. Some organizers feel this is an important restraining factor.

Whatever the reasons, there is

nothing in the record to suggest that private sector unionism will play any larger role in the future than it has in the past.

Elections and rejections

Although the pace of unionization has been slower in recent years, the proportion of elections that has resulted in rejections has remained fairly stable, around 40 percent except for 1976 when rejections occurred in just over half of the elections held that year. (See Table 3) Because some elections involve multi-institutional systems, the number of elections held in a given year may vary widely from the number of institutions participating in the elections. (To take the extreme example, the single SUNY election added 24 institutions to the organized column.) As a result of this fact, the number of elections held each year has been considerably more stable than the number of institutions organized or the number of faculty represented added to the total.

The proportion of elections resulting in rejections is somewhat lower than that of the private sector of the economy as a whole where the rate has hovered around 50 percent. Within the overall total the proportion of rejections in public institutions has been steadily rising while the proportion in the private sector has been well below average since 1976. These trends have been overshadowed by the smaller total of elections in recent years.

Administrators have shown considerable interest in the question of whether unionization is irreversible. So far only two decertifications have occurred, both in small private institutions with less than 100 faculty each, one in 1976 and the

TABLE 4

BARGAINING UNITS BY AGENT, 1979[a]

| | UNITS | | | PERSONS REPRESENTED |
	PUBLIC	PRIVATE	TOTAL	
AFT	11	21	32	42830
NEA	17	12	29	12808
AAUP	19	22	41	21782
IND.	2	7	9	1538
COALITION	3	0	3	6601
	52	62	114	85559

Note that there are fewer units than successful elections principally because some units have been consolidated, e.g. Massachusetts.
[a] As of 9/30/79.

other in 1978. On the other hand, eight election units have been organized after previously voting against unionism in at least one election.

The status of the organizations

The results of a decade of competition for representation rights among the three major faculty organizations are displayed in Table 4. The American Federation of Teachers (AFT), an affiliate of the American Federation of Labor—Congress of Industrial Organization, has the longest and strongest commitment to traditional trade union values and tactics and has recently made some moves toward broadening their organizational base of membership to other professionals.

The National Education Association (NEA) affiliates adopted the tactics of trade unionism in the 1960s. They are the traditional mass teacher organization with a very large membership at all levels of education and the largest financial resources. The American Association of University Professors (AAUP), with membership limited to all levels of higher education, endorsed collective bargaining as a technique of representation at the beginning of the 1970s and, as the latest convert, may still have some ambivalence about the decision.

Analysts of faculty bargaining have developed a consensus about the pattern of representation by faculty organization that is only partially borne out by the current data. Briefly, it has been assumed that the AFT has been most successful in large public institutions, the NEA in smaller public institutions, particularly in former teacher's colleges, and the AAUP in private institutions. The data in Table 4 are generally consistent with these conclusions but the differences are not particularly impressive. The AFT has been much more successful than usually believed in small private institutions and the AAUP has been more successful in winning elections in public institutions than they have been given credit for by analysts.

Case studies and the statistical data indicate that at the local level where elections are fought the competing organizations are not perceived to be nearly so different from one another as the statements and literature that emanate from their national headquarters would suggest.[8] There have been several attempts to work out mergers of the organizations at the national level, but they have been unsuccessful. There seems little prospect that this situation will change in the near future so competition will remain the order of the day.

THE BALANCE SHEET OF UNIONISM

Attempts to evaluate the effects that faculty bargaining has had on the four year sector of American higher education agree in general on the character and direction of the changes.[9] The difficulty is in estimating their magnitude and importance. The principal problem is that the system of higher education has been undergoing dramatic changes for more than two decades and in large part faculty unions have reinforced trends that were already in evidence before they appeared and that continued to operate during the 1970s.

The general trends that can be observed in higher education and, in some instances, in society as a whole are the centralization of decisionmaking, the increasing bureaucratization of administrative processes, and a greater emphasis on due process with regard to individual rights. As the public systems of higher education expanded in the 1960s, decisionmaking moved from individual campuses to the headquarters of integrated systems of institutions or to central coordinating bodies of all higher education in a state. The increases in size of campuses and the growth of multicampus systems intensified the problems of coordination and review and led to an expansion of administrative levels and personnel. The climate of opinion reinforced by court decisions and

8. For an example of a study supporting this view, see Virginia Ler Lussier, "Faculty Bargaining Associations," *Journal of Higher Education* 46, 5 (September/October 1975): 507–518.

9. In addition to earlier citations, major studies of faculty unionism include R. K. Carr and D. K. Van Eyck, *Collective Bargaining Comes to the Campus* (Washington: American Council on Education, 1973); F. R. Kemerer and J. V. Baldridge, *Unions on Campus* (San Francisco: Jossey Bass, 1975); Kenneth Mortimer, *Faculty Bargaining, State Government and Campus Autonomy* (Denver: Education Commission of the States, 1976); and James Begin et al., *Academic Bargaining: Origins and Growth* (New Brunswick: Institute of Management and Labor Relations, Rutgers, 1977).

legislation on open personnel files led to a reduction in secrecy in personnel decisions and subjected some of these decisions to external review.

All of these tendencies have been reinforced by faculty collective bargaining. The need for uniformity of treatment and of procedure in negotiating and administering bargaining agreements for multicampus systems led to a centralization of decision at the top levels of administrative hierarchies. The necessity of uniform application of these decisions to individual cases and the possibility that some form of review of decisions would be made produced an emphasis on formal policy statements, on the development of personnel procedures and extensive documentation that these procedures had been followed. The membership of decisionmaking bodies, the evidence considered in hearings, the reasoning behind the decisions, and the possibility of appeal, sometimes to bodies external to the process, all have been negotiated.

The results have been the familiar conflict between the reduction of arbitrary action and the protection of individuals' rights as seen from the standpoint of the individual and the increased cost and delay, the loss of flexibility and the decline of authority and control from the standpoint of the institution. The assessment of the net effect is essentially a question of the values attached to the two sides of this conflict.

Governance and the unions

No single topic in the literature of faculty bargaining has been discussed more frequently than the impact of unionism on institutional governance. This concern is based on the practice in all bargaining legislation of providing that the chosen agent would have exclusive rights to negotiate issues within the scope of bargaining. Although a few laws have limited the scope of bargaining to protect other governance mechanisms, this provision has appeared to threaten the traditional collegial system of governance usually embodied in a faculty senate. My own conclusion is that organization or the threat of organization has done more to enhance the traditional governance systems than it has to reduce their effectiveness. The level of faculty participation in governance is difficult to judge but it seems clear that the institutions that have been organized have not, in the general case, been institutions with strong traditions of collegial decisionmaking.[10] In some institutions that have organized, faculty senates have been reduced to a minor role; in others, faculty senates have been strengthened by provisions in union agreements; in some, unionism has actually led to the establishment of senates. Of course, the favorable effect of unionism in senates in the aggregate may have been greatest of all in institutions that have not been organized but have felt threatened by the new order.

Whatever the status of governance machinery, in most organized institutions unionization's effect has been limited because the principal concerns of unions have been in areas in which the senates' influence has been limited; for example, pay and personnel decisions. In

10. The most ambitious attempt to classify governance practices in a wide range of institutions was undertaken by the AAUP in 1969; see *Bulletin*, American Association of University Professors (Spring 1971): 68–124.

matters of pay and institutional decisionmaking on academic matters, such as programs, unions do not appear to have affected the powers of senates to any significant extent.

If the concept of governance is extended to departmental or college level personnel decisions, the impact of unionism has been substantial. It is here that the unions have challenged traditional methods of selection, promotion and retention whether these were administrative or collegial, most strongly. The result has been an opening up of the decisionmaking process, the development of explicit procedures and standards, the introduction of procedural safeguards of notification, of review of evidence, of justification of decisions, and of appeal to outside review. In institutions with a genuinely influential peer review or a competent administrative review system, the net effect of unionization has probably been to make the maintenance of standards of performance more difficult. This conclusion leaves unanswered the question of how many unionized institutions had review systems that consistently made distinctions between individuals on the basis of performance prior to unionization.

Compensation and unionization

Due to the relatively low level of unionization in the education "industry" and the short period of bargaining in many institutions, conclusions about the effect of unions on pay are difficult to reach. For an extreme example, how should you estimate what would have happened to the CUNY faculty in the last five years if they had not been organized? It may surprise researchers in higher education to discover that economists have no very good answers to the question of how unions such as the Amalgamated Clothing Workers, the United Automobile Workers, or the International Union of Electrical Workers have affected the compensation of their members over the years.

However, it may be helpful to summarize the conventional wisdom as to how unions in general have affected the pay of their members. The usual conclusion is that in the first years after organization unions raise wages relative to nonunion wages in their industry, but that thereafter the differential remains stable. This seems a reasonable situation when one considers that a long continued increase in the union-nonunion differential would likely result in the elimination of the unionized sector, the organization of the nonunionized units in which case they drop out of the comparison, or the matching of increases in the unionized sector by unorganized firms. The studies in higher education have produced contradictory or inconclusive results so far, but they agree in concluding that the effects, whatever they are, are not substantial.[11] On the other hand, there are clearly individual instances— the Pennsylvania State Colleges— where unions have had substantial impact.

11. A recent study that includes reviews of early studies also concludes that unions have had little effect. Joan L. Marshall, "The Effects of Collective Bargaining on Faculty Salaries in Higher Education." *Journal of Higher Education* 50, 3 (May/June 1979): 310–322. A positive effect was noted by Richard B. Freeman in the most comprehensive study "Should We Organize? Effects of Faculty Unionism on Academic Compensation," Working Paper no. 301, (New York: National Bureau of Economic Research, 1978).

Are there alternative models?

Many observers, particularly administrators, are fascinated by the possibility that alternatives to the industrial model of union-management relations may exist. By this they appear to mean an alternative model that would preserve the traditional faculty-administrative relationships while satisfying the legal requirement that faculty have "the right to organize and bargain collectively through representatives of their own choosing."

It seems to be small comfort to administrators that there is already an alternative model at hand in the form of traditional governance procedures and that the great majority of institutions are still free to use it. The cost of making a system work that produces economic results similar to those in organized institutions and that meets the going standards of academic governance are substantial, but no more and perhaps less than the costs of undergoing organization. Moreover, even under conditions of economic stringency, academics are surely one of the occupational groups with the lowest propensity to organize and educational managers are improving their ability to capitalize on this situation.

The record of the first ten years does not suggest that faculty unionism is likely to sweep the field in the next few years. In public institutions in states with a strong public employee labor movement, faculty unions are nearly universal, but even here the leading institutions have not been organized to date. If they are, it will be through neglect or hostility among the executive and legislative branches of state government and among administrators rather than the shortcomings of traditional governance systems. Having said this, the record of the past decade in this country and abroad indicates that, at least in public institutions, in the long run, faculty organization will probably continue to expand at a modest pace.

Academic Tenure: Its Recipients and Its Effects

By LIONEL S. LEWIS

ABSTRACT: A great deal has been written about the pros and cons of academic tenure but little systematic research has been done on the subject. Through an examination of the dossiers—*vitae*, letters of recommendation, and written assessments—of 115 individuals awarded tenure in 1967 and 1968, this paper attempts to shed some light on the characteristics of those awarded tenure and on its effects. There are large gaps in what writers know about candidates. Still, candidates are portrayed in the most favorable light. Because hard and fast criteria are not applied, the process for awarding tenure seems to be less stringent than evaluation for promotion to Full Professor. It would appear that since tenure does not primarily work either to reduce the intellectual activity of faculty or to protect the idiosyncratic or dissenting scholar, its central function is to insure minimal performance standards and compatibility.

Lionel S. Lewis is Professor of Sociology and Adjunct Professor of Higher Education at the State University of New York at Buffalo. Among some of his more recent publications in the Sociology of Education are Scaling the Ivory Tower: Merit and Its Limits in Academic Careers *and articles in* The International Encyclopedia of Higher Education, The American Sociologist, Social Problems, Sociology of Education, *and* Higher Education.

This paper could not have been written without the cooperation and help of Professor Lawrence A. Cappiello and Dean Robert H. Rossberg (both of the State University of New York at Buffalo) for which the author is most grateful.

THIS PAPER has a double purpose: to shed some light on what it takes to be awarded tenure in an American institution of higher learning and to enlarge the very limited body of existing knowledge of the effects of tenure on individuals.

Academic tenure is an arrangement wherein after a reasonable probationary period of service and upon the achievement of a secure reputation, academic men and women are entitled to a continuing (indefinite) appointment at an institution until retirement due to age, disability, or resignation.

Very few, either within or outside of academia, are neutral about the subject of tenure; it is a topic which arouses a great deal of emotion and controversy and which has claimed more than its share of attention in print. It is also a subject that has been given scant attention by social researchers. Because there has been little systematic study of the subject, most of the writing to be found on the question of tenure has been in the form of discursive essays, focusing primarily on its putative positive or negative effects on academic life.

Advocates of tenure argue that it protects professors from being arbitrarily dismissed for teaching, saying, or doing something that is unpopular by offering freedom of expression through economic security. Opponents of tenure argue that it fosters mediocrity because it makes individuals complacent, indifferent, indolent, inefficient, neglectful, and unproductive. Participants on both sides of the debate assume tenure strongly affects job performance. However, missing from the extended discussion has been concrete analysis—based on systematically gathered evidence—of the actual consequence (on individuals or institutions) of tenure.

It was assumed that materials in the personnel files of those being reviewed for a tenure appointment would provide relevant information on the performance expectations for tenure and its consequences for what appears to be the first empirical study of both of these aspects of tenure.

THE POPULATION

The population under study includes 118 individuals who were reviewed for a tenure appointment to be effective at the beginning of the 1967 or 1968 academic year. Their dossiers, complete with curriculum vitae, letters of recommendation, and written assessments by department chairmen and deans, which had been submitted to a university-wide faculty committee were twice subjected to careful perusal—once to become familiar with their contents and to code and to quantify some of the qualities included on most vitae, and again to complete a formal content analysis of the letters and other written evaluations. These materials were collected by the committee in carrying out its formal function of advising the campus president, prior to his decision, on cases of tenure and promotion after action had been taken by departmental colleagues, the department chairman, a committee advisory to the appropriate college dean, the dean, and the academic vice president. These data were retrieved from the institution's archives.

The institution from which the material was collected is an urban, northeastern university with over 1,200 faculty members, offering degrees to undergraduates, graduates, and professional students. The institution had in the decade become a leading graduate center of a rapidly expanding state system. Given steady growth, the question of tenure quotas did not impose itself in any of the cases under consideration. Although these cases were obtained from a single institution, it is felt that the findings are not unique to it but are generalizable to many other large American universities. In studies in which institutions of higher learning are rated according to one or another criterion, this institution generally ranks somewhere in the top fifty. That it is not one of the top dozen or so most prestigious schools or, on the other hand, could not be fairly characterized as part of the academic hinterlands makes these findings more reflective of conditions in academia than if it fell at one of the extremes.

The majority of cases (93) had been serving at the institution on term appointments: 8 as Instructors or Lecturers, 63 as Assistant Professors, and 22 as Associate Professors. The remainder (25) were to be new appointments, all at the Associate Professor level. Most of these twenty-five apparently received bona fide offers eventually, although not all were accepted.

Of the 118, 12 were females and 106 were males. Thirty-seven were in the humanities (English Language and Literature, Languages, Art), 30 were in the physical or biological sciences (Physics, Mathematics, Biology), 22 were in the social sciences (Psychology, Sociology, Political Science), and 29 were in the professional disciplines (Social Work, Education, Engineering). Faculty whose only advanced degrees were in medicine, dentistry, nursing, or law were excluded from the study.

The advisory committee had been newly created, and in its early years seems to have routinely endorsed departmental and deans' recommendations. Consequently, tenure was expeditiously recommended in over 75 percent of the cases. An additional 10 percent were approved after some debate, delay, or a request for supplemental supporting documentation—there was one individual for whom the record and disposition is unclear—and the remaining 10 percent were recommended for tenure without the anticipated or recommended concomitant promotion. Two additional cases, preceded by weak or negative recommendations, were denied tenure. This cannot be interpreted to mean that almost all of those considered for tenure in the late 1960s received it. It was not possible to develop a comprehensive list of individuals for whom there was so little support at the departmental level that they were terminated without review by the appropriate dean or for some other reason were not evaluated by the central administration.

Given the nature of this population, the focus of the study must be limited to a consideration of only what it might take to be granted tenure. As important as the question might be, it is not possible to compare and contrast the successful with the unsuccessful.[1] The fact that the

1. It is worth mentioning that at another large state university, the University of Utah, in 1967 and 1968 tenure was granted to 81 of 90 (90 percent) individuals formally applying for a continuing appointment. "Report of the University of Utah Commission to Study Tenure," *AAUP Bulletin* vol. 57, no. 3 (September 1971) p. 425.

committee almost routinely approved all cases which it reviewed clearly indicates, however, that in the late 1960s departments and deans could expect their decisions to be readily endorsed by university-wide committees and the central administration. This in turn suggests that if an individual had any constituency in a department or elsewhere on campus who was willing to offer support for a continuing appointment on his or her behalf, he or she had an excellent chance of being granted tenure.[2]

The sub-population

For the 115 individuals granted tenure, it was possible to locate 34 dossiers prepared sometime between 1970 and 1978 for the committee advisory to the president

2. This practice is clearly not unique to this particular institution. For example, the Commission on Academic Tenure in Higher Education concluded from an 81 percent response rate of a questionnaire survey of 511 American institutions of higher learning that:

Tenure is awarded generously. Forty-two percent of the institutions responding to this particular question granted tenure to *all* faculty members considered for tenure in the spring of 1971. Two-thirds of the institutions granted tenure to 70 percent or more of those under consideration. . . . [However] . . . tenure is awarded . . . least liberally in universities . . . only 15 percent of the public and 10 percent of the private universities . . . granted tenure to all those under consideration. . . .

The percentage of public and private universities in which fewer than 80 percent of those considered for tenure did not receive it was only 25.8 and 42.0, respectively. William R. Keast, Chairman, *Faculty Tenure: A Report and Recommendations by the Commission on Academic Tenure in Higher Education.* [San Francisco: Jossey-Bass, 1973]: 6, 223, Table 4.

to support a request for advancement to Full Professor. These cases constitute our sub-population which, of course, is very selective. Specifically, it includes 27 of the 33 who had remained at the institution and had been promoted to Full Professor, 4 of the 40 Associate Professors who continued at the institution at the same rank, their requests for promotion to Full Professor having been denied, and 3 additional individuals who were promoted to Full Professor but subsequently left the university. The files for 6 others still at the university who the records show had been promoted to Full Professor between 1970 and 1974 could not be located. By comparing the original dossiers of these individuals when they were considered for tenure with those submitted when they sought promotion to Full Professor, it was thought that it would be possible to look at the course their careers had taken after they were granted a continuing appointment.[3] First it is necessary

3. Of course, some comparisons might be made between the expectations for a tenure appointment, usually at the Associate Professor level, and for a final promotion to Full Professor. In describing how a distinction is made between "the tenure process and the promotion process" at Indiana University, the sociologist Peter Burke writes:

the promotions committee has to . . . see whether . . . contributions in the areas of teaching, research, and service, in terms of both quality and quantity . . . earn . . . the recognition of promotion. The task of the tenure committee, on the other hand, is to determine whether enough evidence exists to suggest that *in the future* the person in question will continue to be a productive scholar and teacher at a level sufficient to eventually earn the rank of full professor. ("Replies to Scimecca," *The American Sociologist*, vol. 11, no. 4 [November 1976]:202).

to examine in detail the full records that came before the committee penultimately before tenure was awarded.

LETTERS AND OTHER WRITTEN EVALUATIONS: 1967 AND 1968

Before considering the letters of recommendation, it should be noted that the contents of these letters are at least in part influenced by the initial inquiry from a department asking for an evaluation of the candidate's qualifications for a tenure appointment. Most of those charged with soliciting the letters, usually the chairman, saw the institution as a national, rather than a regional or local, university, and this affected the information they solicited and received. Some made it clear in their requests that they would prefer a favorable rather than an unfavorable evaluation. A distinct effort is made in almost all letters to touch the same bases—to provide an assessment of teaching, research, and service—although most are only able to make concrete comments about one or two of these dimensions. The thought that someone might need tenure to protect his or her academic freedom or that the good of society would be served by granting an individual tenure is not expressed in a single letter.

Regardless of what the thrust of an argument might be, in the eyes of most writers it seems necessary to establish not only that a candidate had mastered his or her subject matter but that consistent with the institution's aspirations and formal policy, he or she had developed or is developing professional visibility. In those cases when to one or another committee the granting of tenure was problematic, the deci-

sion, in fact, often seemed to turn on the question of whether or not a reputation was national rather than merely local. Even if someone's strength is obviously in administrative work, this is invariably augmented with a nod towards scholarly accomplishments, and this is commonly done by mentioning that someone's research had opened up other job possibilities or at least had evoked the interest of faculty in the most prestigious institutions. Clearly, someone's visibility, which is thought to reflect the quality of his contribution, is of great importance.

[His] election to the Board of Directors is one more indication that he now belongs to the "inner circle" of the . . . world . . . and I personally take satisfaction and pride. . . .

Even though his five accepted papers are not in print yet, [he] has been professionally active and productive.

As will become evident later on, since it is an explicit consideration in determining the qualifications of someone desiring promotion to Full Professor, the question of visibility takes on even greater significance as academic careers advance. At the earlier stages of a career it is enough simply to hold out promise.

[He] has not yet written a major work. But this is only to say that I expect a major work within the next half decade, for this is the period in which he will really bloom.

Accenting the positive

Most letters and other assessments are highly positive and supportive which, first of all, suggests that it is relatively easy for candidates to get favorable letters. But even more important, this is telling evidence that the academic community is indeed a community. Even someone who has been involved in a public intellectual debate with a candidate, which might be an indication of common membership in both a social and intellectual network, will laud his work.[4] Negative remarks in letters from outside referees often bring forth a refutation in the chairman's or dean's assessment. Most criticism, which is almost always mild, is overlooked. The response, for example, to the observation that a candidate's teaching may be inadequate will likely be "but on balance, his teaching is good."

To be sure, even with all this generosity there seems to be some attempt to offer objective and balanced judgments. Yet, the tendency is to portray candidates as individuals of considerable ability and worth, even when the lack of concrete evidence makes it all very unconvincing. Not only do many cases in the end seem wholly based on a string of extravagant adjectives, the fact remains that, although some faculties may be convinced otherwise, no institution is or could be so ably and uniformly staffed. It would seem that if those in this sample are remarkable, for most it is with reference to activities other than scholarly publication. In any case, in providing such luxuriant social support, academic institutions are quite similar to other institutions. As Robert K. Carr has noted, "it is well to remember that in such fields as the law, the ministry, and many areas of business, justice is also frequently tempered with mercy in dealing with incompetent or neglectful people."[5]

However, it will not be surprising to those familiar with academic culture to find that most individuals are described in at least one letter as "the best" or "one of the best" in some activity. Sometimes the praise is unbounded.

[Her class] in my opinion . . . is probably the best undergraduate course in the country. . . .

I am chary about using the word "brilliant," but I think that [he] is one of the rare specimens to whom it can be applied accurately.

Almost every individual who has published a book has the work described at least once as "excellent," "significant," "important," "distinguished," or "definitive."

. . . it may turn out to be one of the really great books on the subject in this decade.

In the less florid letters, "the best in the country," is transmuted to "the best available." It is not surprising that the shortage of faculty, and the correlative threat of being understaffed, was of obvious concern to many senior faculty and administrators in the late 1960s, and the issue is raised at least once for 32 of the candidates. Most often there is a straightforward reference to "the marketplace."

[We] need to develop a full undergraduate program in . . . and at least a modest graduate program. To do so, we need staff. While [he] may not be ideal, he could not be easily replaced.

---

4. These are never really quarrels, but more like contests of wits, or analogous to a fighting wolf offering his throat as a sign of submission. If the debates were truly acrimonious, it is unlikely that one disputant would be acting as a referee for the other.

5. "Foreword" in Clark Byse and Louis Joughin, Tenure in American Higher Education: Plans, Practices, and the Law (Ithaca, NY: Cornell University Press, 1959) p. viii.

But sometimes the warning is more explicitly ominous.

I would wish those who may cause him to go from us the labor of finding us a comparable replacement.

Only occasionally does this line of argument seem excessive, as this comment for an individual who had yet to publish his first paper.

In any event, promoting relatively early means that the national reputations of people involved are not as great as if we deferred until the papers accepted are actually printed. However, market conditions in our field seem to make that an extremely high risk operation.

Intramural activities are extolled with even more fervor than scholarship. Given the great diversity shown by humans in the performance of any task and the widely held belief that some academics are not always attentive to their institutional responsibilities, this uniformly high praise on dimensions of academic performance other than publishing was somewhat unexpected. Yet, there is little in the dossiers themselves—aside from some teaching evaluations that indicated merely good rather than excellent classroom performance—that would directly contradict it. It is only natural that a writer, who may have been selected or suggested by the candidate himself, would be inclined to put a former student or fellow graduate student or friend of a friend in the most favorable light possible. It would be surprising if it were otherwise.

Thus, when it is evident, as often it is, that a candidate or his or her work is weak, the letters most often emphasize strengths rather than dwelling on weaknesses. The following paragraph reflects the most common tack:

Ultimately, what I am saying is that we cannot hope that every appointment involves every kind of excellence. People differ. They render different kinds of service to the common aims of the university.

The letters, then, attempt to frame this argument in more or less academic terms. A common approach is to point out that the department is large enough to absorb someone who does not measure up on one or another quality before observing that, in any case, everyone does not equally excel in all endeavors. The dossiers suggest that in most cases the candidate is deficient in the publication of research; 45 had written 5 or fewer articles while only 30 had over 11 articles or 2 or more books. Significantly less frequently do the letters digress, as in this appeal to conscience.

His age would *cause* him serious problems in relocating, and on the other hand his continuance would not saddle the department with a harmful or unproductive burden.

And only rarely is the argument totally without merit as when a chairman, who had twice been reminded that a man did not compare favorably with those in the rank for which he was being considered, advocated that "those in that rank should be promoted to the next higher rank."

Although praising strengths and ignoring weaknesses may be laudable, this ardent generosity (charity) or humaneness (compassion) makes it difficult for those who do not share the same perceptions, who are less enthusiastic about a candidate's presumed abilities, to offer a spirited dissent from the groundswell of favorable opinion. There were numerous indications that a review committee or an administrator, usually the dean, saw a positive recommendation of an individual as clearly a mistake. However, in the face of such a heartfelt commitment on the part of so many others, more often than not there was an apparent lack of interest in taking and holding what would be seen as an obstructionist position. It would seem that unless the vote on a candidate was negative at nearly every preceding level (unless there was considerable agreement, beginning with departmental colleagues, and moving up to the department chairman, the dean, and persons representing the central administration, that someone was evidently not up to par) there was reluctance on the part of those at higher levels to make a negative decision—and the granting of tenure seemed almost a foregone conclusion, in spite of endless and tortuous meetings on the matter, all of the accompanying soul searching and bathos, and even the paper shuffling this invariably necessitates.

Parenthetically, it is possible the fiction that the tenure review process is stringent may serve to encourage some of the less able to resign their position in anticipation of being denied tenure. To the degree that this is so, the tenure review process in a very indirect way may eliminate some of the weakest of the academic community.

Floating standards

Although certain themes are predictable in most letters and assessments regarding tenure—"he will continue to remain active [unspecified] and develop"—one is left with a very vivid impression that there are no hard and fast criteria, that not only the letters but the entire process of evaluation and reward in academia

is marked by floating standards. Although it might be taken for granted that the criteria would be different among disciplines, surprisingly there was considerable variance within disciplines and even departments.

The shifting is clearly not random. First of all, expectations will vary among fields: scientists should write articles, and humanists, books, while those in the studio disciplines must show evidence of continued creativity. Moreover, the grounds on which judgments are made constantly move so as to be consistent with the strengths of the candidate under consideration. For some, this is the only way it could be; according to John Perry Miller, it is all for the best.

Anyone who has carefully observed tenure appointments will recognize that scholarly distinction, teaching capacity, administration skills, and service have weighed differently in individual decisions. Conventions of mutual respect and reticence inhibit responsible officials from publicly explaining the weight these various criteria carry in individual appointments.[6]

Joseph Fashing, on the other hand, argues that because there are no clearly established standards of performance, the process of awarding tenure is irrational and inherently inequitable: "Rather, what we have are loosely established criteria of performance which are ambiguous with regard to both their initial application and their interpretation of the evidence. . . . Depending on the prior commitments for or against a candidate by participants on the tenure committee, perceptions, judgments, evaluations of evi-

6. "Tenure: Bulwark of Academic Freedom and Brake on Change," *The Educational Record*, vol. 51, no. 3 (Summer 1970):242.

dence, and the standards themselves will vary wildly."[7] It would seem that after a certain level of minimum achievement, but before a secure academic reputation is achieved, social criteria—"he is very pleasant," "she is very likable"—are most important in the evaluation process.

Thus, there may be a great deal of agreement on what is expected, for example one book or seven articles, to be considered a serious candidate for tenure; the inconsistency surrounds the application of criteria. It is here that the rubber band of measurement is most evident. For example, the effectiveness in teaching and in university service are understood to be necessary but not sufficient conditions for the granting of tenure. One must really be a publishing scholar, it is said. Yet, for some, there is not even the pretense that they would qualify on these grounds. However, in only a handful of cases is there a suggestion that a candidate might be held accountable for a substandard performance. On the contrary, attempts to advance some exonerating conditions to support candidates are quite frequent, and in almost all instances these appeals evidently prove successful. Analysis of other materials to be reported elsewhere reveals that they were somewhat, but not significantly, less successful in the late 1970s.

BEYOND TENURE

Ten years later, in the 1977–78 academic year, 76 of the 115 individuals who were granted tenure were still at the institution under study; of these, only 33 had been promoted to Full Professor, 40 were still Associate Professors, and 3 were Assistant Professors, having gained tenure at this rank after years of service and without a subsequent promotion. Scientists and humanists had the worst record of promotion with only 6 of 20 and 10 of 27, respectively, having reached Full Professor status. Even if it is conceded that nearly all the 39 of the 115, about whom nothing is known beyond the fact that their tenure appointment was approved, had been promoted to Full Professor at some other institution—an assumption here being that inter-institutional mobility in academia often involves promotion—it is still striking that after ten years over one-third are at a rank less than Full Professor.

The belief, common in some academic circles, that promotion to Full Professor rank could be expected after a half dozen or so years as an Associate Professor does not seem to hold more recently and perhaps may never have been so.[8] It may be that those who had not been advanced in rank simply did not work out and the granting of tenure was a mistake. On the other hand, it may be that with the so-called depression in higher education it has been generally difficult to obtain a promotion to Full Professor in the 1970s.

The previous question that could only be answered with more data

7. Joseph Fashing, "Replies to Scimecca," *The American Sociologist*, vol. 11, no. 4 (November 1976):206.

8. Actually, all of this is consistent with Lazarsfeld and Thielens's findings that a greater proportion of high productive than medium or low productive individuals are promoted to Full Professor. Under 40 years of age, the figures are 15 percent, 7 percent, and 2 percent; between 41 and 50 years of age, they are 63 percent, 39 percent, and 23 percent; for those older than 51, they increase to 87 percent, 65 percent, and 45 percent, respectively. Paul F. Lazarsfeld and Wagner Thielens, Jr., *The Academic Mind* (Glencoe, IL: The Free Press, 1958) p. 405, Table A3-2.

TABLE 1

1977–78 RANK OF 1967 AND 1968 TENURE APPOINTMENTS WHO CONTINUED AT INSTITUTION
(PERCENTAGES IN PARENTHESIS)

Rank	HUMANITIES (N = 27)	SCIENCES (N = 20)	SOCIAL SCIENCES (N = 10)	PROFES- SION (N = 19)	TOTAL (N = 76)
Less than Associate Professor	2 (7.4)	1 (5.0)	0 (0.0)	0 (0.0)	3 (3.9)
Associate Professor	15 (55.5)	13 (65.0)	4 (40.0)	8 (42.1)	40 (52.6)
Professor	10 (37.0)	6 (30.0)	6 (60.0)	11 (57.9)	33 (43.4)
Totals of Original Population	27 of 36 (75%)	20 of 29 (69%)	10 of 22 (45%)	19 of 28 (68%)	76 of 115 (66%)

than has been collected for this study, although Figure 1 will shed some light on this matter. There is also no way of determining whether the two-thirds of those who continue at the institution, particularly the 43 who are at a rank below that of Full Professor, would be greatly reduced if there were no protection of tenure. Given the evident pattern of mutual support that colleagues display toward one another, professional judgment may well be suspended for those whom academics find in their midst. It is very unlikely that many would have been made to feel unwelcome, and would have been forced to move.

Publications and Advancement to Full Professor

Only by following the careers of all or some randomly selected individuals of the primary sample can definitive statements be made about the effects of tenure. With this caveat, the dossiers of the follow-up population are now examined. This analysis should increase our comprehension of the course some careers take after tenure is awarded with the hope that this in turn will increase our understanding of the effects of tenure.

That some were promoted to Full Professor within ten years after

tenure was awarded while others were not does suggest that these individuals may have been more careful than others over the years about the performance of their academic responsibilities. Yet, with so few dossiers of those who continued as Associate Professor to examine, this is only conjecture. As is evident from Figure 1, almost all of those promoted to Full Professor had been active researchers before and after being granted tenure.

The thirty individuals represented in this figure are not people who suddenly began publishing after receiving tenure. Promise, hopes, and all the rest notwithstanding, one predictor of continued publication and promotion seems to be early publication. To be sure, on the basis of the limited amounts of materials available for this study, a determination cannot be made about the continued activity of those not promoted to Full Professor. Still it is clear that those with the slimmest publication records at the time they receive tenure are seldom those who are considered for or receive (at least within ten years) the ultimate promotion to Full Professor. This strongly suggests, but by no means proves, that they have not lived up to the assurance found in so many letters that they are on the verge

FIGURE 1

PUBLICATIONS AT TENURE AND AT PROMOTION TO FULL PROFESSOR

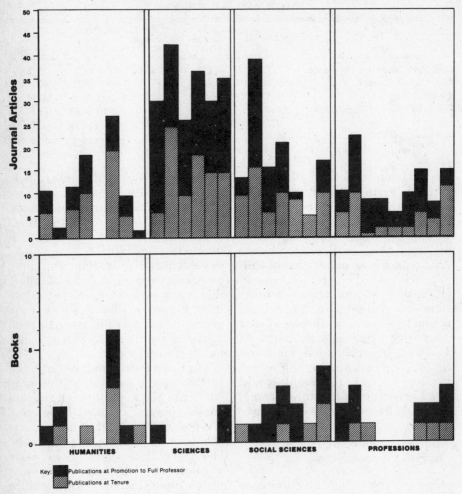

Key: ■ Publications at Promotion to Full Professor
⬚ Publications at Tenure

of publishing a great deal and that once the proverbial ice is broken they will flourish in pushing forth the frontiers of their disciplines. To be sure, it may well be that there are a number with only a few publications at the time tenure was awarded who subsequently became active publishers but for some reason are not deemed promotable to Full Professor. Yet, this seems unlikely.

Tenure Vs. Advancement to Full Professor

It is a widely shared belief that a decision on tenure has greater ramifications for individuals or institutions and as a result is more important than one simply involving promotion. Rationality would seem to dictate, therefore, that the evaluation process for the former would be more stringent than for the latter.

Yet, this does not seem to be the case. Senior faculty, chairmen, and administrators are on the one hand more exacting and obversely less tolerant of professional shortcomings in their expectations of those considered for promotion to Full Professor than for those considered for a tenure appointment. There are only rare exceptions: "Unless the person is so awful that one hopes that he will go away—and such people rarely do!—it seems to me good policy as well as compassionate to promote the individual to Full Professor after a reasonable time." The higher standards are most evident in comments in references to both quality and quantity of publications.

In the first place, the written work of those being considered for promotion to Full Professor is to a slight degree more likely than that of those being evaluated for tenure to be criticized in terms such as "too prosaic," "not greatly innovative," "slight," "in a limited sphere," "only technically competent," "slightly parochial," "not substantial," "not pertinent," "not reveal[ing] . . . a seminal thinker." It is just as likely to be seen as "not measuring up to reasonable expectations," of being "too little," as a "very brief complement," and most commonly as "extremely thin," although the proportion who could be rightly faulted as such is considerably smaller for the population of those being considered for promotion to Full Professor than for those being considered for tenure.

The pattern here seems to be that of fewer apologies and excuses, although unsubstantiated praise is, of course, not absent. All of the supporting arguments received above, and even some new ones, are present in these letters: "Some of my col-

leagues think of him as young. He was 27 when he came to the department, and was 35 last March—old enough to be President of the United States." One simply encounters fewer disingenuous arguments. However, all of it may be irrelevant: in the long run outcomes seem to be positive regardless of what is said. Comments such as the following two examples in effect only delay a positive decision on promotion to Full Professor.

. . . the record is not strong enough to support promotion at this time.

[He is] *adequate* in 52.7 percent by the rating and *inadequate* in one-fifth of the cases. This is the kind of mediocrity we would want to discourage. . . . There is certainly nothing here to suggest an outstanding scholar. . . .

If a candidate is rejected in one year, it is almost a certainty that in subsequent attempts for promotion, his or her dossier will be bolstered with a more supportive complement of letters. As suggested, the fact that a hard look is taken at each candidate and that individuals do not automatically sail through—approximately one-third even of those who in the end are successful are denied promotion by their department or the administration the first time they apply—might dissuade less qualified persons from seeking promotion or convince their sponsors that pressing their cases would be fruitless.

Reputation

According to most of those involved in the process of assessment and promotion, the requisite characteristic for Full Professor rank is reputation, generally expressed as visibility. Ideally, this is achieved by attaining distinction in one's discipline, and one is thought to have attained distinction through continuous publication, being recognized as a national authority, being known by prestigious people in prestigious institutions (sometimes indicated by the source of letters) having one's work cited, having membership on important disciplinary committees, being invited to participate at scholarly conventions, publishing in prestigious journals, being a sought-after consultant, being asked to do research for the government or other organizations, getting research grants, being on editorial boards, obtaining grants, traveling widely, or organizing or being invited to colloquia. The question of reputation is touched, although such information in most cases was solicited, in at least one evaluation for 26 of the 30 individuals eventually promoted.

In addition, the more convincing the case that someone has indeed earned a national, or even more strongly emphasized, international reputation (particularly in Europe) the fewer questions asked about the other merits of a candidate, and the less likely there will be delays in the decision to promote. The argument against the four individuals denied promotion and the approximately one-third of the others in which it was put off, denied sometimes two times, but eventually granted, was invariably that the person was insufficiently "known" as opposed to having "attracted world-wide attention," being a "major figure," being a "presence," a "prominence," or a "world class scientist." As a top administrator puts it:

Certainly, he does not satisfy the criteria of national and international visibility we have used as a bench mark for such promotion. The dossier is extremely weak and deserves no further comment.

In many minds, having earned the respect of disciplinary colleagues in other institutions is the key element that distinguishes those who should be Full Professors from those in lesser ranks. This is why the argument is so dominant in these dossiers and is missing from the majority of letters written on behalf of those merely being considered for tenure.

Teaching and administration

Because the review process appears to be more exacting, that is, standards seemed to be less flexible, for those being considered for promotion to Full Professor than for those granted tenure, there was some expectation that there would be a relatively thorough examination of all aspects of a candidate's performance. This is not the case. As in the evaluations for those in the primary population, very little attention is paid to teaching, the activity which is at the center of most academic careers. Little seems to be known about success in the classroom and what is known does not provide sufficient information on this matter.

I cannot attest directly to his teaching, but can only remark that he is both articulate and conscientious, a combination which generally wears well in teaching.

His teaching style is lively and frequently humorous—one doesn't fall asleep in his classes.

Even when something is known about teaching, it may not count for much as the following excerpts suggest.

Her performance as a teacher and as someone who has rendered university service has been outstanding. Regrettably, her scholarship although of high quality when it has appeared has been quite limited. I sincerely believe that her record viewed without respect to such questions as affirmative action, etc. would not lead to the conclusion that she be promoted. In these circumstances, I recommend that we await. . . .

If competence, devotion to teaching, and length of service were the only criteria to be applied [he] would more clearly deserve promotion to a Full Professorship. However, much as the committee was appreciative of the substantial service which [he] has given, they did not feel that such service was in itself a sufficient basis for his promotion now to Full Professor.

The promotion of the first of these individuals was rejected twice before finally being approved; the second is still an Associate Professor.

On the other hand, the third aspect of their work on which academics are putatively judged, contributions to governance and administration, gets somewhat more attention in the evaluations. From the dossiers, it appears that seventeen of the thirty individuals promoted to Full Professor rank are very active in such matters. Whether this percentage is high or low compared to what would be found in other samples, for example, those who were not promoted, cannot be determined. The argument that someone should be promoted on the basis of administrative work is not uncommon, though rarely successful in the absence of some evidence of publication.

Furthermore he has given years of his life to this university as an administrator. . . . If such service is to have any meaning, [he] richly deserves promotion.

Against this [the small number of supporting articles] it must be said that

[he] worked energetically in this office for some years as associate [dean]. . . .

For these two cases in which the publication record is only marginal, such arguments obviously helped prove persuasive. But for others, especially those who may have served long-forgotten administrations, other achievements might prove necessary.

A final review

In the final phase of the study, the thirty dossiers compiled at the time tenure was granted for those eventually promoted to Full Professor were again reviewed. It was hoped that such an examination would suggest post facto what it takes to have a relatively successful academic career. Were there some common characteristics or qualities evident early on that these individuals seem to possess? To insure the probability that this search for early clues would reveal something noteworthy, these dossiers were compared to a sample, selected nonrandomly but to represent a variety of disciplines, of fifteen of those still at the institution not promoted to Full Professor.

This examination and comparison revealed almost nothing: it was not possible to predict from the tenure files who would first attain the rank of Full Professor, although it was possible to predict who would not be the first to attain the rank of Full Professor. The fact that almost all of those promoted to Full Professor had been involved in research while this is true for less than half of those frozen at the Associate Professor rank—that is, on the average the former had published more books and articles than the latter—is clearly interesting but hardly explains what, so to speak, happened to those in this latter category who in the beginning years of their careers seemed to be fully committed to research and writing. Did they become, as Nisbet has put it, "lazy, incompetent, and delinquent?"[9] Or did they remain active, and their promotions were blocked for some other reason? Did they run out of ideas? Were they involved in a long-range program of research which had not yet begun to bear fruit? Did their intellectual growth stop? Were they, in Logan Wilson's words, "marginal performers . . . shelved in associate professorships . . ."[10] "since many institutions hesitate to reward mere timeservers with full professorships?"[11]

CONCLUDING REMARKS

Given the stated objective of tenure evaluation, which is to cull out those who will not in the future meet the institution's intellectual and performance standards, the process may indeed be more rational than it would appear from the materials in these mostly canonical dossiers, regardless of how closely they are examined and the seemingly contradictory themes that emerge. Organizations reproduce themselves through recruitment; those being selected who are most like those doing the selecting have the best chance of being retained and eventually succeeding. The tenure evaluation process facilitates this in a formal way. The letters, assessments, and dossiers contain enough information so that a reader can make an early, almost unreflective,

determination of how closely a candidate approaches the minimal intellectual and performance standards of an organization, as well as how nearly he or she will fit into a social group.

Moreover, William Goode has pointed out, "groups do not typically expose or expel their members for lesser achievement or talent."[12] This is generally accomplished by: setting standards which essentially everyone can meet and developing techniques that prevent an accurate measurement of output. It is thus common to find that "higher standards are set for obtaining a job than for performance."[13] It is not surprising then that most seem to qualify for tenure under rules that are so adaptable that no one quite knows what it takes to earn tenure.

At the same time, it is not an easy matter to make even the most rudimentary predictions about future performance. Little is known beyond conjecture about how outcomes are produced, or what the effects—positive or negative—of tenure are. Thus, candidates could not be deemed qualified for tenure for possessing or not possessing a certain quality, even one known to produce in the long run certain outcomes. The fact that A always results in Z is of no importance unless we know the relationships between A and tenure *and* tenure and Z. Some who write on the effects of tenure may contend that tenure causes Z, while others may argue that the two are not related.

In any case, a good deal of the concern about the possible effects of tenure may be beside the point.

9. Robert Nisbet, "The Future of Tenure," *On Learning and Change*, Change (1973):47.

10. Logan Wilson, *American Academics* (New York: Oxford University Press, 1979) pp. 67–68.

11. *Ibid.* p. 72.

12. William J. Goode, "The Protection of the Inept," *American Sociological Review*, vol. 32, no. 1 (February 1967):6.

13. *Ibid.*:8.

There is little evidence that tenure is as debilitating to the intellectual life of institutions of higher learning as its critics contend. Katz was able to determine that at the University of Illinois, "productivity declined by about one article per year after promotion to associate professor . . . [and] increased by about the same amount after promotion to full professor." He was persuaded by this that "tenure does not appear to greatly affect lifelong productivity."[14] The findings of this study would support Katz's conclusion.

14. David A. Katz, "Faculty Salaries, Promotions, and Productivity at a Large University," *American Economic Review*, vol. 63, no. 3 (June 1973):475–76.

At the same time, there is also not a great deal to suggest that tenure protects the seemingly idiosyncratic or dissenting scholar. This is only speculation however. There is simply not enough concrete information about the work activities, for example, teaching, in the dossiers to draw a definitive conclusion, although there are indications that such characteristics are not especially valued or cultivated by the professoriate.

To be sure, as anticipated by the founding fathers of the American Association of University Professors, tenure appears to make the academic profession more attractive. Yet, the output of most faculty probably remains largely independent of tenure.

ANNALS, AAPSS, **448**, March 1980

Affirmative Action and the Academic Profession

By ROBERT C. JOHNSON, JR.

ABSTRACT: Affirmative Action in the academic profession must be viewed as a remedial concept designed to ameliorate the present effects of past discrimination. The historical denial of equal access to secondary schools and colleges has limited the number of available black professors. An affirmative action program designed to remedy the results of this past exclusion would be justifiable if the program were properly conceived and implemented.

Robert C. Johnson, Jr., is an Attorney and Director of Affirmative Action, University of Massachusetts/Boston.

AMERICAN colleges and universities are the training grounds for future black professors. Prior to 1960, access to white institutions was either intentionally or unintentionally denied to blacks. The direct result of this historical exclusion has been a paucity of available black doctorates. Currently, blacks comprise only 4.3 percent of all Ph.D. holders.[1]

In the past decade, many institutions of higher education have evaluated their student admission policies and the extent to which black students have been afforded equal educational opportunity. As a result of social pressure, affirmative action programs have been devised to increase significantly the number of black students on primarily white college campuses. Perhaps this increase in access will eventually broaden the pool of available black Ph.D. holders.

However, present employment practices in academe are not designed to encourage black students, whether graduate or undergraduate, to choose the university for a career. Despite a decade of affirmative action legislation and institutional commitment to affirmative hiring, vestiges of racism, manifested through institutional exclusion, still contribute to the denial of employment opportunities to blacks.

A case in point is the Commonwealth of Massachusetts where both institutional racism and the present effects of past exclusion of blacks from public colleges and universities continues to be manifest. Accord-

1. *National Research Council: Summary Report 1977 Doctorate Recipients from United States Universities* (National Academy of Sciences, 1978), p. 24.

ing to the 1977 Higher Education Staff Information Form (EEO-6) which is submitted to federal compliance agencies, the total number of black full-time instructional personnel in the entire state system of public higher education was one hundred forty-three (143) out of a total of five thousand three hundred and fifty-nine (5,359). In percentage terms, blacks comprise 2.6 percent of the faculty. In short, the teaching faculty of public higher education in the Commonwealth of Massachusetts is 97.4 percent white.

In the tenured ranks blacks comprise forty-six (46) individuals out of a total of three thousand five hundred forty-six (3,546). In other words, blacks comprise 1.3 percent of the tenured faculty members in Massachusetts. Although 66 percent of the faculty in Massachusetts public higher education is tenured, blacks are a miniscule proportion of this privileged majority.

It might be argued that if blacks represent only 4.3 percent of all Ph.D. holders nationally, the Commonwealth of Massachusetts is not doing too badly. And the absence of tenured blacks merely reflects historical social conditions for which institutions of higher education should not be held responsible. Indeed, concentration of blacks at the lower ranks represents the system's recent commitment to racial equality.

An affirmative action officer encounters these arguments frequently. It is this line of thought that makes Affirmative Action/Equal Employment Opportunity (AA/EEO) officers positions have one of the highest turnover rates in academic administration. It also contributes to the difficulty in addressing the subject of blacks in the academic profession: there are virtually none (3 percent), and yet no one is responsible. Perhaps most importantly, it overlooks the main thrust of affirmative action legislation in the past decade which requires certain institutions to vigorously recruit and hire minorities as redress for past exclusion.

This paper, will focus on affirmative action legislation as it touches black faculty in higher education. At present such legislation is the major vehicle for increasing the number of blacks in the profession, and the only means of redress in a system of higher education that has not achieved any meaningful degree of integration. This legislation has established racial equality as a just and reasonable social goal. This paper will survey systemic, historical exclusion of blacks from higher education, a condition that prompted AA/EEO legislation and which guides current court decisions on affirmative action and non-discrimination. Institutional commitment to affirmative action will be viewed as of paramount importance if blacks are to become a viable part of the American professoriate.

HISTORICAL JUSTIFICATION FOR AFFIRMATIVE ACTION

Racial exclusion within the academic profession cannot be understood apart from racial discrimination in the United States as a whole. Racial exclusion in the present is the inevitable result of racial exclusion in the past. The denial of access to integrated secondary schools and colleges has had a direct effect upon access to the academic professions. Moreover, the concept of justice embodied in current legal theory touching on equality of employment opportunity is often

based on evidence of institutional practices of past discrimination. A brief overview of historical exclusion allows us to place specific institutional practices in a larger context as well as outline the philosophical and moral justification for vigorous affirmative action programs particularly in predominantly white graduate schools.

Limiting access is a traditional means of controlling minorities. Indeed, teaching slaves was a criminal offense in many southern states. But several northern colleges graduated blacks prior to the Civil War. Bowdoin College graduated the first black, John Brown Russwurm, in 1826. In the same year, Amherst College graduated Edward Jones. The only other colleges in the free states that regularly admitted black students were Oberlin in Ohio and Berea in Kentucky. Despite efforts by blacks to expand educational opportunity, primarily in the North, the racial composition of the nation's student body did not alter significantly before the Civil War. The total number of blacks in 1869 who had graduated from college was a mere 28.[2]

The end of the Civil War brought with it the need for America to resolve its most pressing social paradox: racism and the resultant exclusion of blacks from the fruits of society. Although the Emancipation Proclamation of 1863 purported to give freedom to blacks, nothing short of federal intervention could give blacks the same legal rights heretofore reserved for whites. Consequently, the Thirteenth, Fourteenth and Fifteenth Amendments were

2. Herman A. Young and Brenda H. McAnulty, "Traditional Black Colleges: The Role, Social Benefits and Costs," *The Western Journal of Black Studies* vol. 2, no. 3 (Fall 1978), p. 168.

passed, marking the beginning of a century long and still unresolved struggle to guarantee blacks the rights of national citizenship.

In addition to these Constitutional Amendments, further governmental action was necessary to provide opportunity for the more than 4,000,000 blacks who were freed at the end of the war. Two pieces of legislation did more than any others to advance educational opportunity for blacks—the Morrill Land-Grant Act of 1862 and the legislation establishing the Bureau of Refugees, Freedmen, and Abandoned Lands. Also important was the second Morrill Act of 1890 which led to the founding of black colleges in most of the Southern states. Prior to 1890 only two black colleges were in operation, and these were located in the North—Lincoln University (Pennsylvania, 1854) and Wilberforce University (Ohio, 1856).[3]

The Freedmen's Bureau was one of the earliest agencies to embody the concept that affirmative relief should be granted blacks as a remedy for past discrimination. The purpose of the legislation was explained by Congressman William D. Kelly in a speech before the House:

. . . We have four million people in poverty because our laws have denied them the right to acquire property; in ignorance because our laws have made it a felony to instruct them; without organized habits because war has broken the shackles which bound them, and has released them from the plantations which were destined to be their world.[4]

The first bill did not provide for

the promotion of education among blacks. But an amendment to the original bill, passed over the veto of President Andrew Johnson, authorized the expenditure of funds for the education of blacks. Consequently, from 1886 to June 30, 1872, the year the affairs of the Bureau ceased, education for blacks was a legally required function of a governmentally mandated remedial program. Within this time frame expenditures for the education of blacks increased from a little over $30,000 in 1866 to over $1,000,000 in 1870. By 1870, 4,239 schools were in operation with 9,307 teachers and 247,333 pupils.[5] Many of these schools were run by churches and philanthropic organizations in conjunction with the Freedmen's Bureau. In total a little more than $5 million was expended by the Bureau in behalf of black education. This small sum of money made some impact, but the greatest effect was manifested in the legislatures of the South. Inspired by the Bureau, many states designed public school systems for the first time.[6]

Needless to say, considerable opposition existed toward the education of blacks. Throughout the south, school houses were burned by the Ku Klux Klan and black teachers driven from their schools. With the end of the reconstruction period, a new era of white backlash began. Many of the meager gains made by blacks directly after the war were

3. Alton Hornsby, Jr., "Historical Overview of Black Colleges in the U.S." *The Western Journal of Black Studies*, volume 2, no. 3 (Fall 1978), p. 162.
4. Dwight Oliver Wendell Holmes, *The Evolution of the Negro Colleges* (New York: AMP Press, 1970), p. 31.

5. W. E. B. Dubois, *Black Reconstruction in America* "An Essay Toward a History of the Part Which Black Folk Played in the Attempt to Reconstruct Democracy in America, 1860–1880," (New York: Atheneum Press, 1975); for the most part these figures represent students enrolled in secondary education, rather than higher education.
6. Richard Kluger, *Simple Justice* (New York: Vintage Books, 1977), p. 51.

slowly eroded in the U.S. Supreme Court decisions in *Plessy vs. Ferguson*, 163 U.S. 537 (1896).[7] At issue in *Plessy* was the constitutionality of a Louisiana statute which required separate railway carriages for white and black passengers. The case was significant because it represented one of the first Constitutional challenges to segregation brought under the post-war amendments. The legal issue raised in the case was whether federal constitutional rights guaranteed to citizens by the Thirteenth and Fourteenth Amendments prohibited segregation required by Louisiana law. The U.S. Supreme Court upheld the Louisiana statute and ushered in an era of legalized segregation which effectively barred blacks from many of the benefits of American society, including education.

Eight years later, segregation in higher education was sanctioned by the United States Supreme Court in the case of *Berea College vs. Kentucky*, 211 U.S. 45. On October 8, 1904, an indictment was brought against Berea College charging that it violated Kentucky Acts 1904, Chapter 85 which prohibited white and black students from attending the same school. The Act was pervasive in its regulation of higher education. It prohibited any instructor from teaching in any school where students of both races were received. The Act did allow, however, a private school, college or university to operate a black institution if it was separated from white schools by a distance of at least twenty-five miles.

Berea College challenged the constitutionality of the statute but lost at trial and on appeal to the Federal Circuit Court of Appeals. Ultimately, the College appealed to the Supreme Court of the United States where that court held in a 7 to 2 decision that the legislation of Kentucky prohibiting all racial contact in schools fell within the power of a state to regulate its corporate creatures. Justice Harlan, who dissented in *Plessy*, also filed a dissenting opinion in *Berea* in which he maintained that the Kentucky statute constituted an arbitrary invasion of rights guaranteed by the Fourteenth Amendment.

By 1910, segregation and unequal educational opportunity at primary, secondary and higher levels was the supreme law of the land. Higher education reflected the segregative nature of society. By 1900 the total number of black college graduates had risen to 2,500, but only 800 students were enrolled in that same year. This number increased to approximately 23,000 in 1932, of which 21,383 reflected enrollments in traditionally black institutions.[8] Due to the low capitalization of these institutions and the lack of high school training for most black students, the curricula for many schools was limited to industrial training.

Despite political leaders like W. E. B. Dubois, the Pan-African Movement and the Harlem Renaissance, the situation of blacks in higher education did not change appreciably. Even the 1954 *Brown vs. the Board of Education* decision failed to open the doors of white schools to blacks in any significant manner. It was not until black students working in the Civil Rights Movement engaged in protest that

7. *Plessy vs. Ferguson*, 163 U.S. 537 (1896).

8. *Quarterly Review of Higher Education Among Negroes*, vol. 1, no. 1 (January 1933), p. 29.

changes in access patterns to higher education began to occur.

On February 1, 1960, four freshmen from North Carolina A&T, Greensboro entered a segregated department store and refused to leave until they were served. This protest against the discriminatory practices of Woolworth's soon spread as hundreds of students staged protest sit-ins at lunch counters. The sit-in idea spread to other cities as protests were recorded throughout the South. Eventually this student activism precipitated the development of the Student Nonviolent Coordinating Committee (SNCC). In 1964, in response to black agitation, the Civil Rights Act, basis of current affirmative action, was passed. It represented a monumental step toward full equality for blacks by providing affirmative relief from acts of discrimination, both individual and institutional.

The end result of this social activism and the resultant legislation was the widening of the doors of opportunity in higher education. Prior to 1965 most white colleges and universities had only a sprinkling of black students enrolled. However, due to increased recruitment efforts which included a drain upon student enrollments in traditionally black colleges, the number of blacks on white campuses increased dramatically. For example, between 1960 and 1974, black enrollment in colleges increased by 188 percent, as compared to 102 percent for whites. In four years alone the percentage change in black student enrollment, from 1970–1974 was 59.5 percent, compared to 15.1 percent for whites.[9] In a five year period between 1965 and 1970, the enrollment of blacks shifted from predominantly black schools to white ones. In 1965, 50 percent of all black college students attended predominantly black colleges, while in 1970, 72.4 percent of blacks were in white institutions.[10]

In absolute numbers, the change in black enrollment in American colleges between 1960–1976 was from 227,000 to 1,034,680. If enrollment figures are analyzed according to regions, then the southern states outranked the other three regions in total numbers of black full-time undergraduate enrollment with 13.9 percent of the total in 1970. The northern and western states registered the lowest percentage (4.5) of blacks.[11] The higher percentage in the South was undoubtedly a reflection of enrollment figures in traditionally black institutions.

Although the number of black students increased dramatically, the number of black faculty has not. The point at which blacks disappear from academe is between completion of the B.A. and enrollment in graduate school. The reasons for black students not continuing are the subject of much controversy and many interpretations. However, the resulting paucity of black Ph.D. holders accounts for the dearth of blacks in the profession. Continued development of affirmative action programs in higher education according to reasonable federal/state guidelines may, in time, change this situation.

10. Frank Brown and Madelon D. Stein, *Minorities in U.S. Institutions of Higher Education* (New York: Praeger Publishers, 1977), page 29.

11. U.S. Department of Health, Education and Welfare, *Racial and Ethnic Enrollment Data From Institutions of Higher Education* (Fall, 1970), p. 116.

9. U.S. Department of Commerce, *Statistical Abstract of the United States*, 1978, p. 141.

LEGAL REDRESS FOR
INSTITUTIONAL RACISM

During the 1970s a process of legal redress for discrimination was developed through commissions, federal agencies, and the courts. In a study issued in May, 1976, the U.S. Commission on Civil Rights found that overt and institutional discrimination operated to limit employment opportunities of blacks within the construction industry.[12] Although this report dealt with access of blacks to apprenticeship programs, the definition of institutional discrimination developed by the Commission has broad applicability to other facets of institutional life, including the university.

According to the Commission, institutional discrimination represented the most common form of discrimination against blacks. The most prevalent example of this discrimination was the use of seemingly neutral practices and policies that had the effect of excluding blacks from employment opportunities. This adverse impact need not be a result of the intent of an employer to discriminate, but may be caused by ". . . economic, educational and social disparities in the society. . . ." The ultimate test of whether institutional discrimination exists revolves around the question of utilization of blacks within the academy. Although the absence of blacks in the academic profession does not in and of itself mean that the institution discriminates, it does raise an inference that institutional policies and practices may contribute to the paucity of black instructional personnel.

In addition, the absence of blacks

on the faculty may constitute irrefutable statistical evidence of a pattern or practice of discrimination. This would be particularly true if the institution's applicant flow data indicated that blacks applied for employment in sufficient numbers but were denied employment at a higher rate than were whites. Furthermore, if blacks, once employed, encountered greater difficulty in obtaining tenure than did whites, then this statistical evidence would raise an inference that blacks suffered discrimination in the tenure review process. The test in these tenure decisions as well as in the employment application process would be whether a seemingly neutral policy or practice had a disproportionate adverse impact upon blacks. If however, the institution could demonstrate that such policy or practice was job related, then the inference of discrimination might be rebutted.

This method of analyzing institutional policies and practices to determine whether they produce a discriminating impact has evolved into a legal theory of discrimination which was first sanctioned by the United States Supreme Court in a 1971 decision known as *Griggs vs. Duke Power Company*. It is through the Griggs analysis that institutional racism has been legally challenged under Title VII of the Civil Right Act of 1964.

In *Griggs*, the United States Supreme Court was faced with its first major challenge to institutional discrimination (racism), brought under Title VII by black employees.[13] Prior to the passage of Title VII,

12. U.S. Commission on Civil Rights, *The Challenge Ahead, Equal Opportunities in Referral Unions* (May 1976), p. 92.

13. Although the court does not use the language "racism," it nevertheless is appropriate since discrimination is an effect of racism.

Duke Power Company discriminated against blacks by relegating them to the least desirable positions which were concentrated in its Labor Department. The salaries for this department were the lowest in the entire company. After the passage of the Civil Right Act, Duke Power Company allowed blacks to transfer to other departments, but conditioned such transfers upon the receipt of a high school diploma and the successful completion of two aptitude tests.

Black employees who had previously been segregated in the labor department filed a civil law suit challenging the conditions imposed upon transfer. The Court held that an employer's use of tests which disqualified a disproportionate number of black applicants and could not be shown to be job related violated Title VII. According to the Court, the thrust of the Act was directed at the consequences of employment practices and not at the motivation or intent of the employer to discriminate. In addition, the Court reasoned that Congress in passing the Civil Rights Act had ". . . placed on the employer the burden of showing that any given requirement (has) a manifest relationship to the employment in question. . . ."[14] In determining whether a job requirement or criterion has a manifest relationship to job performance the Court sanctioned the use of the *EEOC Guidelines of Employee Selection Procedures*,[15] which in the Court's opinion expressed the will of Congress, and must be given great deference by the Judiciary.

14. *Griggs vs. Duke Power Co.*, 401 U.S. 424 431 (1971).

15. 29 C.F.R. 1607, 35 Fed. Rge. 12333 (August 1, 1979).

As a result of *Griggs*, blacks (other minorities) and women have a legal redress for discriminatory employment policies and practices. Although the great bulk of this litigation has involved non-academic employment, such employment—including the tenure review process—is not immune to similar challenges. For eight years following the passage of the Civil Rights Act of 1964, universities and colleges were exempt from coverage, which reflected a traditional aversion to the federal regulation of education. This exemption, however, was repealed by the Equal Employment Opportunity Act of 1972, which made universities and colleges both public and private, subject to the legal prohibition against discrimination on the basis of race, color, religion, sex and national origin.

The inclusion of educational institutions under Title VII of the Civil Rights Acts afforded women and minorities legal redress for discriminatory employment practices in the academe. Legal theories of discrimination such as disparate impact and, more importantly, disparate treatment found broad applicability in lawsuits filed by women and minorities. One of the earliest lawsuits against a university was *Green vs. Board of Regents*, which was brought by a female associate professor under Section 1983 of the Civil Rights Act of 1871. Dr. Green began work as an instructor at Texas Tech University in 1954. In 1955 when she received her doctorate, she was promoted to assistant professor. In 1959, she was promoted to associate professor and applied for full professor in 1962, but was denied this promotion. On several occasions she reapplied for promotion to full professor, but each time was denied the promotion. In 1969 she filed suit against the University alleging discrimination on the basis of sex. The United States District Court for the Northern District of Texas held against plaintiff, holding that the University had established definite criteria for evaluation of a candidate's qualifications and that it would not substitute its judgment for that of the faculty. The court reasoned:

Decisions of this nature that have been made by proper authorities of a University, including its administrators and its governing board, are not justiciable in the absence of abuse of discretion, capricious action or discrimination of such a nature as to constitute a violation or deprivation of constitutional rights.[16]

In *Green* the plaintiff did not prevail due to the reluctance of Courts to interfere with the internal operation of Universities. However, in *Johnson vs. University of Pittsburgh*, this hands-off approach was rejected by the United States District Court for the Western District of Pennsylvania in a lawsuit involving similar fact patterns. In this case a female biochemistry professor at the University of Pittsburgh Medical School brought a Title VII action against the University alleging sex discrimination for its failure to grant her tenure. Although the defendants argued that the case was not subject to the 1972 Amendments which became effective on March 24, 1972, the Court rejected this argument and reasoned that the Amendments were designed to be remedial in nature and thus subject to broad interpretation. Therefore, the Court concluded, largely the basis of statistical evidence, that the University of Pittsburgh had

engaged in a pattern and practice of discrimination against women in the tenure review process. The Court was persuaded by statistical evidence that a significant disparity existed between average salaries held by tenured males ($37,500.00) and tenured females ($27,000.00).[17] Viewing the tenure process over the past six years, the Court was disturbed that seventy (70) men were granted tenure, compared to three (3) women. Finally, in regards to the affirmative action plan established by the University, the Court found that little progress had been made since its adoption.

A more recent case involving Dr. Carolyn F. Hunter, a black biochemist, indicates that judicial relief under Title VII can be obtained for discrimination. Dr. Hunter brought her lawsuit to prevent the University of Arkansas Medical School from denying her employment on the basic science faculty as an instructor. Dr. Hunter was a lifetime resident of the State of Arkansas with a reasonable amount of experience as a researcher in biochemistry, but no teaching experience. She alleged that her denial of employment was premised upon her race and sex.

In deciding the case, the Court reviewed statistical evidence which exhibited the stark absence of black female faculty employees at the Medical School. For, example, the statistical evidence established that the Medical School had never employed a black person as a full-time faculty member,[18] despite the University's verbal commitment to equal employment opportunity. The University contended that it was

16. *Green vs. Board of Regents*, 335 F. Supp. 249, 249, aff'd 474 F. 2nd 594 (5th Cir. 1973).

17. *Johnson vs. U. of Pittsburgh*, 359 F. Supp. 1002 (U.D. Pa. 1973).

18. *Hunter vs. Ward*, 20 FEP Cases 1644, 1649 (1979).

unable to attract black female faculty members because of the small pool of candidates who were available. Mr. Charles Wadkins, Chairman of the Biochemistry Department, testified that there were only 13 black members in the American Society of Biochemists. The Court answered the defendants' arguments with the following:

. . . If all of these assertions are true, and we have no reason to suspect that they are not true, the defendants' treatment of the plaintiff appears to be quite inconsistent with their verbal commitment to equal employment opportunity. If, as a matter of fact, a qualified black biochemist is such a rarity, it would appear that the employment of Dr. Hunter as an instructor would have presented an irresistable prize, for not only is she a qualified biochemist, but she is black, a female and a native Arkansan. . . .[19]

The Court concluded that Dr. Hunter had suffered discrimination and therefore ordered that she be employed.

Other cases involving application of Title VII to Universities and Colleges have been Sweeney vs. Bd. of Trustees of Keene St. Coll., 18 FEP cases 520 (1978), and Lamphere vs. Brown University, 16 FEP cases 748 (1979). These cases were brought initially in the federal district court which applied the current legal theories regarding discrimination. In Wheelock College vs. MCAD, the Massachusetts Supreme Court adopted the federal standard for the proof of discrimination based upon disparate treatment.[20]

19. *Hunter vs. Ward*, 20 FEP Cases 1644, 1649 (1979).
20. *Wheelock College vs. MCAD*, 20 FEP Cases 1457 (1979) This federal standard was first enunciated by the United States Supreme Court in the case of *McDonald Douglas vs. Green* 411 U.S. 792 (1973).

There appears to be a trend for state court adoption of the federal court definitions of discrimination.

THE CASE FOR AFFIRMATIVE ACTION IN FACULTY HIRING

At the heart of the legal redress process are affirmative action programs. These programs are designed to provide self-evaluation so institutional discrimination can be identified and, if it exists, rectified by preferential hiring of minorities. Such programs have been developed to aid institutional compliance with federal/state laws and regulations and to offer employers limited liability by facilitating identification of any employment factor that has a "disproportionate impact" and could render the institution vulnerable to costly and potentially damaging civil law suits.

However, it is unsettled as to whether the self-evaluation that is the key to a successful affirmative action program is in and of itself sufficient justification to withstand a challenge alleging reverse discrimination. At issue is the degree to which institutions may act unilaterally, proactively, and affirmatively to establish access for minorities. The Bakke and Weber cases dealt tangentially with affirmative action programs in which self-evaluation studies revealing an underutilization of blacks moved institutions to set specific quotas or grant racial preferences in hiring. While the decisions in these cases caution against over-zealous and carelessly designed programs to enhance minority access and employment, they do not pose a legal barrier to the development and implementation of strong voluntary affirmative action plans.

Under Bakke, a university subject

to Title VI of the Civil Rights Act or the Fourteenth Amendment may take race into account as one factor of many involved in an admissions process if the purpose of such arrangement is to achieve a diverse student population. In this case, the United States Supreme Court considered the question of whether diversity in the university student population was a goal which could be legitimately achieved through an affirmative action program. Justice Powell, writing for a majority of the court, stated that the attainment of a diverse student body was a permissible goal. Yet the Court found unlawful the reservation of sixteen (16) medical school seats to blacks out of a total of one hundred (100), even though it upheld the use of race in admissions decisions.

In *Bakke* the issue decided by the Supreme Court involved a class of individuals whose underutilization at the medical school was primarily a function of historical discrimination. The majority opinion, however, rejected arguments of societal discrimination and instead reasoned that an affirmative action program such as the one at issue in *Bakke* would only be lawful if there had been a legal determination of past discrimination.[21] In effect, *Bakke* slows down but does not halt legal redress for institutional racism, and points to future case by case consideration of discrimination, closely supervised by the Courts.

21. However, the Court strongly hinted that an affirmative action program designed to create a "diversity of perspective" among the student population might be lawful given the First Amendment considerations involved in academic freedom, which includes the right to select the student body. Furthermore, four of the Justices would have allowed the racial quotas, to stand despite the lack of finding of past discrimination.

Like *Bakke, United Steelworkers of America vs. Brian Weber* is not an obstacle to the development of affirmative action programs. In this case the Supreme Court reviewed an affirmative action program involving employment. The issue the court had to decide was whether Title VII of the Civil Rights Act of 1964 forbids private employers and unions from voluntarily agreeing upon bona fide affirmative action plans that grant racial preferences. The court ruled that Title VII does not forbid the kind of affirmative action program established by Kaiser Aluminum. The court reasoned that the program was designed to eliminate "traditional patterns of racial segregation" and that Civil Rights Act must be read in historical context.

This decision marked an important milestone in that the court explicitly sanctioned the use of history as a measure for gauging the legality of affirmative action programs. According to Justice Brennan, who wrote the majority opinion, it would be ironic for a program designed to carry out the purposes of the Civil Rights Act, to be in violation of the Act. Furthermore, he stated that since the purpose of the affirmative action program was consistent with that of the Act, it did not violate the Act.[22] In the 5-2 decision he explained that the purpose of the Civil Rights Act was to

22. *United Steelworkers of America vs. Brian Weber*, 20 FEP Cases 1 (1979) This plan reserved for black employees 50 percent of openings in craft training programs. The program would operate until the percentage of blacks in the craft training program approximated that in the local labor market. Prior to 1974, when the program was first instituted, blacks comprised only 1.83 percent of the skilled craft workers, even though the local work force was 39 percent black.

integrate blacks into the mainstream of America through full participation in the workforce. Relying upon legislative history, in particular the debate of the late Senator Hubert Humphrey, the court recognized the relationship between jobs and education. For example, the court quoted Senator Humphrey in a debate on the senate floor in which he explained:

. . . How can a Negro child be motivated to take full advantage of integrated educational facilities if he has no hope of getting a job where he can use that education. . . . Income from employment may be necessary to further a man's education, or that of his children. If his children have no hope of getting a good job, what will motivate them to take advantage of educational opportunities.[23]

Currently, court decisions pertaining to institutional discrimination remain cautious and somewhat contradictory. As a result, institutional racism persists even though mechanisms for handling complaints have been developed. Federal administrative agencies have made an attempt to clarify the situation. The Equal Employment Opportunity Commission (EEOC) has tried through the release of its *Affirmative Action Guidelines* (1979) to reassure institutions unnerved by Bakke. The expressed reason offered for the guidelines was to ". . . encourage voluntary action to eliminate employment discrimination. . . ."[24] The Guidelines are the Commission's interpretation of Title VII. The Commission does not believe that there is a legitimate concept of "reverse discrimination" under Title VII, but that discrimination against

all people is what the statute proscribes. The Commission postulates that Congress enacted Title VII to ". . . overcome the effects of past and present employment practices which are part of a larger pattern of restriction, exclusion, discrimination, segregation and inferior treatment of minorities and women in many areas of life. . . ." Most importantly the Commission stated:

. . . It is essential to the effective implementation of Title VII that those who take appropriate voluntary affirmative action receive adequate protection against claims that their efforts constitute discrimination. . . .

The effect of this particular Guideline is that the EEOC will issue a determination of no reasonable cause against a plaintiff who is challenging an affirmative action program which was founded in reliance upon the Guidelines.

Affirmative Action as defined by the federal civil rights enforcement agencies should be applied in all areas of employment, including tenure. Unless affirmative action is vigorously persued at all levels of appointment, the university will never make substantial progress towards its goal of full utilization of black faculty members. Compliance with affirmative action at all levels will insure that the faculty is able to relate effectively with urban student populations and to serve as role models for individuals from economically depressed communities.

CONCLUSION

The underutilization of blacks in the academic profession cannot be understood apart from the historical reality of racial discrimination in higher education, particularly in the admission of students. It is through the education of qualified black stu-

23. *Weber*, p. 5.
24. EEOC, *Affirmative Action Guidelines* 42 F.R. 64, 826.

dents that the nation develops a pool of candidates from which future professional employees can be drawn. Due to the exclusion of blacks from primarily white institutions of higher education, a predominant number of available professional employees are graduates of black institutions. These institutions shouldered the national responsibility for educating black students at a time when the doors of opportunity were closed to most blacks. As a result, graduates of these institutions account for seventy-five (75) percent of all black Ph.D.s and eighty (80) percent of all black doctors.

If higher education is to move affirmatively in the hiring of black professors, this pool of highly qualified talent must be continually drawn upon and expanded. This nation cannot expect to move toward an integrated faculty if it does not insure the survival and development of the predominantly black institutions of higher education. A national policy that mandates the desegregation of black colleges, rather moving against the segregated educational systems of the North and West, places in grave jeopardy the educational resources that have been solely responsible for generating the largest pool of qualified black faculty.

To insure the continuation of this available pool, vigorous enforcement of civil rights laws must be undertaken against institutions that continue to exclude and/or limit advancement of blacks into the academic ranks. Institutional policies and procedures that have the effect of limiting opportunities for both black students and faculty should be vigorously studied. This review should focus upon both student admission and faculty employment. Black students must be insured a good faith opportunity to graduate from college. Institutional self-evaluation of admissions and retention practices may reveal problems that can be voluntarily rectified rather than be made the subject of a lawsuit.

A vigorous affirmative action effort on the part of this nation's institutions of higher education can have considerable impact in broadening educational opportunities. After the *Brown* decision in 1954, institutions failed to develop affirmative action programs even though there were no legal barriers to their development. The civil rights movement provided the impetus for their development. In the next decade, colleges and universities must renew their commitment to greater levels. They must actively lobby for the survival and expansion of black colleges, and make greater efforts to retain and advance black faculty who are currently employed. The scope of these efforts, however, should be determined by a self-evaluation study conducted pursuant to federal and state affirmative action regulations and guidelines. As such, universities and colleges can become instrumental in moving this nation closer to its social goal of equal opportunity and economic justice.

Untenured and Tenuous: The Status of Women Faculty

By LILLI S. HORNIG

ABSTRACT: Issues of equity in higher education have assumed prominence with the development of laws seeking to abolish sex discrimination. The status of women on faculties thus has become a subject for widespread study and debate. A historical sketch of women's participation in the professoriate is followed by a more detailed overview of the positions they hold, how they are distributed among institutions, what they are paid, and what functions they perform. Numerous studies in this field agree that women faculty are overconcentrated in the least prestigious institutions and in the lower ranks, carry a disproportionate share of teaching loads especially at introductory levels, and are seriously underpaid at all levels when rank, field, Ph.D. cohort, type of institution, and work functions are held constant. Evidence is adduced which suggests that such faculty distributions and reward systems may adversely affect the quality of education and of scholarly research. Implications for higher education policy are discussed.

Lilli S. Hornig is Executive Director of Higher Education Resource Services (H.E.R.S.) at Wellesley College. H.E.R.S. conducts research on women in higher education, and programs designed to improve the status of academic professional women. Dr. Hornig, a graduate of Bryn Mawr College, holds a doctorate in chemistry from Harvard and has been a faculty member at Brown University and at Trinity College, Washington, D.C., where she chaired the chemistry department. She is a member of the National Academy of Sciences' Commission on Human Resources and chairs its Committee on the Education and Employment of Women in Science and Engineering.

DURING the past decade, a heightened awareness of equity problems in higher education awakened a good deal of interest in the status of women faculty and made available a large though inchoate body of data concerning them. They are now more than a quarter of all instructional faculty, but because their share of faculty positions has grown faster recently than the total professoriate, they are on the average younger, more recently trained, and in more junior positions than their male colleagues. They are also distributed differently among institutions, more likely to be in four and two year colleges than in universities. Certain disparities between male and female faculty stem in part from their very different distribution among academic disciplines and from the fact that a larger fraction of the men hold doctorates. However, major disparities in rank, tenure status, and salary remain even when factors such as field, level of degree, and years of experience are held constant.

Beyond the obvious problems of equity which these imbalances present for women, for the institutions in which they serve, and for the profession as a whole, they may have additional importance in a period of changing enrollments, shrinking faculty openings, and decreasing research support. By and large, male enrollments at both undergraduate and graduate levels have begun to decline while women's are growing; among entering freshmen, women now outnumber men and the overall sex balance is likely to be even in the near future if present trends continue. The question of whether predominantly male faculties can in fact provide equal education for women students thus becomes increasingly important. The largest numbers of women are among the younger, more recently trained faculty who are likely to be at the forefront of research. Retaining them will be necessary to the continued vitality of their fields and their institutions as well as to a full complement of women students. At the same time, the abnormally high concentration of women in untenured and off-ladder positions makes them especially vulnerable to the "academic depression" and arouses concern that colleges and universities are not giving adequate attention to many of these issues.

Although only about one-third of all faculty hold doctorates, most of the research directed toward elucidating the disparities between male and female faculty has centered on Ph.D. holders, and reliable comparisons are therefore best made at this degree level. Much of the detailed discussion which follows is focused on doctorate faculty.

THE HISTORICAL FRAMEWORK

As a proportion of faculties in higher education, women have had their ups and downs. A century ago (when universities in the modern sense did not exist in the United States) "college" faculties were reported to be well over half female but by 1890 the fraction of women had dropped to about one quarter. After 1910 it began to rise slightly, to a high of 27.6 percent just before World War II, dropping subsequently to about 22 percent.[1] Over the last six years it has risen to 25.5 percent.[2]

1. *Digest of Education Statistics 1977–78*, National Center for Education Statistics, 1978, p. 94.
2. "Memorandum on Selected Statistics on Salary and Tenure of Full-Time Instructional Faculty" National Center for Education Statistics, 15 April 1978, p. 5.

Patricia Graham has suggested that the emergence of the research university as the model for higher education, a development paralleling the post-World War II flowering of the sciences, created a climate unfavorable to women in part because of their historic connection with teaching and in part because the sciences were less attractive and less hospitable to women.[3] Certainly the proportion of women taking advanced degrees in the sciences during this period declined, principally as the result of rapid growth in the numbers of men.

To what extent this disproportionate increase in male over female students, and subsequently faculty, was fueled by the G.I. Bill and by the explosive growth of Federal graduate student support remains a subject for speculation. G.I. benefits were unavailable to women, and many other types of both undergraduate and graduate scholarships were designated exclusively for men. Unlike their male counterparts, women as a rule could pursue advanced study only at their own expense. Decreasing opportunities for women in research universities were offset to some extent by the growth of two year colleges during this period.

Detailed assessments of historical trends are difficult because there are insufficient data about the distribution of women faculty within universities, about precise definitions of faculty status, and about distinctions between full and part time faculty. Most of the leading research universities had virtually no women on their strictly "academic" faculties before 1970, at least

in senior positions. However, that fact is obscured in aggregate data, which may include divisions or schools of home economics, education, library science, or nursing; such divisions typically had largely female faculty. Data collected in the last decade, with more reliable definitions of positions, demonstrate slow but definite growth in the proportion of women faculty in the arts and sciences, the core fields of higher education.

The exploding undergraduate enrollments of the sixties, when the baby boom generation reached college, created an inflated demand for teachers which many women with master's degrees and doctorates helped to meet. They "returned to teaching" in considerable numbers, many of them unaware that the ancillary slots open to them as lecturers, instructors, or adjunct assistant professors were not generally a route to tenure, security, and highly respected professional status. Along with their male colleagues, they were also unaware that the boom could not last and that their untenurable positions made them particularly vulnerable to potential cutbacks.

The resurgence of feminism during this period both reflected and contributed to the astonishing growth of advanced graduate education for women which has augmented the pool of women doctorates enormously in the last fifteen years. The pipeline to senior faculty positions, reduced to a trickle for more than two decades, seemed to be open. Concurrently, the mandate for unbiased hiring and promotion policies imposed by equal opportunity legislation appeared to ensure the fuller use of women on faculties. The sections which follow examine the extent to which these expectations have been realized.

3. Patricia Albjerg Graham, "Expansion and Exclusion: A History of Women in American Higher Education," Signs, vol. 3 (Summer 1978), p. 759.

TABLE 1

DISTRIBUTION OF WOMEN FACULTY IN HIGHER EDUCATION INSTITUTIONS, 1976

	TENURED FACULTY		UNTENURED FACULTY		TOTAL FACULTY	
	NUMBER	PERCENT WOMEN	NUMBER	PERCENT WOMEN	NUMBER	PERCENT WOMEN
Total, All Institutions	208,168	18.3	168,989	31.6	377,157	24.3
Universities	71,939	11.1	48,009	26.6	119,948	17.3
Other 4-Year Institutions	94,939	19.0	79,911	31.0	174,850	24.5
2-Year Institutions	41,290	29.2	41,069	38.7	82,359	33.9

Source: *Salaries, Tenure and Fringe Benefits of Full-Time Instructional Faculty in Institutions of Higher Education 1975–76*, National Center for Education Statistics, 1977, (NCES 77-318), pp. 26–27.

THE STATISTICAL FRAMEWORK

The data which describe the growth or decline of faculties, the shifting field mix within them, and the people who compose them are varied and copious but imperfectly correlated. It is seldom clear in large-scale surveys what the sources and magnitude of errors are, and different surveys rarely yield strictly comparable data; faculty data are often flawed by imperfectly defined positions and variously drawn distinctions among full and part time or tenure, tenure track, and off-ladder posts. These problems suggest particular caution in interpreting data concerning women who hold disproportionately high shares of such ill-defined positions. As pointed out above, it is also necessary to distinguish between doctoral faculty and those holding lower degrees.

Faculty size and distribution

The total number of full time faculty and the percent of women in the three types of higher education institutions in 1976 are displayed in Table 1. The single largest block of women, as of all faculty, is found in four year colleges; but women are a larger fraction, about one third, of faculty in two year colleges than in other types of institutions. They are least represented in universities. In all cases they are significantly less likely than men to be tenured, but the discrepancy is smallest in two year colleges and largest in universities. These overall relationships have remained essentially constant over a number of years.

Balance among academic fields

While the total size of faculty by fields is not readily determined, some indication of the overall distribution across disciplines can be gained by examining data available for doctorate holders. Table 2 illustrates both the total size of doctoral faculty in a range of fields and the distribution of women among them; the latter reflects fairly closely (but in no case equals) the proportion of doctorates earned by women in most of the respective disciplines and cohorts. It should be noted that engineering and certain other physical sciences, which account for large numbers of male Ph.D.s and faculty members, are not included here because they have only small fractions of women.

Taking into account these strongly male fields, however, it is evident that the balance of numbers

TABLE 2

SIZE OF DOCTORAL FACULTY AND PERCENT OF WOMEN FACULTY
IN SELECTED FIELDS, BY PH.D. COHORT

	MATH.	CHEM.	BIOSCI.	PSYCH.	SOC.SCI.	HIST.	ENG/AM. LIT.	MOD.LANG. & LIT.
Total Number of Doctoral Faculty	11,936	15,339	33,353	16,498	31,867	12,911	14,776	8,552
Percent Women Faculty								
1934–49 Ph.D.s	8.4	4.2	11.9	16.6	9.8	12.4	18.6	13.4
1950–59 Ph.D.s	3.8	7.6	10.3	11.6	7.6	8.0	11.9	17.7
1960–69 Ph.D.s	6.5	9.0	14.9	19.8	10.5	9.2	23.1	27.9
1970–74 Ph.D.s	8.8	11.6	21.2	27.4	17.1	16.0	31.9	36.4
1975–76 Ph.D.s	10.8	13.3	23.1	32.7	25.1	24.1	47.2	48.7

Source: Betty D. Maxfield, Nancy C. Ahern, and Andrew W. Spisak, *Science, Engineering, and Humanities Doctorates in the United States: 1977 Profile*. National Academy of Sciences, Washington, D.C., 1978, pp. 21 and 48.

among faculties is heavily weighted toward the sciences, where women are found in decreasing proportions as the fields become more quantitative or technological. Conversely, the highest concentrations of women are in a small number of relatively small fields. This imbalance, which is indeed obvious on casual inspection of most faculties, contributes to a number of controversial issues which are discussed below.

It is not clear to what extent the distribution of doctoral faculty among fields actually parallels that of all faculty. Somewhat surprisingly, Ph.D.s are a minority in all types of institutions, with the likely exception of research universities, constituting only one third of total faculty (but almost half of university faculty). Women faculty members overall, however, are only half as likely as men to hold a doctorate; in two year colleges, where Ph.D.s are infrequent in general, almost equally small fractions (3–4 percent) of men and women hold this degree, but in universities the likelihood of a male faculty member having a Ph.D. is almost three times

that for a woman, with four year colleges occupying an intermediate position.[4]

This distribution has been interpreted widely as reflecting a greater degree of anti-female bias in universities as compared to colleges, but that is not necessarily a valid conclusion. On the one hand, those science fields which have few women are likely to be dominant in universities while the humanities areas in which women are relatively well represented have become more peripheral, especially in graduate schools. On the other hand, predominantly female professional fields like home economics, library science, education, and nursing are more likely to be part of comprehensive universities rather than colleges and should thus augment the proportion of women on these faculties.

Rank, tenure, and salaries

The degree to which institutions draw gender based distinctions

4. *Digest of Education Statistics 1977–78*, National Center for Education Statistics, 1978, p. 96.

among their faculties is reflected most vividly in the proportions of women and men at different ranks, with and without tenure, and in the salaries paid to each of these categories. While differences in these factors are characteristic of all faculty in all institutions, they are demonstrated best for doctoral faculty, where precise data permit detailed comparisons.

The details of rank distribution for men and women doctoral faculty by field and Ph.D. cohort have been investigated for faculty in the sciences[5] and in the humanities,[6] and yield essentially similar sex distributions among fields. In all disciplines, about two-thirds of the men are in the two senior ranks, but only about 40 percent of the women; for 1960–69 Ph.D. cohorts, men are about two to three times as likely as women to be full professors. Summed over all cohorts, about 40 percent of men are full professors while less than a quarter are assistant professors; the fraction who are instructors or lecturers is below 2 percent. By contrast, the single dominant rank for women of all cohorts is assistant professor, which alone accounts for nearly 40 percent of all female doctoral faculty. Conversely, the proportion of women at full professorial rank is smallest, less than that in unranked faculty positions.

Tenure is a more reliable in-dicator of true senior faculty status than rank per se. The frequent assumption that all full professors, almost all at associate rank, and no assistant professors are tenured turns out to be invalid. Even among doctoral faculty in the sciences, no single rank is fully tenured; nearly 96 percent of male full professors are, but only 92 percent of females. The sex difference is markedly larger at the associate professor level, where almost 82 percent of men but only 71 percent of women hold tenure. Among assistant professors, nearly 13 percent of men and 10 percent of women are tenured. For associate professors of identical Ph.D. cohorts, after 1960 these differences are greatly magnified in some fields, reaching 25–30 percent in some of the physical sciences.[7]

Over the last few years, the proportion of men achieving tenure has exceeded that of women by about 5–20 percent among recent doctoral cohorts, depending on field. They are five to seven years beyond the doctorate and may thus be regarded as the "fast movers" among young faculty. This difference may be partially ascribed to the women's somewhat greater propensity to accept postdoctoral appointments and to hold them for somewhat longer periods than men—or to be forced to take such positions because they cannot get faculty posts. In either case, it is a cause for concern.

Salary differences between men and women are widespread in all occupations and at all educational levels; the professoriate is no ex-

5. *Climbing the Academic Ladder: Doctoral Women Scientists in Academe*, (Washington, DC: Committee on the Education and Employment of Women in Science and Engineering, National Academy of Sciences, 1979), pp. 60–61.

6. Betty D. Maxfield, Nancy C. Ahern, and Andrew W. Spisak, *Science, Engineering, and Humanities Doctorates in the United States: 1977 Profile* (Washington, DC: National Academy of Sciences, 1978), pp. 20–22 and 47–49.

7. *Climbing the Academic Ladder: Doctoral Women Scientists in Academe*, (Washington, DC: Committee on the Education and Employment of Women in Science and Engineering, National Academy of Sciences, 1979), pp. 82–86.

ception. The salaries of male faculty exceed women's by about 20 percent overall—a difference which follows in part, but only in part, from their different pattern of distribution among institutional types, fields, and ranks. Even when these variables—in addition to Ph.D. cohort—are held constant, men's salaries continue to exceed women's by amounts ranging up to almost 15 percent for assistant professors hired within the last few years. In chemistry, a field which shows evidence of sex bias in many forms, the median annual salaries of male and female full professor in 1977 differed by an astonishing 28 percent, or $6,200.[8]

Functional distinctions

Do men and women on faculties perform the same functions—teaching, research, service to the academic community, and administration—so that in fact they should be eligible for the same rewards of rank, tenure, and salary? The answer is a very qualified yes, depending on how each function is weighted; male and female faculty do the same things, but in varying degrees.

First, one of the canons of conventional wisdom must be dispelled; women faculty are not predominantly or even substantially part time workers; 92 percent of them, compared to 96 percent of men, work full time. Part time faculty of both sexes are fairly evenly distributed among institutional types. About 3 percent more of the women are employed for 9–10 months, and correspondingly fewer for 11–12 months, but the overall sex difference in part time and part

year appointments is surprisingly small.[9]

These data must be viewed with some caution, however, since there is much anecdotal evidence to suggest serious under reporting of part time faculty employment. This arises from an apparently fairly common institutional practice of not carrying part time appointees on the faculty rolls unless they have long-term contracts, which most part time teachers do not; under the circumstances, such persons are not readily accessible to surveys. What the sex balance among them is remains to be studied, but general employment data suggest a preponderance of women in this group.

Considerable differences occur in principal work activities. Overall, about half again as many men (12 percent) as women are primarily engaged in administrative work, while 5 percent fewer are teaching. Three times as many men list "research" as their principal activity— but less than 5 percent of total faculty are in this category. The sex differences are again magnified in universities, where almost 10 percent of male faculty are primarily researchers.

Well over half of all male university faculty—53 percent—teach eight hours or less per week, but only 35 percent of women enjoy such a light schedule; conversely, 28 percent of women university faculty teach 13 hours or more weekly, but only 15 percent of the men carry such a load. In four year colleges teaching loads are much more equitably distributed, but significantly more of the women

8. *Ibid.*, pp. 88–94.

9. *Digest of Education Statistics 1977–78*, National Center for Education Statistics, 1978, p. 96.

carry the heaviest teaching loads, 17 hours or more per week.[10]

Scheduled teaching loads alone do not, of course, define adequately the nature and extent of a faculty member's obligations. The unscheduled portion of time may be spent in various ways—on research, on teaching and supervising graduate students, and on administrative or service activities. An exceptionally heavy scheduled load may include several sections of a single course, or several different courses; short hours may be assigned to those teaching very large classes—or very small seminars. Data to sort out these questions do not exist. Nonetheless, the preponderance of men with low teaching loads is striking.

The level of courses taught is an important criterion of a faculty member's status, quite aside from formal rank definitions. In modern language departments, where women are an average 34 percent of faculty, they are 45 percent of those who teach only first- and second-year courses. However, they are only 12 percent of those who teach graduate courses exclusively.[11]

Combined with the inequitably distributed teaching loads cited above, this finding suggests that male faculty not only have considerably more time for research but also enormously better access to the graduate students who facilitate a faculty member's research effort.

Service to the academic community, either within an institution or outside it in scholarly associations, is not readily quantified, nor is it clear how much importance attaches to it either for promotion and tenure decisions or for general professional recognition. There is some evidence that women may devote more time to such activities than men, possibly because their relative isolation in many departments makes it harder for them to assess the actual benefits to be derived.[12]

Quality and productivity

Marked differences in the status and rewards of male and female faculty would be justified and indeed expected if the two groups were not of equal quality. Definitions of "quality" for faculty members are elusive but for new Ph.D.s at the outset of their academic careers certain fairly objective measures may be applied. Among these are academic records, test scores, elapsed time between bachelor's and doctoral degrees (considered indicative of drive and motivation), and quality of the doctorate-granting department. When these factors were examined for women scientists, they indicated that women doctorates on the average showed somewhat greater academic ability than men, studied in highly rated departments in comparable proportions, and completed their doctorates as fast as men or faster.[13]

The situation of women doc-

10. *Ibid.*, p. 97.

11. Florence Howe, Laura Morlock, and Richard Berk, "The Status of Women in Modern Language Departments: A Report of the Modern Language Association Commission on the Status of Women in the Profession," *Proceedings of the Modern Language Association* 86 (1971), pp. 459–468.

12. C. S. Widom and B. W. Burke, "Performance, Attitudes, and Professional Socialization of Women in Academia," *Sex Roles* 4 (August 1978), pp. 549–562.

13. *Climbing the Academic Ladder: Doctoral Women Scientists in Academe*, Committee on the Education and Employment of Women in Science and Engineering, (Washington, DC: National Academy of Sciences, 1979), pp. 19–31.

torates in the humanities has not yet been explored in such depth. In the major humanities fields, however, women generally take slightly longer than men to complete Ph.D.s[14] This difference between the sciences and the humanities may well derive from different patterns of financial support. Most graduate students in the sciences receive considerable financial aid, and while the sources of this aid differ somewhat for men and women, there is no reason to believe that support as such has been a problem. In the humanities, on the other hand, fellowship support is rarer and most students must teach, part or full time, during the course of their graduate careers. If women have greater difficulty getting such positions, as we have reason to believe, and if they are paid less than men when they do, as has been demonstrated, it is not surprising that they need more time to complete their degrees.

One aspect of faculty "quality" is scholarly productivity, usually measured by some combination of publication and citation counts, both of which are known to be somewhat unreliable because of differing usages in ordering authors' names, inordinately high numbers of citations to faulty or controversial papers, and other difficulties. A number of contradictory studies exist, comparing men's and women's productivity; some show different productivities and some equal ones. All are flawed by the absence of controls for teaching loads, access to graduate students, or to facilities and funding. Until there are many

14. *Summary Report 1978, Doctoral Recipients from United States Universities*, (Washington, DC: National Academy of Sciences, March 1979), pp. 30–33.

more women in senior positions of research departments, it is unlikely that a meaningful sample for such an investigation can be assembled.

IMPLICATIONS OF THE DATA

Women occupy the lower reaches of the national academic pecking order. Disproportionately concentrated in the untenured and non-tenurable ranks, underpaid by all institutions, in all fields, and at all ranks, and overloaded with introductory courses, they constitute a valuable marginal labor supply for colleges and universities. The burdens of financial stringency and fluctuating enrollments are likely to fall more heavily on them; involuntary unemployment among women Ph.D.s is three to five times that of men. The positions women faculty hold, regardless of their abilities, do not give them effective access to the tools of research, neither the facilities nor the graduate students they need. In effect, women discover that something disqualifies them for advancement, but if that something is scholarly research, the possibility of remedying the situation is also blocked. They weigh very lightly in the balance of academic power.

It is often assumed that women do more teaching because that is their preference, and indeed a few studies do appear to show either that women have a greater commitment to teaching than men or that they attach more importance to it. No studies have explored the possibility that women "prefer" teaching only because it is their sole realistic choice if they cannot gain access to positions which provide the students, facilities, or intellectual climate necessary for research.

Among the pragmatic implications for colleges and universities to consider is whether they are buying the best faculties they can afford and making optimal use of the ones they have. It is statistically obvious that the quality of faculties must improve if the recruiting base of equally qualified personnel is broadened while total numbers of those selected must remain constant or decrease. This simple logic has been used in the past to "upgrade" traditionally female professions—nursing, librarianship, and elementary education—by recruiting more men into them. There is some evidence that universities have already applied such reasoning: women on science faculties increased about three times faster than total faculty growth between 1973 and 1977, and growth in the proportion of women at all ranks was fastest in research universities which traditionally had the fewest women.[15]

Undoubtedly some of this growth is also attributable to affirmative action pressures which have forced faculties to assess potential women members objectively for the first time in history. In most universities, however, resistance to affirmative action has been so explicit that there is no reason to believe compliance alone is directly responsible for increased numbers of women. Rather, compliance efforts may have brought to light the high quality of women candidates. However, much anecdotal evidence suggests that women's credentials and performance continue to be evaluated more stringently than men's.

Such stricter scrutiny may account in part for the "revolving door" phenomenon, the rotation of women faculty through junior appointments without serious consideration for tenure. How much of the recent net growth in number of women junior faculty is attributable to this effect remains uncertain. Statistical reports from a number of research universities indicate lower rates of retention for women assistant professors than for men, but these reports do not take into account comparative teaching loads, research productivity, or length of service. There is an urgent need for detailed comparative studies of junior faculty retention rates.

Whether the present maldistribution of women faculty does or does not represent optimal use of faculty resources depends on one's point of view. The freedom of male faculty to choose an individual balance of teaching and research commitments is not available to women; they must teach primarily. It is entirely possible that their disproportionately high share of teaching loads and introductory courses contributes uniquely to the quality of undergraduate education. It is equally possible that if they are miscast in this role, undergraduate teaching suffers as does the quality of academic research, denied the talent of those with strong aspirations to create new knowledge.

There is only scattered evidence to suggest that predominantly male faculties may not be able to provide an optimal education for the female half of the student body; this area needs further investigation. M. E. Tidball has found that faculty members tend to be more supportive of the aspirations of students of their own sex, and to hold higher expecta-

15. *Climbing the Academic Ladder: Doctoral Women Scientists in Academe*, Committee on the Education and Employment of Women in Science and Engineering (Washington, DC: National Academy of Sciences, 1979), p. xiii.

tions for them.[16] In a study of six graduate departments, Carolyn Perrucci
found that the extent to which faculty
members believe career goals to be
held primarily by men is inversely
related to the career commitment
of their women doctoral students.
Yet female students whose male professors were supportive of their
career goals were more likely to
attain their goals.[17] S. D. Feldman
demonstrated that male faculty and
students believe women students to
be less dedicated than men, regardless of the women's actual performance.[18] In view of the special
problems of chemistry departments
with women's salaries (see above),
it is interesting to note that both of
the latter two studies found chemistry departments to be most markedly
"male-oriented."

One of the tasks of higher education is to broaden a student's outlook and insight by teaching her or
him to examine evidence objectively
and to draw independent conclusions rather than accept traditional
views unquestioningly. What are
universities and colleges doing about
sex stereotyping, that oldest of social
traditions? Are they examining their
precepts, let alone the examples they
are setting?

Will the presence or absence of
women on faculties influence where
students go? In the coming era of
competition for fewer students, that
may be an important question for
institutions. We have only a straw
in the wind to answer it: enrollment
in selective women's colleges, which
have by far the largest proportion
of female faculty, is rising faster than
in any other type of institution,
despite the leveling and imminent
decline of overall enrollments.

The response of colleges and universities to these issues to date has
been largely at the elementary level
of fighting legal battles. Anti-bias
regulation has been met with unthinking anti-regulation bias, a perspective whose most vocal pro-
ponent was Richard Lester.[19] Higher
education institutions became mired
in self-serving argument about their
rights to be above the law, while
making grudging efforts to comply
with it. There are few signs that they
have begun to deal with the profound ethical issues which discrimination raises, especially when practiced by those who proclaim themselves a meritocracy; there are even
fewer signs that the educational and
scholarly issues interest them.

Despite the blame for these omissions so often heaped on administrators, it is faculty members who
hold power and exercise leadership
in autonomous faculties who are
remiss in addressing issues of equity
in higher education. They are the
ones who make and carry out decisions about the nature and composition of the professoriate; these
decisions should reflect a greater
degree of concern for the enhance-
ment of education and the improvement of scholarship that may result
from greater equity.

16. M. Elizabeth Tidball, "Perspectives on
Academic Women and Affirmative Action,"
Educational Record 54 (Spring 1973), pp.
130–135.

17. Carolyn Perrucci, "Sex-based Professional Socialization Among Graduate Students in Science," National Research Council,
Research Issues in the Employment of
Women: Proceedings of a Workshop, (Washington, DC: National Academy of Sciences,
1975), pp. 83–123.

18. Saul D. Feldman, Escape From the
Doll's House, Carnegie Commission on
Higher Education (New York: McGraw-Hill,
1974), pp. 70–71.

19. Richard A. Lester, Antibias Regulations of Universities: Faculty Problems
and Their Solutions (New York: McGraw-
Hill, 1974).

African Academics: A Study of Scientists at the Universities of Ibadan and Nairobi

By THOMAS OWEN EISEMON

ABSTRACT: This paper analyzes how western academic and intellectual traditions are being transformed at two African universities, the University of Ibadan (Nigeria) and the University of Nairobi (Kenya). It is argued that the academic and intellectual culture of these universities must be understood in terms of the accommodation of conflicting influences on African academic life: authority and autonomy; individualism and collectivism, and, finally, cosmopolitanism and specificity. While Ibadan and Nairobi are described as faithful to the traditions of Western universities in many ways, these traditions are influential selectively. Moreover, the academic and intellectual culture of these universities is shown to comprise traditions which are indigeneous and unreconciled with their colonial inheritance.

Thomas Owen Eisemon is Associate Professor at the Department of Social Foundations of Education, McGill University, Montreal, Canada. He has been on the staff of the UNESCO Institute for Education, Hamburg, West Germany. He is author of U.S. Educated Engineering Faculty in India *and has contributed to such journals as* Interchange, Higher Education, Teachers College Record *and others.*

THIS PAPER will analyze how Western academic and intellectual traditions are being transformed at two African universities: the University of Ibadan (Nigeria) and the University of Nairobi (Kenya). These universities are among Black Africa's most prominent institutions of higher learning and are acknowledged centers of excellence within East and West Africa respectively. They are the leading producers of scientific research in their respective countries and in Black Africa as a whole.[1] Both were established during decolonization under the supervision of the University of London.

Since independence, the universities of Ibadan and Nairobi have evolved from affiliated institutions oriented to undergraduate instruction and comprised mainly of European academics, into autonomous, complete universities, increasingly staffed by Africans. These transformations, which are very recent in the case of the University of Nairobi, have given new and uniquely African meanings to academic work, meanings that arise from the accommodation of Western academic and intellectual traditions—autonomy, individualism, and cosmopolitanism transplanted during the colonial period—to African conceptions of academic life emphasizing generational authority, collectivism, and involvement in national development.

The observations presented here are derived from interviews carried out with mathematicians and zoologists during the Spring term of the 1978 academic year.[2] Mathematics and zoology were selected to compare scientists working in disciplines which differ in their potential for applied science and, thus, in their relationship to national science policy in qualifying for financial support.

These departments are among the oldest, largest and most internationally visible in the science facilities of the two universities.[3] Thirty-four scientists were interviewed, a little more than half of the members of the mathematics and zoology departments, sixteen at the University of Ibadan and eighteen at the University of Nairobi.[4] All were African scientists, the term African comprising in Kenya, Ugandan expatriate scientists as well as Asians who have become Kenyan citizens. Special importance was attached to interviewing scientists who obtained post-graduate degrees from African universities (14), all but four of whom were affiliated with the University of Ibadan where opportunities for post-graduate training have existed for a longer time and Africanization has proceeded more rapidly.[5] For instance, white expatriates account for almost half (43 percent) of the staff members of the mathematics and zoology departments studied at Nairobi. They represent only 22 percent of the staff in these departments at Ibadan.

Locally trained African staff constitute the second generation of African scientists.[6] Collectively, they represent the achievement of a measure of self-sufficiency in ad-

1. J. D. Frame, et al. "The Distribution of World Science." Social Studies of Science 7 (1977), p. 507.

2. See also T. O. Eisemon, "Emerging Scientific Communities: A Study of Nigerian and Kenyan Academic Scientists," Minerva (Autumn 1979, forthcoming).

3. Ibid.

4. Ibid.

5. See T. O. Eisemon et al., "Collective Scientific Self-Reliance: Possibilities and Limitations." in I. Spitzberg. Universities and Collective Self-Reliance (forthcoming).

6. See T. O. Eisemon, "African Scientists: From General to Generation," Bulletin of Atomic Scientists. (forthcoming).

THE ANNALS OF THE AMERICAN ACADEMY

vanced scientific training, a preoccupation of science policy in Nigeria and Kenya in the independence period. The interviews conducted at Ibadan and Nairobi elicited information about the academic and intellectual life of scientists and focused on their careers, the factors influencing their selection of research topics, and the possibilities for communication and collaboration in their research field, institutionally, regionally, and internationally.

Although some references will be made to differences between Ibadan and Nairobi, as well as between mathematics and zoology, their commonalities will be emphasized. In many important respects the academic and intellectual culture of the two universities is similar. The colonial inheritance in each is being transformed by circumstances which are African rather than specifically Nigerian or Kenyan, namely, their peripherality vis-à-vis the international production and dissemination of knowledge as well as the need to satisfy expectations generated by independence for rapid advancement, individual and societal, cultural self-assertion, and international recognition. It will be argued that the process through which the universities of Ibadan and Nairobi are being transformed into African universities involves a dialectic between western academic and intellectual traditions, on one hand, and transcedent African values and obligations, on the other. This dialectic is perhaps most evident in the interactions of autonomy with authority, individualism with collectivism, and cosmopolitanism with specificity in African academic life.

Autonomy and authority

The conception of academic work as a profession characterized by a high degree of autonomy and of the university as a self-governing association of scholars was transplanted to Africa through foreign training and continuing contact with expatriates; it was imbedded in the patterns of governance and collegial traditions of the universities of Ibadan and Nairobi. Yet, autonomy and collegiality compete with another conception of academic life, derivative of the colonial experience but African in its application, which is also imbedded in the patterns of governance and traditions of these universities—a conception of academic life emphasizing generational authority and hierarchy. Autonomy and authority influence different dimensions of the academic culture of Ibadan and Nairobi, simultaneously suggesting fidelity to and important departure from colonial legacies.

In his book *Power and Privilege in an African University*, Pierre Van den Berghe depicted the senior academic staff of the University of Ibadan as a "mandarinate."[7] "Historically," he notes, "they are the successor class to the colonial administrators whose privileges they inherited," education having supplanted color as a source of social differentiation. Van den Berghe observes that to the mandarinate, "the university is not simply a place to work—[it is] their raison d'être —they largely regard the university as theirs in a quasi proprietary sense."[8] This is in part reflected in the strong commitment to the traditions of participation in university governance acquired during the period of expatriate pre-eminence.

At Ibadan and Nairobi, the Senate is the most important instrument of

7. P. Van der Berghe. *Power and Privilege in an African University* (Cambridge, MA: Schenkman, 1974).
8. Ibid., p. 112.

academic governance, though it is nominally accountable to the university council. In contrast to, say, the Indian universities which have somewhat similar patterns of governance, the Senates of these universities are much more influential in matters of academic policy ranging from decisions concerning resource allocation to individual promotions. Not surprisingly, meetings of the Senate are well attended and membership on important Senate committees is highly coveted and sometimes campaigned for.

As in the British universities, academic management and academic work are considered as complementary and governance a collective obligation. Academic responsibility is rarely delegated to the administration, or Council, and jealously defended against encroachments by the university's administrative officers. Academics are appointed to most senior posts in the university administration on the advice of Senate, usually for brief terms subject to periodic review of a substantive rather than a ritualistic nature. Deanships, for instance, are two year appointments. At Ibadan and Nairobi, in what is a conscious effort to offset the considerable power the university statutes confer on the Vice Chancellor, those selected as Deputy-Vice-Chancellors, who manage the day-to-day affairs of the institution, have often been known rivals of the Vice-Chancellor.

Traditions of professorial autonomy and collective governance embodied in the British universities and transplanted to Ibadan and Nairobi have contributed to the politicization of these universities. Institutional politics is serious business, or at least seems to preoccupy many of the staff interviewed, especially at the University of Ibadan. In the Faculty of Science

at Ibadan, for example, controversy last year focused on the recommendation of the Dean to promote a staff member who was reputed to have an undistinguished publication record. Ethnic favoritism was alleged. The controversy was resolved at a Faculty meeting called while the Dean was in Europe attending a professional conference at which time a new Dean was selected. Although a dramatic illustration of the intensity of academic politics at Ibadan, this event was not exceptional and demonstrates the influence of academic staff in university governance. So routine are such upheavals that lasting bitterness rarely results at least insofar as working relationships among staff and between staff and the university administration are concerned.

Ibadan and Nairobi are federal, multi-ethnic universities and the necessity of managing ethnic tensions enhances their traditions of professorial autonomy and collective governance. Of the two, Ibadan would seem to have a stronger commitment to ethnic cosmopolitanism in the recruitment and promotion of African staff.[9] While Ibadan has become less ethnically cosmopolitan in recent years, owing to the Civil War and the expansion of Nigerian higher education, it is still anxious to maintain its status as a national university. However, the potential for academic conflict along ethnic lines is increased both by the commitment to being a national university and by the fact that Ibadan Africanized its staff very rapidly, leading eventually to competition for scarce senior positions. The number of senior positions al-

9. For comparative data relating to the science departments of the two universities see Eisemon "Emerging Scientific Communities . . ."

located to departments has been augmented to provide some scope for professional advancement as well as to permit Ibadan to compete more favorably with the newer Nigerian universities in the recruitment and retention of professionally ambitious younger staff. Still, the competition for senior lectureships and professorships is intense.

The University of Nairobi, because it Africanized more slowly, has not experienced similar problems. At Ibadan, the result is a climate of intrigue accompanied by suspicion of ethnic favoritism. On one hand, these circumstances promote the use of meritocratic criteria for professional advancement as will be discussed later. On the other, they reinforce traditions of professorial autonomy and collective governance. Intrusions from government into university affairs or administrative interference into the affairs of faculties and departments are strongly resisted, even by staff who might presumably derive short-term benefit, since this would exacerbate ethnic tensions at either of these universities.

While the autonomy of the professoriate is valued at Ibadan and Nairobi, collegiality competes with authority and hierarchism in ways that express the African academic and intellectual culture of these universities. The mandarinate, to use Van den Berghe's term, is itself highly segmented. Differentiation of academic staff according to rank is very pronounced. Professors at Ibadan and Nairobi are allocated more spacious university housing—bungalows with servants' quarters surrounded by well-kept gardens—than academics of lesser rank.[10] Pro-

fessors have more access to research funds either generated internally or from such external sources as government departments and international agencies. They are represented on the university Senate and hold almost all important academic committee posts.

Within departments, professors and senior lecturers or associate professors constitute an oligarchy responsible for assigning work loads, evaluation of staff for purposes of promotion, and dispensing such scarce resources as office and laboratory supplies. The departmental headship rotates among the professors if there is more than one. Because of staffing difficulties, resulting from austerity at Ibadan and a shortage of qualified senior staff at Nairobi, the tenure of a department head can be very long with no formal provision for review.

Younger staff are conspicuously less well-off materially, have more substantial instructional and supervisory responsibilities, and are virtually without power in the university. The professors, senior lecturers, and associate professors interviewed were generally outgoing and self-confident, almost invariably either involved or very concerned with university affairs, and active internationally in their professional field. In contrast, lecturers were quiet, unassuming, committed to advancing themselves professionally through their scholarly research and hopeful that some day their patience and reticence would be rewarded. Junior staff apprentice themselves to powerful senior colleagues, acknowledge them as co-authors of papers they have written, and solicit their advice on professional and personal matters, including marriage.

Occasionally, junior staff members expressed resentment about these

10. For a discussion of this point see Van der Berghe, *Power and Privilege*, Ch. 4.

discrepancies in power and privilege. But resentment was rarely expressed in terms of the desire for greater democratization. Instead, resentment focuses on individual abuse and often implicitly on a staff member's eventual access to authority and influence in the university. The system which supports the privileges of senior faculty is not the target of resentment.

However, resentment directed toward individuals sometimes surfaces in acrimonious intradepartmental conflicts. In Ibadan, for instance, junior members of one department in the Faculty of Science attempted to depose the Head of that department whom they accused of misappropriating funds, sexual exploitation of women students, a wide spread practice accompanied by much sanctimoniousness, and even physical intimidation of staff, specifically, instructing a laboratory technician to vandalize the offices and cars of dissenting colleagues. The department head, an internationally known scholar and one of the most senior members of the university, was perceived to be vulnerable because he maintained the ethnic balance in his department through engaging expatriates to fill senior posts. The controversy quickly subsided when junior staff were unable to elicit support from other professors outside the department whose complicity was needed to initiate a formal inquiry.

When the universities of Ibadan and Nairobi were created, expatriate staff functioned as members of the colonial civil service. As Ibadan and Nairobi became Africanized, African staff sought the privileges accorded Europeans of similar rank. They opposed any effort to treat Africans differently. At Ibadan this was a particularly contentious issue during de-colonization.[11] Moreover, in Nigeria, Kenya, and other African societies, age is highly valued and in the colonial, hierarchial traditions of their universities, seniority is more closely related to autonomy and responsibility than in our own universities. Consequently, the interrelationship of age, rank, and privilege is not as controversial as it would be in a Western university.

Among the junior scientists interviewed, there was not only an acceptance of inequalities in professional and material privileges based on age and rank, but also a feeling that this was appropriate. Some junior staff, for instance, with financial resources sufficient to permit them to live more lavishly than their university, and outside, income would allow, were reluctant to do so. As one scientist remarked about his selection of an appropriate automobile, "though I can afford to drive a Peugot or a Volvo, it wouldn't be right for a person my age." Indeed, young expatriate professors holding senior appointments often experience resentment that stems as much from their status as individuals privileged beyond what their age would indicate as from the fact they are seen to displace Africans from such positions. And though staff sometimes grumble about governmental efforts to put academics on the same footing as civil servants, as is increasingly the case in Nigeria, it is the possible erosion of privilege, such as the shortening of vacations, rather than the routinization of academic life that arouses concern.

Traditions of autonomy and authority co-exist but influence different aspects of academic life at

11. J. F. Ade Ajayi and T. N. Tamuno, *The University of Ibadan 1948–73* (Ibadan: University of Ibadan Press, 1973).

Ibadan and Nairobi. Autonomy is influential insofar as it affects patterns of governance and the activities of the senior academic staff, specifically. Despite collegial patterns of governance, authority relations are hierarchial. Autonomy is a privilege distributed like material privileges, according to an academic's rank.

Individualism and collectivism

African scientists at the universities of Ibadan and Nairobi are typically individuals from humble circumstances who dedicated themselves to scholarship as a means of social and economic advancement and succeeded.[12] They take obvious pride in their success, showing no reluctance to recount their careers or to total their accomplishments. Their allegiance is to the social and economic system that permitted their mobility. Their homes and offices are often cluttered with pictures of important events in their careers and souvenirs of trips abroad.

Most of the scientists interviewed at the universities of Ibadan and Nairobi were the first in their families to have received secondary and higher education. In many cases, they were the first to attend school at all. In Kenya, the majority were from village backgrounds. In Nigeria, most were from small towns. They walked long distances to primary school and usually boarded at a secondary school. The schools they attended were impoverished, the curriculum demanding, the selection process more rigorous than in most parts of the world. Most started their scientific careers in the colonial period, long before science became a national priority. Science was

12. See Eisemon, "African Scientists: From Generation to General."

something studied in a textbook—often seriously out of date—presented in science classes at dictation speed by a teacher with little or no training in science, to be memorized and recited at examinations. The Bunson burner was sometimes first encountered by older scientists at a foreign university where instructors assume that all students possess the requisite laboratory skills.

The younger generation of African scientists, who received secondary and university training in the 1960s, were, of course, more fortunate. But even today, with the emphasis on science education at the primary and secondary school level that followed independence, schooling is scientifically deficient in important respects. African scientists are first of all, survivors. For them, hard work and dedication were rewarded materially and professionally as science became a national preoccupation.

While it may be meaningful in describing the social structure of Western scientific communities to focus on the status obtained through intellectual discovery and its recognition within the international scientific system, the rewards of a scientific career are much more tangible in Africa. This is especially the case for the older generation of African scientists whose social mobility was dramatic. Indeed, many research senior scientists have abandoned scientific activity to pursue careers in government, the international civil service, or in university administration. Too often this is deplored by Western colleagues who lack appreciation not only of the difficulties of contributing to science under conditions which require ingenuity and perseverance, but also of the social context of an African scientific career.

Academic life is a reward in itself, signifying entry into the governing elite of Nigerian and Kenyan society, and conferring an opportunity to accumulate wealth. Hence, in Nigeria and Kenya, academics are part of the entrepreneurial class. Many have substantial business investments and consulting commitments which demand their attention. In Kenya, this is explicitly encouraged; the government recognizes that the pool of entrepreneurial talent is too small to separate the public and private sectors in the manner of Western countries. Such outside activities are not considered distractions from academic work but part of the entitlements of academic life, even a responsibility of academia in a developing economy. Nigeria's Federal Military Government has taken a different view and in 1978 issued regulations requiring reportage of consulting activities and a division of professorial fees received from such activities.

Although individual attainment—both in terms of intellectual pursuits and social mobility—is embedded in the academic culture of Ibadan and Nairobi, so also are important professional and social obligations to one's family and society. Wealth accruing from a university appointment, for instance, is in the African tradition to be dispersed among one's kin group rather than used solely for individual enjoyment. Many Nigerian and Kenyan scientists pay the school fees of distant relatives—fees which are as high, relatively, as the cost of private schooling in North America. The material privileges of academic life are shared as well. Staff housing originally designed for nuclear expatriate families, now accommodate African extended families. There is little that is personal or private about privilege and wealth, so strong are the responsibilities of kinship.

African academics only partly belong to an academic world. A university is a place where they live and work, but it is never their home. Home is always the network of social relationships of childhood which cannot be replicated elsewhere. For this reason, as soon as they become prosperous enough, many African academics will build homes in the small towns and villages from which they came. They never regard themselves as belonging to Ibadan or Nairobi unless that is where they were born and even then they tend to refer to their mother's or father's village as home.

Professionally, Nigerian and Kenyan academics exhibit a consciousness of the collective aspirations of their societies that is seldom encountered in universities in more developed countries. Characterizations of scientific activity in developed countries place great importance on the recognition of individual scientific accomplishment and on the cosmopolitan, transnational professional affiliations of scientists which supercede particularistic loyalties. Where scientific recognition is shared, for instance, it is with those who participate in whatever merits recognition: colleagues; funding agencies; employers—not with such entities as a nation or a people. Thus, in 1977, when Americans virtually swept the Nobel prizes awarded to the scientific community this reflected the accomplishments of individuals or research teams rather than the collective accomplishment of the American nation.

The scientists studied at the universities of Ibadan and Nairobi spoke of themselves and their work as African. Invitations to professional conferences abroad, publications in international scientific journals, research funds obtained from international scientific organizations, and so on, were presented as African and/or Nigerian and Kenyan accomplishments, to be recognized as such by others. This is particularly noticeable in the department of many African scientists attending international professional conferences. They are acutely aware of their collective identity, frequently made more conspicuous by their adoption of national dress sometimes irrespective of climactic conditions. While many Western colleagues doubt the existence of African science, few Africans do, though they readily acknowledge the universality of science and have an ill-defined concept of the specifically African nature of their work. The peripherality of African academic life fosters common identities and mitigates against individualistic tendencies to depict scientific accomplishments without reference to the collective aspirations of African societies.

Cosmopolitanism and specificity

The universities of Ibadan and Nairobi were developed in affiliation with the University of London to implant metropolitan standards of excellence. Today, both are autonomous universities. Yet, they have consciously sought to retain their cosmopolitanism in the recruitment of students and staff, in their curricula, which is still influenced by the practices of metropolitan countries and monitored by external examination, and also in regard to the encouragement given to staff to seek international recognition

through their research. Scientists at the Universities of Ibadan and Nairobi profess to be very much committed to a research ethos. Among those interviewed not a single scientist felt that research and graduate training activities are better left to the metropolitan countries. In the international scientific division of labor, African scientists have no intention of remaining "hewers of wood."

The commitment to publish and obtain international recognition is deeply imbedded in the rhetoric of academic life. To be sure, the level of research activity of the African scientists is modest, about one article per year in refereed scientific publication since initial appointment, and their research obtains little international visibility. Between 1962 and 1976, 77 Africans on the staff of the science faculty at Ibadan and Nairobi received 204 citations to their research from North American and British colleagues compared to 272 citations to the research conducted by 27 European expatriates.[13]

Nevertheless, research and international recognition are highly valued especially among the foreign trained "first generation" of scientists and those from ethnic groups which are numerically and/or politically uninfluential in the two universities. For the former, including many senior scientists who have abandoned a research career, commitment to the research ethos is an assertion of their desire to participate in the international scientific system into which they were socialized through post-graduate studies in metropolitan countries and sub-

13. See Eisemon et al., "Collective Scientific Self-Reliance . . ."

sequent apprenticeship to expatriate professors. This commitment must also be understood in terms of their experiences with unsympathetic foreign colleagues who confidently predict that African science will decline as Western scientific traditions are weakened in the independence period by policies favoring Africanization and science for development.

Among junior scientists, particularly those whose ethnicity makes them vulnerable to efforts to produce demographic "balance" in the academic profession, the research ethos is seen to ensure the application of criteria of scholarly accomplishment. Indeed, the research ethos supresses overt application of ascriptive criteria in such matters as promotion. This is especially evident in the promotion of several professionally ambitious, influential scientists at both institutions whose ethnicity might have otherwise presented an impediment to their professional advancement. It is, likewise, evident in the retention of some highly productive, internationally visible expatriates for as long as institutional regulations permit.

While African scientists seek to participate in the international scientific system and voice adherence to the cosmopolitan research traditions of metropolitan universities, importance is also placed on scientific research formulated in light of local needs and resources which accelerates the development process—specificity. In Nigeria[14] and Kenya[15] science and technology are considered instruments of social and

economic change. Both countries are integrating national science planning into development planning. Most local funding available for scientific research is stipulated for work that has some kind of immediate pay-off. In Nigeria, and to an extent also in Kenya, academic scientists desiring to carry out research must have "applied" interests, posing difficulties for instance, for many mathematicians. Of course, research in mathematics often necessitates only pencil, paper, a quiet office and a good scientific library. However, since research support improves the conditions of academic life, providing funds to purchase books, and travel abroad, the attractions of such areas of applied mathematics as statistics, operations research, and functional analysis are considerable. A field like zoology affords more scope for application of the scientist's research interests to development. Among research projects initiated by the zoologists interviewed were studies of the harvesting potential of *telepia* (a tropical fish), bush rats, grass cutters, and antelopes, all important sources of protein in the African diet.

But, there are strong differences of opinion between academics and science administrators in regard to what should constitute applied research. More specifically, many scientists complained that funds could not be obtained for applied research which was either long term in nature—three to five years—or addressed to theoretical as well as practical concerns. Projects which were described as having important developmental implications, proposed by senior scientists with much research experience, were rejected by government authorities for these reasons. In the view of many Nigerian

14. Unesco, *National Science Policies in Africa* (Paris: Unesco, 1974) pp. 245–256.
15. Ibid., pp. 133–150.

and Kenyan scientists, funds should be available for research which offers a developmental pay-off as well as affords the possibility of international recognition. In health related fields such as parasitology, this is possible in light of the historic interest in tropical medicine on the part of Western countries with a colonial experience. In several other scientific fields it is not possible, thus requiring many African scientists to give their attention to a subsidiary research interest if they desire research funding or consulting.

The task of developing scientific communities with an infrastructure of scientific institutions, sources of professional recognition, and financial support sufficient to provide a counter attraction to Western scientific influences is difficult. The scientific communities of Nigeria and Kenya, Black Africa's largest, are nonetheless very small. The number of Nigerian scientists engaged in research slightly exceeds two thousand (2,083) for a population of more than 70,000,000, yet the country has thirteen fully functional universities, several government research institutes, and an incipient network of scientific societies and journals. Kenya's "stock" of scientific manpower and scientific infrastructure is even smaller. There are not enough research scientists (569 in total) to support scientific societies and publications organized along disciplinary lines in Kenya, a situation made more difficult by the break down of the East African community and with it, the dissolution of important regional scientific and educational organizations. Nigeria is slightly more fortunate in these respects, but it too lacks economies of scale in science.

The universities of Ibadan and Nairobi, like many other African universities, have, in seeking to offer scientific training in many fields at the undergraduate and now post-graduate levels, overextended themselves in ways that fragment their limited scientific resources. Duplication of expertise is considered a luxury to be afforded only in times of abundant scientific manpower with the result that few scientists share the same research interests. Furthermore, since Nigerian and Kenyan universities have just recently elaborated graduate programs and much advanced scientific training is still undertaken abroad, those scientists who share scientific interests often experience difficulties in collaborating because they have received their training in countries which vary enormously in their approach to graduate education. The absence of opportunities for collaboration reinforces feelings of isolation and lack of international recognition that are in turn compounded by problems in communicating with colleagues within their country or abroad. There are few opportunities to attend professional conferences locally. Opportunities for foreign travel have constricted. Ibadan, of the two institutions, the most generously financed, can no longer afford to send its staff abroad to attend professional conferences. Postal communication, particularly in Nigeria, is problematic. Manuscripts are sent to North America and Europe with travelling friends. Access to foreign scientific publications, very important in fields like mathematics where communication is essential to avoid anticipation, is increasingly a source of complaint. Foreign exchange restrictions introduced in Nigeria and now Kenya complicate scholarly communication further. Such circumstances impede participation in the international scientific system as well as efforts to create specifically African scientific communities.

Conclusion

This paper has sought to delineate some important dimensions of the social context of academic life in African universities. It has been argued that the academic and intellectual culture of the universities of Ibadan and Nairobi must be understood in terms of the accommodation of conflicting influences on African academic life: authority and autonomy; individualism and collectivism; and, finally, cosmopolitanism and specificity. The two universities studied were established in the colonial period in preparation for decolonization. Today, they find themselves intimately involved in the development of their respective societies.

The universities of Ibadan and Nairobi are no longer exotic institutions, but institutions which are African and, in unique ways, have assimilated foreign influences. Traditions of autonomy, individualism and cosmopolitanism—the academic and intellectual legacies of the colonial period—have been successfully transplanted but given African expression in the authority patterns of these universities, the sense of collective responsibility exhibited by staff, and in the articulation of scientific work with aspirations for national development.

The academic culture of the two universities studied, as this paper has shown, is not a replication of what prevails in metropolitan countries. While Ibadan and Nairobi are faithful to the traditions of western universities in many ways, these traditions are influential selectively. In other words, they only partially describe African academic life. And where western traditions are influential, they are given distinctly African meaning—that is illustrated for instance, by the commitment to the research ethos as a mechanism of differentiation permitting the allocation of professional rewards on the basis of universalistic criteria in the situation fraught with ethnic tension. What is important is the functionality of conceptions of academic life instilled in the colonial period. That they remain a fixture of African academic life is more indicative of their instrumentality than reflective of habits of deference acquired from the colonial experience and mindlessly perpetuated.

The academic and intellectual culture of Ibadan and Nairobi cannot be understood simply in terms of African adaptation, however ingenious, of Western traditions. Much of the academic and intellectual culture of African universities is not adapted but African. The intrusion of kinship responsibilities into African academic life is an example. This is not an adaptation but an assertion of African traditions that would have primacy in almost any circumstance. The sharing of the material privileges accruing from academic work is not a reconciliation of individualism with African communal obligations. It is, instead, a statement of what is African in the academic and intellectual culture of these universities. Similarly, the oligarchial, almost patriarchal authority structure of African universities is neither a local aberration produced by incomplete tutelage nor a transitional phenomenon likely to disappear when new universities become old universities.

The academic and intellectual culture of African universities comprises traditions which are indigenous and unreconciled with their colonial inheritance or contemporary educational influences. In sum, African academic and intellectual culture is shaped by the mediation of antagonistic conceptions of academic life, some transplanted and reinterpreted, some African in inspiration and operation. Despite the tension which this dialectic sometimes creates, African academic and intellectual culture is best described in terms of the harmony of seemingly contradictory traditions.

ANNALS, AAPSS, 448, March 1980

The Indian Academic: An Elite in the Midst of Scarcity

By SUMA CHITNIS

ABSTRACT: Indian academics constitute the third largest academic community in the world. As university graduates in a country in which 70 percent of the population is illiterate, and as heirs to one of the most ancient traditions of learning, they are a highly privileged elite. As guardians of the intellectual and political formation of youth in one of the world's largest democracies and developing nations they hold a unique position of influence and power in the Third World. This paper describes the situation, the functioning, the satisfactions, and the frustrations of these academics in the context of development.

Suma Chitnis is Professor and Head of the Unit for Research in the Sociology of Education at the Tata Institute of Social Sciences, Bombay. A sociologist, Dr. Chitnis has written extensively on problems of the scheduled classes and castes in India, on higher education, and on issues relating to education and equality. She is co-author of Field Studies in the Sociology of Education in India, co-editor of Papers in the Sociology of Education in India and of The Indian Academic Profession. She serves on the Senate of the S.N.D.T. Women's University and on the Governing boards of three colleges.

THERE ARE about 180,000 academics in India spread through some 3,000 colleges, 105 universities, and a number of specialized institutions for technology, engineering, management, and other fields. Responsible for the education of 2,500,000 students, they constitute the third largest academic community in the world.[1] As university educated scholars in a society in which 70 percent of the population is illiterate, they are a privileged elite. Yet the vast majority of academics are not part of a confident community of intellectuals. Instead, they are confronted by an absence of autonomy, a decline in status, erosion of academic standards, and consequent low morale.

In searching for an explanation of the problems faced by many Indian academics, this paper focuses on the structure of higher education. It is argued that this structure reflects patterns of political economic development—pre-colonial, colonial and, currently, neo-colonial—that are uneven and often contradictory. Each major phase of development called forth an institutional expression in higher education, and these disparities have never been resolved. Most glaring are the disparities between British model universities, which account for approximately 98 percent of the enrollment, and a small set of institutions that are post-independence transplants from the industrialized world. The latter are "deemed" universities, but account for only 2 percent of enrollment. Yet they are provided with funds and facilities far in excess of the British model universities,

and are consciously recognized to be responsible for the education of the technical, professional, and managerial elite.

THE ORGANIZATIONAL STRUCTURE OF UNIVERSITIES

The university system as it operates today was inherited from the British. It dates back to 1857 when the first three universities were set up in Bombay, Calcutta, and Madras by the colonial rulers as institutions for European higher learning in India. These universities were mainly established to provide administrative, supervisory, and clerical manpower for the British Government in India, and to spread and generate European culture among the Indian elite. They were also expected to provide a small cadre of professionals, mainly lawyers and doctors. Accordingly, they concentrated on providing a broad liberal arts degree considered appropriate for the first two of these three purposes and on providing some professional education in medicine and law.

Although they were supposed to have been modelled after the University of London, these universities were not designed to be major centers of research or of advanced post graduate level education. Rather, they were conceived of as centers of undergraduate studies, and as peripheral adjuncts to the centers of advanced university education at Oxford, Cambridge, London or elsewhere in Europe.[2] And yet, they

1. All statistics are approximate and are based on information supplied by the University Grants Commission. See *Report for the Year 1977-78*, (New Delhi: University Grants Commission, 1978).

2. Irene Gilbert, "Autonomy and Consensus Under the Raj," in S. and L. Rudolph, eds., *Education and Politics in India*, (Cambridge, MA: Harvard University Press, 1972), pp. 172–206; see also Aparna Basu, "Policy and Conflict in India: The Reality and Perception of Education," in P. G. Altbach

were highly exclusive institutions designed to serve only the small fraction of the population that would eventually constitute the administrative, professional, political, and social elite.

With the attainment of Independence, and the national commitment to provide facilities for all those who aspired to higher education, the university system, initially established to serve a small elite, had to be expanded phenomenally. The scale of this expansion may be gauged from the fact that there were only 28 universities with a total enrollment of about 400,000 in 1951, at the outset of the First Plan Period; today there are 105 universities with an enrollment of 2,500,000.

In the process of expansion, there has been considerable diversification of courses, both in the non-professional fields, such as the liberal arts, commerce, humanities, physical and social sciences, and mathematics, and in professional areas which include education, law, dentistry, medicine, and engineering. However, very little has been done to develop the universities as centers of advanced study or of research. Research is mainly located in separate institutes and the universities primarily continue to be responsible for undergraduate and graduate-level teaching. Nor have there been significant changes in the organizational structure of universities.

Except for a few teaching universities, most Indian universities are organized on the federal or affiliating

principle. The main function of federal and affiliating universities is to provide able governance for their constituent or affiliated colleges. Their teaching responsibilities are confined to the provision of instruction and facilities for master's and doctoral level education. All undergraduate teaching, which in fact amounts to about 90 percent of the teaching done by universities, as well as some graduate and post-graduate teaching, is done by the constituent or affiliated colleges. A single federal or affiliating university may be responsible for the governance of as many as two hundred constituent or affiliated colleges. Each college is a separate administrative entity organized to provide instruction in a specific field or fields of study. On the basis of their fields of instruction, colleges are somewhat loosely classified into non-professional and professional colleges.

ACADEMIC REALITIES

University academics function as employees either of the universities or of the constituent and affiliated colleges. Thus, there are two categories of university academics: university teachers who are employees of universities and who teach either at one of the teaching universities or at the university departments of federal and affiliating universities; and college teachers who are employees of colleges and who teach at the constituent or affiliated colleges. University teachers constitute barely .05 percent of all academics, while college teachers account for 99.95 percent.

Each of these two categories is further stratified into a hierarchy of statuses. The hierarchy of university teachers consists of professors

and G. Kelly, eds., *Education and Colonialism*, (New York: Longmans, 1978), pp. 53–69; and Edward Shils, "The Academic Profession in India," in Amrik Singh and P. G. Altbach, eds., *The Higher Learning in India*, (New Delhi, Vikas, 1974), pp. 205–206.

at the top, followed by readers, and by lecturers. College teachers are organized into a hierarchy headed by professors, followed by lecturers, and tutors/demonstrators.

Unlike their counterparts in societies which organize universities on the collegiate principle and where academics enjoy full rights as professionals, university academics in India are treated purely as employees in a bureaucracy. Although there is some provision for their participation in bodies like university senates or college academic councils, academics have, in reality, very little control over policies and decisions relating to the management, administration, and organization of universities and colleges or to their own functioning within these institutions.

Absence of autonomy

University academics have very little autonomy, regardless of whether they teach at the undergraduate level or the graduate level. The syllabus for each course, as well as the books and reference materials to be used for teaching the course, are minutely defined and categorically specified by universities. These specifications are drawn up with the help of small committees made up of university and college teachers. Few academics have the chance to function on these committees; thus, most do not participate in the deliberations concerning courses and syllabi.

Academics at the undergraduate level do not have much choice with regard to mode of instruction. They are required to provide instruction through lectures consisting of 40 to 50 minute monologues that cover the themes in the syllabi. Lectures are supplemented by "practicals" and laboratory experiments for science courses and some professional courses, and with tutorials for courses in commerce or arts. Universities decide upon the number of lectures, practicals, and tutorials to be allocated to each course and time tables for teaching are set accordingly.

Degrees and certificates are awarded not on the basis of a continuous evaluation of students by their teachers, but on the basis of students' performance at annual examinations, over which universities exercise total control. They design and conduct examinations, organize the assessment of papers, declare results, and award degrees and certificates. The practice of external examination is followed to obtain objectivity and fairness for students from the various colleges. But it also means that teachers are categorically excluded from the evaluation of their own students.

Reduction of academics to lecturers

Thus, excluded from decisions on course content and from authority over evaluation, university academics teaching undergraduate or graduate courses are reduced to lecturers who, over the course of the year, are required to deliver a fixed number of lectures that cover the topics specified in syllabi. The task of lecturing is monotonous and exhausting. Each faculty member is required to deliver eighteen to twenty-four lectures per week. The burden of this heavy workload is somewhat relieved by the fact that syllabi remain unchanged for several years, with the result that lectures once prepared can be used from year to year with minor updating and revision. The workload is also lightened by the fact that the system of evaluation is such as to favor learning by rote, a cramming of facts, figures, and referral information regarding the viewpoints of authorities, rather than the cultivation of critical, analytical and creative thought. This system reduces teaching to a monotonous and a mechanical task, devoid of the joy of interaction and the adventure of helping young minds unfold and scholars grow.

Inasmuch as lectures are expected to be rich in information and instructive in acquainting students with a variety of viewpoints, there is challenge in their preparation. Teachers can, within limits, use creativity and imagination in teaching. Despite the definition of the lecture as a one-way process, teachers who are gifted can, if the class is reasonably small, generate a rich and lively interaction with and between students. However, with the massive expansion of higher education and the consequent pressure to accommodate increasing numbers of students, university departments and colleges are forced to stretch their facilities to a point at which classes, which formerly consisted of twenty-five to fifty or at the most seventy students, may now easily have one hundred or even one hundred and fifty. This reduces the classroom lecture to a mass oration and inhibits even the limited interaction that is possible with smaller numbers.

Erosion of standards

The quality of lectures is further affected by the continuous lowering of academic standards. In some cases, particularly in non-professional undergraduate courses, the standards have been lowered so far that the bachelor's degree is reduced to the level of a high school diploma.

Similarly, the quality of lectures has been affected by the mechanization of evaluation that has come about with expansion. Universities have responded to the pressure of numbers by encouraging all kinds of practices that facilitate the task of evaluation. Since coordination of examination work is easier if examination papers follow a set pattern, paper setters are required "to conform to established conventions" with the result that it is now possible for students to anticipate questions with reasonable probability of a correct guess. Students work out possible questions and press for dictation of notes that can easily be memorized, organized into suitable answers to anticipated questions, and reproduced at examinations. Teachers who are able to provide such notes are not only popular with students but prized by college authorities for the good results they help the college obtain at university examinations.

These structural constraints have created expectations and reward systems that inhibit productive scholarship. Academics hardly expect their colleagues to be scholars— and there have been instances in which those who have been enterprising enough to publish or do research have received a cold reception as norm busters. This, together with the decline of the social status of academics described below, leads to a continuous erosion of scholarship.

Decline of status

In the value system of the British era, heavily dominated by the concept of caste, the academic profession was considered equal to the sacred learning of the highest castes.[3]

3. See Edward Shils, "The Academic Profession," pp. 220–22.

Since both students and teachers at colleges and universities came exclusively from the higher castes, this equation was more than notional. The position of academics was further elevated by the fact that they were recognized to be the privileged custodians and promoters of the culture of the ruling elite. Thus, the profession of university academics combined the sacred function of the guru in the native tradition with the equally prestigious but more secular function of the formation and grooming of a loyal elite to uphold the imperial power.

At a more mundane level the academic profession was prestigious because it was among the most lucrative and comfortable occupations available. As years went by, the profession gained in worth as, somewhat unexpectedly, academics contributed significantly to social reform in the country and came to be recognized as intellectuals strategically placed to influence India's political destiny.[4]

Much of this has changed since Independence. With conscious efforts to secularize occupational rating and to build a healthy respect for manual work and labor, university teaching has ceased to enjoy its earlier status as a high caste occupation. The new emphasis on egalitarianism, concretized in the commitment to mass education, has rendered obsolete the self-conscious elitism and the proud exclusiveness which characterized the profession only two or three decades

ago. Meanwhile, with the growth of industrialization there has been a burgeoning of new lucrative and prestigious occupations; the profession has lost disastrously in relative occupational ranking, power, and economic status. The political worth of academics has not remained quite the same either. Responsible for socializing the educated youth to shoulder the responsibilities of democracy and development, academics are no doubt placed in a new position of political power. But in the post-independence politics of manipulation they are less effective politically, or as agents of change, than they were as reformers in the pre-independence politics of sacrifice, and of moral confrontation with the British.

BOMBAY COLLEGE TEACHERS —A CLUE TO THE MORALE OF THE OTHERS

All this has serious implications for the morale of university and college teachers. They rate themselves poorly as scholars and rank themselves low in the hierarchy of occupations, as may be seen from the following data from a study of college teachers in the city of Bombay.[5]

Asked to state their impression on how many of their colleagues continue to be scholars, 40 percent of the respondents to the study replied that less than 5 percent of their colleagues are scholars, 36 percent believe that less than 20 percent are scholars, and 11 percent believe that between 20 percent and

4. College teachers played a major role in the reform movements. In the last decades of the nineteenth century and the first three decades of the twentieth century, Jambhekar, Chiplunkar, Ranade, Firdonjee, Naoroji and others all came from the teaching community and were active in reformist and nationalist efforts.

5. These data have been obtained from a case study of three of the most prestigious Arts and Sciences colleges affiliated to the University of Bombay. See Suma Chitnis, "The Teacher role in the University System," (Ph.D. Diss., Tata Institute of Social Science, Bombay, 1973).

50 percent are scholars. Barely 13 percent believe that more than 50 percent of their colleagues are scholars.

In response to a question asking them to state their opinion on whether the status of college teaching as an occupation has declined since they themselves were students, as many as 66 percent of the respondents categorically stated that is has. Asked to rank their own profession in terms of one of the following categories—at the apex of the occupational hierarchy, equal to other professions like medicine and engineering, a class by itself, equal to Class II or Class III government service —only 3 percent of the college teachers placed themselves at the apex of the occupational hierarchy. Barely 22 percent placed themselves in the second category, alongside doctors and engineers. The majority, 42 percent, placed themselves in the third category as a class by themselves or equated their status with that of Class II and Class III government servants (33 percent).

Surprisingly, the same college teachers seem to be a fairly satisfied and committed body of functionaries within the university system. Asked to state whether they would like to change their occupation if a suitable opportunity presented itself, 68 percent of the teachers said that they would not. This 68 percent is made up of 42 percent who say that they are happy in the occupation, 18 percent who have given no specific reason, and 8 percent who say that it is a convenient base for some other activities such as politics, community service, or literary pursuits, in which they are engaged. Obviously there are benefits from the profession that sustain college teachers in spite of the erosion of their academic role.

Sources of satisfaction

These satisfactions are highly varied. The Bombay study reveals that many teachers find an outlet for their talents as faculty in charge of the National Social Service Scheme, through which college students are involved in social service and social work. Others find satisfaction in organizing students' music circles, plays, debate or drama groups, or in supervising the training of students for competitive sports and intercollegiate activities.

A general observation of academics suggests that regardless of the deterioration in the status of the profession since Independence, there are some college teachers for whom the profession continues to carry a halo from its earlier ranking as a high caste occupation and as one of the most prestigious of the white-collar occupations in the British regime. But by far the most important returns from the profession seem to be in the rewarding personal relationships that many teachers have with their students. This is particularly true in situations in which teachers are able to guide students with respect to their personal lives and careers. Deprived of the opportunity to function significantly as academics, college teachers seem, nevertheless, to enjoy the pastoral function of the socialization of the younger generation—much in the fashion of high school teachers.[6]

College teaching also provides a convenient base for community service and political work. For instance, college teachers located in some of the backward regions are

6. S. Filella, "College Teaching in India: An Academic Function, A Personal Relationship, or Coaching for Examinations?" *Journal of Higher Education (New Delhi)* 3 no. 3 (1978), pp. 321–31.

known to have made a unique contribution to development by travelling to remote villages, informing high school graduates and their uneducated parents of the new opportunities available in nearby educational centers, and drawing young men and women from the highly backward rural, tribal, and former untouchable sectors of Indian society into higher education. It also provides them with long vacations, a steady income, valuable contacts and a respectable identity.

The foregoing is a broad profile of college and university teachers in the country. However, there are major variations within this picture. These variations are partly determined by structural differences between the specific organizations in which academics function—for instance, between universities and colleges, between non-professional and professional colleges, between colleges managed by one type of agency and another, or between the situation of undergraduate and postgraduate teachers within the same college. Other influential components are contextual and societal factors: rural or urban location of a college or university; backwardness or development of its region; or the marketability and occupational ranking of the profession in which the institution specializes.

Due to these structural and contextual variations, university teachers enjoy advantages that are far beyond the reach of college teachers; and academics at colleges owned and managed by relatively liberal, progressive, or democratic managements enjoy rights and privileges unknown to teachers at colleges with orthodox or authoritarian managements. Similarly, academics at professional colleges enjoy a respect and an authority seldom available to non-professional college teachers. Somewhat unexpectedly, academics in rural areas, who are privileged, influential, and respected in the communities in which they function, enjoy satisfactions which stand in sharp contrast to the frustrations of academics in metropolitian cities who are visibly disadvantaged in the matter of income, influence, and social status relative to other professionals, such as engineers or doctors.

College teachers: the large majority

On the whole, non-professional college teachers, particularly those teaching at the undergraduate level at arts and science colleges in large towns and metropolitan cities, such as those in the Bombay study described above, are most hard hit by the pressures of expansion and by the devaluation of higher education that has occurred in the process of development. They account for practically 85 percent of the academics and are responsible for teaching about 70 percent of the total student population.

The situation of teachers at professional colleges such as law, medicine, and engineering is distinctly superior to that of undergraduate teachers at non-professional colleges. In principle, the organization of education is largely similar at both types of colleges. However, there are three major differences. Firstly, the content of instruction at professional colleges is far more specialized and advanced than the content of instruction at the non-professional colleges. Secondly, enrollment is conspicuously smaller and more selective. Thirdly, the course requirements—particularly in fields such as medicine, dentistry, veterinary science and engineering—are such that they call for a great deal of practical work, and teaching does not depend completely on the lecture method.

All three factors contribute to elevating the quality of teaching at professional colleges and to making the academic role of the teachers at these colleges more effective and meaningful. The position of these teachers is further enhanced by the fact that education in the professions does not easily lend itself to the process of mechanization.

However, it would be mistaken to imagine that all professional fields of education are equally favorable to the elevation of the academic role. There is marked variation between the situation in the different fields. The conditions at medical or engineering colleges are, for instance, visibly more favorable to advanced scholarship and involvement on the part of teachers than are the conditions at law colleges or colleges of education. These differences are partly the outcome of the state of specialization in the field. However, they are also related to factors such as the ranking of a profession in the occupational hierarchy and, by implication, to the kind of qualifications practitioners in the profession are generally expected to hold.

Thus, the contrast between professional and non-professional college teachers illustrates the manner in which the societal context may make for variations in roles which are otherwise identically structured and organized.

University teachers

University teachers constitute a category of academics that are distinctly different from college teachers. University teachers are largely responsible for graduate and postgraduate teaching. As such they enjoy all the advantages of teaching at an advanced level. As employees of universities they enjoy salary scales and terms of work that are distinctly superior to college teachers. In fact, the difference between the facilities, the conditions of work, and the overall social and academic status of university teachers is so far superior to that of college teachers that one well known commentator on higher education in India describes University teachers as Brahmans, in a system, which, according to him, treats college teachers as "Shudras."[7]

University teachers are advantaged in many other ways. They have better library and laboratory facilities and have ample opportunity to participate in academic events like seminars, conferences, and other professional meetings. Centrally located in the university, they have better access to information of openings and facilities available for further study and research within the country and abroad. They have better access to information regarding international academic exchange programs, and better opportunities for meeting with visiting academics and for making valuable professional contacts. Most of the research, writing, and publication done by academics in India is done by university teachers. The academics who are invited or picked to function on public bodies or official and professional committees are almost invariably university teachers. And yet, university teachers are by no means as well placed as the faculty at the new institutions,

7. P. G. Altbach, "The Distorted Guru: The College Teacher in Bombay," in S. Chitnis and P. G. Altbach, eds., *The Indian Academic Profession*, (Delhi: Macmillan, 1979), p. 6.

deemed universities, as may be seen from the following.

FACULTY AT THE NEW INSTITUTIONS OF SCIENCE AND TECHNOLOGY

As institutions specially set up to produce highly qualified technical, professional, and managerial personnel for the more sophisticated manpower needs of development, the new institutions deemed universities are unique. Unlike most of the universities which are primarily designed to serve the states in which they are located, these new institutions are conceived of and designed as national in scope. Although funded by the government, as are the universities, their funding is far more generous. Eager to ensure that they do not fall short of the facilities necessary for the production of highly qualified manpower, the government has spent lavishly on their establishment and maintenance. Moreover the government has made conscious efforts to obtain foreign aid, advice, and expertise to assist with the establishment of these institutions and to collaborate with them. It has helped them to forge linkages with renowned centers of study and research in the U.S.A., the U.K., Germany and the U.S.S.R.[8] Given their generous resources and their emphasis on the technological and professional fields which are in great demand in India and abroad, these new institutions are able to obtain the cream of the student population. Equipped to offer salaries and service conditions that are

superior to those available at university departments and colleges, they are able to attract a highly qualified faculty.

There are also major differences between the organizational structures of universities and of these institutions. They are conspicuously smaller than universities and zealously guarded from the pressure to expand. They focus on a single field or a set of related fields. Moreover, they are not merely conceived of as centers for undergraduate and graduate study and instruction. Rather, the new institutions are designed to be advanced centers of learning and research in their respective fields.

Accordingly, library, laboratory, computer, and other facilities are generously provided; as are opportunities for interaction with and exchange between scholars and academics at other universities and institutions to ensure that both students and faculty are able to maintain high standards of study and of research. The courses that are offered are advanced in content and highly rated, even by international standards. They are frequently revised and updated to remain abreast of new developments. Faculty are not only actively involved in the design and revision of courses but held responsible for their high standards.

The methods of instruction at these institutions are also noticeably different from those commonly adopted at university departments and colleges. Lectures continue to be important to teaching, but discussions, seminars, and guided reading are also extensively utilized. There is a conscious effort to promote interaction between students and teachers, and to encourage students to do research and refer-

8. The Indian Institute of Management at Ahmedabad has links with Harvard University. Of the five Institutes of Technology, one has had Soviet assistance, another British, a third American, and the fourth has been aided by the West Germans.

ence work on their own. Students are evaluated on the basis of a continuous assessment of the work done over the course of the year. Moreover, in contrast to the practice of external evaluation at universities, evaluation at these institutions is almost exclusively internal and faculty are fully involved. Faculty are respected as professionals and granted considerable autonomy for decisions and action.

All this has a positive result. It is reflected in the academic output and involvement of faculty from these institutions which is distinctly superior to that of university teachers and college teachers teaching at the same level, undergraduate or graduate, in the same fields. It is also reflected in the visible self-confidence in intellectual horizons and in the extension of frames of academic reference nationally and internationally, which contrasts sharply with the largely provincial identities and orientations of most universities and colleges.

CONCLUSION

The wide variations in role structure and performance in the Indian academic hierarchy reflect the disparate levels of development at which the country operates. At the lowest level, professional college teachers, although valuable to the country's needs, would hardly be accepted as university professors according to industrialized countries' standards. Their participation reflects at least two phases of development. First, college teachers function in a highly authoritarian structure that accords a disproportionately high importance to certification because higher education retains some of the elements of traditional her-

itage in which learning is considered sacred and in which rote assimilation of sacred texts is the accepted form of learning. Second, they work in a highly bureaucratized university structure rooted in a British regime where higher education was at least partially a device for transference of culture and obtaining clerical, supervisory, and administrative staff for colonial government.

The university system adapted to post-independence pressures for the expansion of higher education with increasing bureauracratization of form and function. While popular demand has been met, the structural adoption of a colonial system to the pressures of post-independence development has reduced the academic function of college teachers to a point of marginality.

The faculty of the new institutes for higher education in science, technology, and management fulfill a totally different need in development. They have effectively met the challenge of providing education to meet the country's new needs for engineering, scientific, and managerial manpower for industry, and for the various services. They have been effective in elevating Indians, both to compete in the international market for employment in these fields, and for participation as equals in the world community of scholars and researchers. The more open and democratic structure of these new institutions may be explained by the fact that they are fresh transplants from societies in which higher education is expected to be organized on collegiate rather than bureaucratic principles.

There are some doubts about the functioning of the faculty at the new institutions. These doubts arise out of the fact that these institutions have not yet been able either to relate themselves satisfactorily to the development of an appropriate middle level technology or to gear themselves fully to the country's medical or management needs. Doubts also arise because these institutions seem to lean heavily upon their parent institutions in the industrialized countries, as is evident both in the recurrent need of the faculty to refresh themselves with short-term or long-term spells at universities in the industrialized countries and in the strong inclinations of their alumni to migrate to these countries.

India is grappling with the problem of arresting polarization and of integrating the multilevel development in different spheres of life. In higher education the impact of forces making for polarization is evident in the fact that while the college teacher's role is increasingly unacademic and moves closer to that of the high-school teacher, faculty at the new and prestigious institutes are isolating themselves in pockets of excellence with links abroad. The integration of academics moving in these different directions into an academic role system that is redefined and more purposively integrated to meet the needs of development is one of the principal challenges for higher education in India in the decade of the eighties.

Book Department

International Relations and Politics 151

Africa, Asia, and Latin America 161

Europe 170

United States History and Politics 174

Sociology 184

Economics 193

INTERNATIONAL RELATIONS AND POLITICS

WARREN I. COHEN, *The Chinese Connection.* Pp. x, 322. New York: Columbia University Press, 1978. $16.50.

In this fascinating and well executed study, Professor Warren I. Cohen has analyzed how three nonofficial individuals influenced U.S. foreign policy attitudes toward East Asia during the first half of the twentieth century. The three principals—Roger Sherman Greene, Thomas W. Lamont and George E. Sokolsky—were all substantially different in background, temperament, interests, motives, ideology, and profession. For each of these men, East Asia represented quite divergent opportunities and problems.

Roger Sherman Greene had a family pedigree and long experience in Japan and China. He was initially in the U.S. Department of State and from there moved to the Rockefeller Foundation. He is portrayed as a "humanitarian internationalist" who had too little impact upon U.S. policies.

Thomas W. Lamont did not have a family pedigree but his position in the highest echelons of the J. P. Morgan banking and financial interests made him a person of influence in several circles. He is interesting because of his often conflicting loyalties to country and company. Cohen does a good job presenting this aspect of his subject. Indeed, Cohen's discussion of the process through which Thomas Lamont balanced and maneuvered these interests makes for some of the most interesting and relevant parts of the book. In most cases, it is important to note, company interests informed his perspectives.

George E. Sokolsky was also without a family pedigree and seemingly spent most of his life trying to gain prestige and influence. He is portrayed as bright, energetic, and capable of either enlightened or vicious self-serving commentaries on Asian affairs. He ended up in China during the 1920s and as a journalist made a mark by his insightful, farsighted writing. The other side of Sokolsky was his personal opportunism which led him to hold a string of generally unprincipled ultra-right positions stretching from the 1930s to the McCarthy Inquisition during the early 1950s in which he played an important role.

In this effort Professor Cohen set an ambitious and important task for himself. The weaving of personal influence and policy together is most significant for our understanding of U.S. foreign policy toward Asia as well as the rest of the world. This book is an informative assessment of one set of very noteworthy connections.

CARL F. PINKELE
Ohio Wesleyan University
Delaware

A. W. DEPORTE. *Europe between the Superpowers: The Enduring Balance.* Pp. xv, 256. New Haven, CT: Yale University Press, 1979. $18.50.

For many theorists of international relations, the principle of the balance of power is as incontrovertibly important to the viability and stability of the modern European state system as eighteenth century thinkers believed the principle of the invisible hand was indispensable to the well-being of the economies of that system. Accordingly, in A. W. DePorte's work the balance of power, much like the invisible hand, is regarded as an inexorable principle of system behavior which policymakers are free to ignore only at their own risk and peril. From this point of departure, DePorte, a member of the State Department Policy Planning Staff, analyzes the intriguing historical antecedents of our contemporary bypolar system. Its structure, he points out, was fixed by the outcome of World War II, and can be understood properly only against the background of the devolution, beginning in 1870, of a relatively stable four century old European state system.

The long view, then, of the confrontation between the two superpowers and their client states begins with the Prussian victory over France which undermined the traditionally dependable balance of power. Thereafter, the growth and consolidation of German power led to the first World War. Germany's initial war successes brought forth intervention by the United States. But the subsequent defeat of Germany settled few of the overriding issues of power mainly because the defeat was far from decisive. The lull between the two world wars and the national division of European territory therefore had no basis in power realities.

Asserting herself again in 1940, Germany quickly became the hegemonial master of Europe. Germany's final defeat this time was made possible only by the combined forces of the Soviet Union and the United States. The war, DePorte observes, was not fought simply against the Nazis but against a Germany much too powerful to be contained in any balance of power equation. Defeat and inadvertent partition solved the German problem and prepared the way for a new bypolar system.

The new system would first be tempered by the cold war which, contrary to the popular impression of rivalry, strife and crisis, was a period of constructive though painful adjustment by the superpowers to the reality that their respective policy options were limited by a new balance of power. A balance, that is, which neither side was strong enough to alter. Interestingly, the balance and its post war territorial arrangements are seen to be as much the result of the free momentum of events as of deliberate planning.

However, DePorte implies that major responsibility for the cold war belongs to the United States. The failure of the United States to perceive such elemental facts as that the Soviet Union too had won the war and that it too had spheres of interest helped harden attitudes and exacerbated cold war tension. Americans, DePorte explains, were not conditioned historically to think in terms of international power realities. Given their liberal democratic idealism they were not inclined to accept Soviet domination and subjugation of Eastern Europe. For that matter, Soviet interests and actions, whatever they might be, were not likely to be accorded much legitimacy. On the other hand, the Soviets tended to exaggerate the hostility of the West.

Despite all these difficulties—including the mistaken judgments and calculations of men like Truman and Kennan—the warp and vicissitudes of the cold war permitted the formation of a stable Euro-Atlantic–Euro-Asian bypolar order. DePorte estimates that this order is resilient enough to survive well into the twenty-first century.

Within a framework of Hobbesian assumptions and logic, the conventional wisdom of most international relations theory, DePorte has written an articulate and sober account of United States and Soviet relations. Because the Soviet Union has been, in his opinion, more mindful of the principles of *Machtpolitik*, its policies are judged less harshly than those of the United States. The latter, in this regard, is criticized for simplistic idealism. For example, the American post-war wish for free Polish institutions is described as more naive than disingenuous. American postwar goals in general are dismissed as excessively ambitious in light of the available power of implementation.

While admitting personally to liberal democratic preferences, DePorte like many of his political science brethren, finds power to be the ultimate arbitrator of values. Therefore, such an important political concept as legitimacy is reduced simply to an appraisal of what is possible. Theorizing in this fashion, DePorte concludes that present power arrangements represent the best of all possible worlds. In support, he stresses that the bypolar balance of power has produced peace and has insured the national survival of member states—an assertion which has to be read of course in the context of American violence in Southeast Asia and the Soviet rape of Eastern Europe. Whether the politics discussed here are in point of fact those of the best possible world, or whether that world instead remains, because of these politics, far from reach, is a question that needs to be pondered.

PAUL L. ROSEN
Carleton University
Ottawa
Canada

GLEN FISHER. *American Communication in a Global Society*. Pp. ix, 165. Norwood, NJ: Ablex Publishers, 1979. $17.50.

Most examinations of American communication in the world tend to concentrate heavily on the content and technology of the mass media. Such a focus is understandable as it takes account of the most tangible aspects of a pervasive and subtle process. In this book, Glen Fisher paints a more richly complex picture of the factors involved in international communication.

Fisher takes pains to point out that international communication is not communication between monolithic societies. Individual citizens as well as private and governmental organizations of the United States are engaged in communicating with their counterparts abroad. And the messages purveyed by America are perceived quite differently by various segments of the receiving culture. The middle class may respond favorably to American communication while other segments of the same society form less positive impressions. Successful international communication strategies thus depend on policymakers' attention to much more than the content of some message; they must begin to weigh such factors as the psychology of information processing and image formation, interpersonal and organizational communication, political ideology, social structures, and the cultural milieu in which communications are received and interpreted.

The author seems most comfortable when discussing the role of communication in the conduct of foreign affairs. Communication should be considered when laying the groundwork of foreign policy and is not just the concern of technicians charged with implementing completed plans. Fisher is cautiously optimistic that the International Communication Agency may figure more prominently in contributing to policy formation than the bureaus from which it was recently created. He forthrightly offers other recommendations and suggests that some painful changes are in order—changes which may not be palatable to Americans eager to export the country's ideology and values.

The vagueness of Fisher's methodology detracts slightly from his effort. The book is largely a work of synthesis, though it also draws conclusions from pilot studies of several developing nations which Fisher conducted for the State Department's Bureau of Educational and Cultural Affairs. He fails to make the nature of these studies explicit, noting only that they involved systematic interviews with more than 200 professional communicators and knowledgeable observers. The upshot is that the book strikes the reader as being impressionistic, probably distilled from the author's experience as a foreign service officer; he is now at Georgetown University's School of Foreign Service.

The shortcomings of *American Communication in a Global Society* may be excused as those typical of an exploratory study. The book is a timely reminder that many of the crises America faces in dealing with other nations, especially those of the Third World, are compounded by breakdowns in communication.

RICHARD B. KIELBOWICZ
Iowa State University
Ames

LESLIE H. GELB and RICHARD K. BETTS. *The Irony of Vietnam: The System Worked.* Pp. xi, 387. Washington, DC: Brookings Institution, 1979. $14.95. Paperbound $5.95.

It is the basic theme of this book that the United States did not "stumble" or somehow "blunder" into the Vietnam war but, rather, that given the need to limit Communist expansion in the world, itself a legacy of World War II's costly lesson of isolation, escalating American commitments in Indochina by successive administrations were preceded by careful institutionalized processes of decision making, during which tactical doubts and qualms were openly expressed by various responsible officials and the relative benefits and disadvantages of each policy were closely scrutinized. This is what is meant by Gelb and Betts when they say that the "system worked"; that is, that in the American determination to become more and more involved in the Vietnam fighting, an attempt in fact was made to arrive at something of a consensus in the U.S. policy making establishment, particularly in relations within the executive agencies and in relations between the President and the Congress. Contrary to the belief held especially in the

antiwar movement that criticism of U.S. involvement in Vietnam was ignored, it is the contention of Gelb and Betts that among the "general criteria" by which the American foreign policymaking process may be said to have worked is that—"virtually all views and recommendations were considered and virtually all important decisions were made without illusions about the odds for success."

Both Gelb and Betts have been well placed to develp their principal thesis, the former having been director of the U.S. Defense Department's Pentagon Papers project, while the latter, beginning his work as a Harvard University faculty member, like Gelb completed this study while associated with the Brookings Institution. The book is thoroughly researched and not only have the authors been able to use portions of the Pentagon Papers that have become available, but they have also drawn on declassified Presidential documents in the Kennedy and Johnson libraries, and carefully have tapped available secondary sources. The result is an altogether impressive contribution to the growing body of literature on the "why" of the Vietnam war, as seen not from the perspective of the ground in Vietnam itself but rather from the perspective of American policymakers.

We are taken step by step in successive chapters through the long tunnel of the gradually deepening American involvement in the Indochina problem, beginning with Roosevelt's concept of an "international trusteeship" for the area and Truman's dilemma of dealing with the implications of the "fall" of China, through Eisenhower's equivocal policies of assistance to the French and later to Ngo Dinh Diem, and ultimately the growing U.S. military commitment "in force" under Kennedy and Johnson. The authors rightly note that until 1965 a "dominant moderate-liberal consensus," sufficiently wide so as to "include just about everyone," appeared to prevail in domestic American political thinking, with "only the fringes of opinion"—some on the Left, others concerned with an excessive strategic and financial U.S. burden, on the Right—in opposition.

Not the least valuable section of the book is the brief analysis (pp. 220–226) delineating the "practical political considerations" which after the pre-1965 consensus began to break down, nevertheless compelled the Chief Executive, his advisors, and party, and congressional leaders to persist in augmenting the U.S. military presence in Vietnam even as public opinion not only in the United States, but also among America's allies, rapidly came to consider that presence to be a dreadful mistake. As the authors note in their review of the "lessons" of Vietnam, U.S. Presidents found it much more difficult to drastically alter established policies than many in the Congress did. The very weight of the Presidential office made dissenting bureaucrats in the vast policy-making establishment particularly loath to buck official White House policies, thus further contributing to the fatal inertia of continuing the war.

But perhaps the real villain of the piece, as the authors see it, was the very premise of the Cold War era itself, the self conceived American mission of "containing" Communism, wherever and whatever its forms. From this premise it seemed to follow that the fall of Vietnam (like the fall of China before it) could only mean that one part of the Free World after another would await a similar fate. Gelb and Betts caution Presidents not to adopt doctrinaire policy positions and then strive for broad if not unanimous public support for them. But how else are U.S. chief executives to govern effectively? It may be the weakness of leadership institutions in constitutional democracies that policies cannot be implemented without such doctrinaire policy and consensus seeking, and that the need for pragmatism which the authors counsel as desirable becomes an invitation to disarray and inaction. The crisis and debate over U.S. policy in Iran once again would seem to confirm this.

JUSTUS M. VAN DER KROEF
University of Bridgeport
Connecticut

LOUIS HENKIN. *The Rights of Man Today*. Pp. xiv, 173. Boulder, CO: Westview Press, 1978. $14.50.

JAMES AVERY JOYCE. *The New Politics of Human Rights*. Pp. xi, 305. New York: St. Martin's Press, 1979. $19.95.

Both these books describe the development of the concept of "Human Rights" and stress its international scope as represented by the various declarations of the United Nations. Professor Joyce is more concerned than is Professor Henkin with the actual state of the world and the widespread ignoring of the written guarantees.

Actually, Professor Henkin's book is grounded on Thomas Paine, as its title suggests. He summarizes the recent expansions of human rights by the courts and legislatures in the United States. While aware of remaining imperfections, he concludes that they "are alive and rather well." He is not so optimistic about their existence in Socialist-Communist states, noting that the words of the constitutions are "deceptive" and enjoyed "only by political grace." He gives special attention to Castro's Cuba and finds it wanting in the absence of an independent judiciary to see that the promises in its constitution are kept. He finds the Third World constitutions in much the same state, particularly when the constitutions permit "emergency rule."

Professor Henkin treats the development of the idea of international obligations with special emphasis on the European Human Rights Convention and its court. Recognizing the inadequacies of the international aspirations, he applauds the attitude of the United States.

While Professor Henkin merely indicates the gaps between promise and performance, Professor Joyce starts right off with specific instances of the violations of human rights. His first subject is slavery, which still exists in many parts of the world, especially with regard to children as laborers and young girls as wives, instancing a case in Italy in 1976. After a discussion of attempts at amelioration, he describes some of the violations in chapters entitled "Mobilisation of Shame" and "Raising a Double Standard." He gives great credit to Amnesty International for its activities in bringing many of these horrors to light and also to the International Commission of Jurists. He is critical of the West's failure to recognize Israel's violations of human rights. In a chapter dealing with self determination, he calls the rape of the Sahara by Morocco and Mauritania the "gravest setback" that the movement has suffered. Throughout runs the thread of the 1948 "Universal" Declaration of the United Nations and its later additions; the full texts are appended.

Professor Joyce takes a look at the impact of modern technology: on the right to privacy, on the right to know, and on the right to die, as well as on genetic engineering, on the ethics of transplants, and on crimes by computer; that is, the use of computers by criminals.

Finally, Professor Joyce points to a new Committee that is independent of the U.N., which was set up to investigate complaints, and to the European Court of Human Rights as assuring greater attention to violations. He suggests the appointment of a High Commissioner to coordinate efforts, but reaches no conclusion on the desirability of the enactment of a modern Bill of Rights in England. He concludes by insisting that the purpose of human rights is the protection of the individual, not the state.

Both books have notes: the first citing many decisions of the United States Supreme Court; the second referring to the literature of the subject. Only the second has an index.

OSMOND K. FRAENKEL
New York City

LYNN KRIEGER MYTELKA. *Regional Development in a Global Economy*. Pp. xvi, 233, New Haven, CT: Yale University Press, 1979. $17.50.

DAVID K. WHYNES. *The Economics of Third World Military Expenditure*, Pp. xiv, 165. Austin: University of Texas Press, 1979. $13.50.

Whynes' book is a brilliant and topical one that fills a long-standing need in the area of defense economics vis-à-vis the prospects for economic development in the Third World—developing or less-developing countries (LDC).

The focal point of this book is an assessment of the cost-benefit analysis and moral implications of the staggering defense expenditures of the Third World in face of the human degradation, squalid conditions, and the penury of the peoples. It argues that LDC's might reduce their cost of human destruction, therefore improving their welfare, by adopting policies of civic action or sociomilitary integration—"non-military defense" (NMD).

While the LDC economy is agrarian with a 2.4 percent annual growth rate from 1971–76, manufacturing balloons at a phenomenal 7.3 percent rate; the GNP grows at 5.3 percent annually while population grows at a rate of 2.1 percent. The military sector expansion rate is 6.5 percent or twice the average capacity of the people to produce (per capita incomes). This priority for defense causes the misallocation of economic resources. It provides suboptimal living standards, lowered economic growth, malnutrition and a shortened life-expectancy at the treadmill of daily existence. The raison d'être for the military-industrial complex varies from security to the vested interests of the military establishments (Chapter 2). Thus military expenditure correlates positively with manpower, employment, and population growth, but not as much as in the developed countries (DC) (Chapter 3).

Professor Whynes further discusses the arms proliferation with the attendant moral implications of trade and aid thus engendered. The LDC's have become dumping grounds, therefore sources of employment opportunities for the DCs. He analyzes and provides ample models, data (from NATO, Warsaw Treaty Organization, and others), references, and tables to prove his thesis on this sensitive topic. There is intuitive appeal in his recommendations but they are iffy at best.

Mytelka's book is about the drama and tragedy of the Andean—Bolivia, Chile, Columbia, Ecuador, Peru and Venezuela —experiment of regional economic integration with the multinational corporations (MNCs).

The post-World War II monopolistic growth of the giant MNCs in the product and factor, technology, markets propelled the internationalization of their operations for markets, particularly in LDCs, to defray the high costs of production. This action unveiled transmission mechanisms of technologies, economic and political opportunities that should have promoted import-substituting industrialization to tilt the extractive consignment of the international division of labor, full-employment and socio-economic equality.

The industrialization process saw the formation and failure of the Latin American Free Trade Association (LAFTA) to promote national development or equitable distribution of gains from integration among Andean countries. It produced underdevelopment, despite increased per capita incomes and technologies in the region: a well-off minority gained at the expense of social costs to the poor majority.

By the mid-1960s, the rise of new social forces in the region led to conflicts between national and international capital. The result was new integrative policies by the Andean leaders to reduce dependence on foreign capital and technology through regional regulation and planning.

These books are most erudite in the development and defense economics of LDCs. They address and assess issues primal to these nations. Ipso facto, they should be of interest and aid to the politico-economic observers of the Third World and their policymakers in particular.

JOHN B. ADESALU
Loyola College
Baltimore

FREDERICK C. MOSHER. *The GAO: The Quest for Accountability in American Government.* Pp. xx, 387. Boulder, CO: Westview Press, 1979. $24.00.

MARTIN PAINTER and BERNARD CAREY. *Politics Between Departments: The Fragmentation of Executive Control in Australian Government.* Pp. xii, 132. Lawrence, MA: Queensland University Press, 1979. $21.75.

How do representative democracies successfully protect their citizens' investments? What institutional mechanisms are available and how effectively do they function? Such questions are addressed in these books, which deal with two types of government: the American or Presidential model and the British or Parliamentary model.

The links between both books include treating legislative-executive relationships, viewing agency liaison arrangements, and focusing on management of public policy. As political scientists, the three authors show awareness of the power inherent in institutional patterns that afford some people more access than others.

Australia is the locale for the fast paced Painter/Carey book, which draws on material from 1972–75. At first the authors seem to have constructed a maze of acronyms representing the Canberra government. A closer look at such IDCs (interdepartmental committees) as SANMA and SIDCURD reveals an intriguing governmental scheme. We learn that IDCs are bureaucratic forums which can overcome policy coordination problems among governmental departments. The 30 to 50 IDCs which exist at any time impose consensus norms on their participants, some of whom have "watching brief" roles while others have delegate roles.

The authors' humor ("IDC members do not . . . throw paper clips at one another . . . ," p. 70) helps to restrain a bracing criticism of Australia's application of the British model. Painter and Carey allude to "fragmentation and departmentalism" in a model that "oversimplifies and distorts," applying "primarily to roles rather than processes" (pp. 83–85). They even say that "IDCs are doing jobs they should not be doing," as they point to "ad hoccery" (p. 100) inherent in cabinet organization.

Mosher's encyclopedic treatment of the General Accounting Office is a tome that belongs on the reference shelf. As a well-indexed history, it provides the reader with a mass of information. As a readable account, it lacks a critical analytic framework.

Instead, Mosher has divided a 58-year history into three sections: 1921–1945 (the years for railroad carloads of documents), 1945–1966 (when emphasis was placed on getting information at its source), and 1966–1978 (a time for legislative-executive conflict). Unfortunately, the political interactions of GAO over the years do not seem to be evaluated sufficiently in Mosher's first part, a seven-chapter evolutionary report.

Only in the four-chapter second part, "Emerging Roles of the GAO," does Mosher appear to evaluate GAO as a social scientist should. Early on (p. 71), Mosher had spoken of a model, but it was the old, authoritarian model, with a requirement for "the ringing of bells" when GAO employees began and ended lunch breaks. In the latter section, though, Mosher cites a recommendation that GAO adopt a "project team approach" for its business (p. 354). Perspective is provided also on GAO's systemic roles, such as its help with New York City's budget and its overseas reviews for such operations as the Marshall Plan and the Vietnam War.

Mosher's book should be required reading for the new Comptroller-General to be appointed next year. Chapter 7 especially can warn GAO's next head of impending political conflict. It tells of GAO reports on Watergate that were "too effective for some congressional stomachs" (p. 216) and of GAO actions on impoundment control that forced President Ford to release funds for a housing program.

Both books make notable contributions to political science literature. Their impact could be strengthened by closer linkage to decisionmaking research, such as Alexander George's multiple advocacy model and Graham Allison's organizational process paradigm. Why not view activities of Australian IDCs and the U.S. GAO within the framework of small group research? Such a perspective should enable the Painter/Carey and Mosher approaches to be applied to analyses of other bureaucracies around the world.

CHARLES T. BARBER
Indiana State University
Evansville

YITZHAK SHICHOR. *The Middle East in China's Foreign Policy.* Pp. xiii, 268. New York: Cambridge University Press, 1979. $25.00.

For China, the Middle East, sub-Saharan Africa, and other parts of the Third World are important keys in Peking's effort to build an "international united front" against both superpowers, Russia and America. But China's interest in the whole northwest sector of the Indian Ocean goes beyond ideological warfare in the name of proletarian internationalism. Since the Peoples Republic of China (PRC) reentered the world of conventional state-to-state diplomacy, about 1969, and repudiated the paramilitary tactic of Lin Piao and the Gang of Four, China has begun to view the world through geopolitical spectacles.

Not that China has ceased being an exporter of revolutionary ideas to restive countries bordering the Indian Ocean, a highly unstable littoral to begin with. Much of Chinese policy is still governed by the motives of the 1955 Bandung Conference. The PRC has, in fact, reinvigorated its network of friendship societies, print-media outlets, international broadcasts in north and sub-Saharan Africa, and throughout the world generally. But in the present era, *raison d'etat* has apparently superseded Maoism, or perhaps the latter is at least abetted by expansion of Chinese trade and diplomatic and other ties with countries in the "intermediate zone" (according to the Three Worlds formula). Of this zone, as Yitzhak Shichor writes, the Middle East occupies an "extremely important strategic position, as the main battlefield against the West"—and against the Soviet hegemonists.

Mr. Shichor, of the department of East Asian Studies at the Hebrew University of Jerusalem, has dedicated his book to the proposition that while China may be considered by some to be an outsider in the Middle East, the Chinese never "lost sight of [the importance of the Middle East] in their strategy and foreign policy considerations."

After 1971, Peking's Middle Eastern effort accelerated noticeably, and Egypt appeared to be the kingpin. Particularly with Egypt's expulsion of the Soviet technicians and the reorientation of Egyptian policy away from cooperation with Moscow since 1973, Peking has sought close relations with the Sadat government. It even welcomed the Egyptian-American rapprochement. As to Chinese long-standing support for the Palestine Liberation Organization—which continues today—the Soviet comrades have had this to say: as quoted by Shichor, from monitoring Radio Moscow): "Despite loud anti-Israeli propaganda, [Peking is] playing a dishonest double game; their only contribution to the Palestinian struggle has been a supply of books of quotations and Mao badges."

Indeed, according to the author, "continued Chinese support for some revolutionary struggles [against governments whose friendship Peking sought] became incompatible with Peking's new orientation." The PRC particularly resented the manner in which national liberation movements, once installed in power, turned to Moscow for political and military support. Peking even advocated "political bargaining," between "liberators" and the regimes they sought to replace, as an "intrinsic part" of the military and political struggle. Various Palestine liberation organizations, as well as some in the Persian Gulf, have been advised by Peking not to forego the peaceful route to power. Terorism, likewise, has been condemned. Peking spoke up firmly against the forcible detention of the 50-plus Americans in their embassy in Teheran at the U.N. Security Council meeting of Dec. 1, 1979.

In short, Mr. Shichor's excellently

researched and wide-ranging book documents the fascinating process by which the Middle Kingdom, under the post-Mao leadership, has reentered the rest of the world, particularly that extension of it lying among the most strategic "rim-lands" of what the Chinese call "West Asia and Africa," which in their geographical perception includes the Middle East. While the author is well aware of the way ideology follows the flag in Peking's diplomatic and trade activity in the Middle East, he also cautions against an exaggeration of the strength of this activity. China is too weak militarily to make its power felt in the region. Also, despite isolated trade deals of considerable magnitude, the PRC lacks the economic means to acquire really significant leverage. Judged in terms of traditional power politics, Shichor writes, "China's Middle East policy must be admitted a complete failure." Yet, he asserts, China's political voice is significantly effective in its opposition to imperialism and hegemonism of whatever stripe, and in its fervent support of national independence.

ALBERT L. WEEKS
New York City

A. P. THORNTON. *Imperialism in the Twentieth Century.* Pp. xii, 363. Minneapolis: University of Minnesota Press, 1978. $20.00.

GEORGE LISKA. *Career of Empire: American and Imperial Expansion over Land and Sea.* Pp. xi, 360. Baltimore, MD: Johns Hopkins University Press, 1978. $17.95.

These two books provide an intriguing complementarity. Professor Thornton is a historian of scope and imagination, a skilled detector of linkages, with a strong and immediate sense of reality, generous in his provision of insights and information. Professor Liska also has a strong historical dimension. But his object is to reduce his observations to system, with a view to using system to illuminate the present, together with future policy choices and prospects. Thornton is much easier to read; his work is structured, but not seriously confined by its structure. Liska, with his "analogico-historical" method, expressed in compacted polysyllables and contracted syntax, makes stiff reading for those seeking to follow him in his "effort to uncover both a common and a coherent basic anatomy of superficially diverse empires" (p. 350). But the discipline necessary to accompany Liska is worth the very considerable effort.

Thornton sets the terms of his discussion with a brisk definition: "An imperial policy is one that enables a metropolis to create and maintain an external system of effective control. . . . Imperialism is a critical term for activity let loose" (p. 3). He sees imperialism almost as an inherent phenomenon, practiced by states that have, by the mysterious processes of history, achieved autonomy and coherence, but not equilibrium. Their situation thus impels them to impact outward upon other societies that have failed to achieve a matching status. In so doing they alter themselves, assuming the characteristic attitudes and outlook appropriate to their role, and imposing a kind of reciprocal of these upon the societies they are able to dominate. "A Great Power that denies any capacity for or intention of imperialising," says Thornton, is "itself an anomaly" (p. 245).

To argue thus is to push the attendant questions back a stage. They center around the problem: what are the circumstances that award to some states the core or metropolitan role, and to others that of the impacted upon periphery? This aspect Thornton does not directly discuss in his present book. He writes of the twentieth century, taking his pattern of imperialisms as already established. He is thus chiefly concerned with the way in which the configuration set in the nineteenth century and earlier has evolved further in the present one. But his treatment is perhaps not so complete as his title implies.

It is of the imperialisms of Britain and France that he chiefly writes, imperialisms that had the time and scope to generate something approaching an ideal type. The United States enters the story in a somewhat secondary way. The imperialisms of contiguity and assimilation of the Soviet Union and China are largely left to one side. The USSR is discussed mainly in terms of the reciprocal attitudes between itself and the West, although the point is made that a peculiar situation exists when imperialism is, and must always remain, by definition, unknown to Soviet policy (p. 266). Japan receives barely more than incidental mention. These relegations and omissions are perhaps indicative of the limitations that attach to any attempt to conduct a generalized discussion of imperialism. This is true especially of the feedback effects on the life of the metropolitan country: these have been very different as between the European imperial powers, the great land-mass empires, and Japan.

Moreover, in more recent years the kind of outward thrusting coherence attained by Britain and France in the past has been superceded in parts of the world by arbitrary factors having little to do with internal societal structure, namely the sudden realization of a critical industrial input: oil. This change is taken into account in a sense: the new masters who want to "change the deal," Thornton tells us, will act as their predecessors have done: but "the game," he says "would remain the same."

In a sense this is true. But whereas former imperialisms arose largely from the on-going logic of internal societal factors, the new oil imperialism is not generated within the oil states. Instead it derives from the fact that the classic imperialisms blindly created for themselves a state of dependence on their former clients, while at the same time adopting a code of international behavior, reinforced by a stand off between the great powers, which denies them the traditional relief of being able to seize the resources they require. The former clients, for their part, are confronted with the disruptive societal implications of their new wealth. Their imperialism will, presumably, in spite of Thronton's dictum, be very different in many senses from that of their predecessors.

Liska's focal interest is American imperialism, largely since World War II; in order to elucidate it he turns to the empires of Rome and Britain as analogues. This three-part approach inevitably carries yet further overtones, opening up the prospect of formalizing imperialism on a generalized basis. To what degree is this the objective?

For some purposes Liska seems to envisage a generalized dynamic and its accompanying necessary set of conditions which allows of universal conclusions. For other purposes he distinguishes between Rome, land based, and Britain, maritime based, with different relationships to the other societies in their respective systems; this he does in order to elucidate different phases in American experience and responses. Of the universal factors, the nature and reactions of the ruling élites are important. But these, when placed under scrutiny in the three cases, seem to be almost arbitrarily determined, arising from circumstances so complex and time-lagged as to make them almost autonomous in terms of the situations in which they were called upon to act. Are such élites independent entities or must their responses be in terms of the demos? Whichever way the national state of mind is determined, it may be characterized by "slackening of energies" or by vigorous "responses to danger" (p. 336). These again are not necessarily intrinsically determined, but may depend upon the threat behavior of the other imperialisms.

Because the approach offered by Liska is so largely contingent it is not predictive in any general sense over all imperialisms and their responses. But his anologico-historical method does go some way toward setting out the choices in a given context at a given time, and the consequences likely to follow from the selection made from among them. Historically, an imperial power would seem to have had three choices; namely an attempt at parity with rivals,

the pursuit of some kind of agreed equilibrium state, or the extension of her own empire in pursuit of a stabilizing hegemony. The anologico-historical method is offered as an aid in assessing which choice is the most likely, by helping to define the comparative configuration present at the time.

Liska is able to stand back from immediacy to express a truth which, though very high on the scale of generality, is nevertheless a profound one. Presumably Professor Thornton would agree with it. "The sources of the expansion of states are the vital, if latent, springs of all statecraft," Liska writes, "They keep alive, as it were, the timeless mysteries which surround the pursuit and exercise of power" (p. 3).

S. G. CHECKLAND
University of Glasgow
Scotland

AFRICA, ASIA AND LATIN AMERICA

MICHAEL ADAS. *Prophets of Rebellion: Millenarian Protest Movements Against European Colonial Order*. Pp. xxvii, 243. Chapel Hill: University of North Carolina Press, 1979. $19.00.

Historian Michael Adas' *Prophets of Rebellion* is an interesting but not entirely successful attempt to use some of the theoretical ideas of contemporary social science to understand millenarian protest movements against colonial rule. He focuses on five "revitalization" rebellions that took place in Java, New Zealand, East-Central India, German East Africa and Burma at various points between 1825 and 1932. As revitalization implies, these prophet led, peasant based revolts were efforts to repel colonial intrusion and to reconstruct a culture founded on traditional, indigenous principles.

Adas finds the causes of these revolts in the feeling of relative deprivation born of the destructive impact of the European commercial-industrial revolution on the customary culture and structure of power in these colonial areas (pp. xix–xxx, 42). Faced with the corrosive political-ideological power of obdurate colonial authorities, the colonized were left no alternative but violence in their efforts to re-establish their own cultural and political norms (Ch. 3). As they rebelled, so racial and ethnic antagonisms bubbled to the surface, since "in colonial societies power was monopolized by and most of the economic benefits went to the European rulers and their immigrant, and at times indigenous, allies" (p. 79).

The central figures in these revolts were the prophets who led them. Their personalities and their ability to formulate millenarian visions, even where traditionally none had existed, were vital factors, says Adas, in mobilizing the populace. But mobilization alone could not guarantee success. The revolts failed largely because their leaders remained backward looking and were unsuccessful in formulating the kind of modern strategy and tactics that marked the campaigns of later anticolonial nationalists. And one of the chief reasons for this failure was that the prophets misjudged or simply did not understand the European colonists (p. 182 and ch. 7 *passim*).

In a short concluding chapter Adas assesses "Prophetic Rebellion as a Type of Social Protest." It is here, by omission, that the main problem of *Prophets of Rebellion* becomes clear. Adas has to this point given us an engaging theme and developed it well enough. But the importance of revitalization movements surely lies in their connection to anticolonial revolts and revolution as a whole. Adas never explores these connections, particularly the Janus-like character of violence and revolt that has been so ably examined by such authors as Charles Tilly, who does not appear in the bibliography, Eric Hobsbawm and James C. Scott (who do, but whose ideas Adas has not used to advantage. Nor, in the end, does Adas really illuminate what he claims to be the vital role of the prophets themselves (pp. 92–3). He gives us potted biographies of them and a short analysis of prophetic leaders (ch. 4) but, apart or

together, these things are insufficient to substantiate his claim.

Adas' *Prophets of Rebellion* is a stimulating, if incomplete work: long where it could be shorter, as in its discussion of the role of talismans in revolutionary mobilization, and short where it could be longer, as in the concluding chapter cited above. Nevertheless, it is a good start to this new series, edited by Philip Curtin, on Comparative World History.

PETER COCKS
State University of New York
Albany

HANNA BATATU. *The Old Social Classes and the Revolutionary Movements of Iraq*. Pp. xiv, 1283. Princeton, NJ: Princeton University Press, 1978. $75.00.

Dr. Batatu has undoubtedly written a major work on the social history of modern Iraq which will be an essential source for all future students and scholars of the Middle East. While the work contains a comprehensive introduction to the old regime, as well as a brief history of post-1958 revolutionary movements, such as the Free Officers and the Ba'th Party, the core of the book is a history of the Communist Party in Iraq from its origins to 1958. About twenty years of research and revision have gone into this study, the result of which is a monograph of mammoth size, rich in information and source material, much of it published here for the first time.

The work is really three books in one. The first describes Iraq's classes and divisions under the monarchy, with a wealth of detail on the structure of Iraqi society, the social groups which comprised it and the influence of these groups on Iraqi politics. The second book focusses on communism in Iraq in the same period, tracing the origins of the movement, detailing the merging structure of the Party, articulating its internal divisions and conflicts, and relating the Party to other political groups such as the Istiqlal (Independence) Party, the left-wing National

Democratic Party and the Ba'th. The third book deals with the transformation of Iraq in 1958 from a monarchy to a republic and its introduction to socialism and twenty years of political instability. Here the author fails to show the impact of the political transformation on the structure of traditional social classes as he did in the first book.

The amount of information compiled in this work is truly awe inspiring. It includes statistics, tables, and voluminous data on the tribal linkages and family backgrounds of political leaders as well as exhaustive bibliographical data. But the data frequently overwhelms the reader. The result is a work that is more of an unorganized encyclopedia than a systematic and methodological approach to the subject. Some chapters run on for a hundred pages without subtitles; meanwhile the reader loses his train of thought.

A second criticism is more substantive. The heavy use of Communist sources, and the natural sympathy of the author for his subject have often led him to overemphasize the impact of communism on Iraq. The Iraq Communist Party (ICP) has simply not played the leading role assigned to it by Batatu. For example, it played little or no role in the fall of the monarchy in 1958, the removal of Qassim in 1963, the end of the first Ba'th regime in 1963, or the removal of the Arif regime in 1968. In fact the ICP has always represented a minority—although an active minority—among Iraq's political parties. The driving force behind Iraqi public opinion, and especially its politicized elements was, and is, nationalism, to which little space is devoted in Batatu's discussion of revolutionary movements.

Two of the author's most interesting conclusions are contained on p. 351 and p. 1134. The first is the leftist interpretation that the old regime fell mainly because of its failure to accommodate the forces of social change. No one today would deny the absence of social change, but again the conclusion minimizes the fact that the driving force behind the revolution of 1958 was political and economic independence from the West, not social change. Moreover, Batatu completely overlooks the compelling influence of Nasser and the 1952 Egyptian revolution.

His second conclusion is that the present Ba'th regime cannot survive unless it shares power with the ICP and the Kurdish Democratic Party. He sees these three—the Ba'th, the ICP and the KDP, as the three "principal political powers in the country." While he is correct in grouping these left-wing parties together, they cannot be considered the principal political forces in Iraq unless, by forces, he means organized political parties. The rural population, the urban lower classes, and the lower echelons of the army and the bureaucracy, which constitute the majority of the country, remain essentially conservative and nationalist in orientation. To politicize these groups the left has a long way to go.

LOUAY BAHRY

University of Tennessee
Knoxville

LEONARD BINDER. *In a Moment of Enthusiasm: Political Power and the Second Stratum in Egypt.* Pp. xxii, 437. Chicago: University of Chicago Press, 1978. $22.50.

Long awaited by scholars of Middle East studies, Binder's new study on rural Egypt is must reading for those who remain concerned about modernization and social change in Third World countries. It is not easy to do justice to a book of such scholarship as this in a short review. Professor Binder has written a superb piece of historical reconstruction of the social and political continuity that appears to characterize the pre- and post-1952 revolutionary elite structure of rural Egypt.

Utilizing Mosca's "second stratum" as the crucial instrument through which the ruling oligarchy maintains its control over the broad masses of society, Binder seeks to emphasize the significance of Nasser's party elite in rural Egypt. Binder's general hypothesis points out "that the rural middle class in Egypt was able to capture the support of the Egyptian masses in a moment of enthusiasm . . . (this) second stratum does not rule but is the stratum without which the rulers can not rule."

One can approve of his "revisionist" orientation which focuses on social structure and not just political culture, which seeks greater clarity in the political processes between elites at the center and periphery of power instead of the more static demographic description of such elites. His concern is with the ways in which central politics impinge on local politics and vice versa, emphasizing interaction and relationships that exist between and among levels of party organization and government bureaucracy in Egypt.

In what must be classified as a masterly job of social science detective work and an exemplary form of political inquiry, Binder documents the still indomitable impact of family ties and kinship relationships in rural Egypt. In reviewing the importance of social class and the impact of traditional families across the hundreds of villages which are included in his sample, Binder reinforces the notion that such families still play the dominant role in the political life of most villages of rural Egypt.

Although this study seeks to document the progressively significant position of the middle class in Egypt under Nasser and presumably now under Sadat, Binder goes several steps beyond that notion observing that while "the outstanding characteristic of the second stratum is its agricultural base . . . our general picture of the second stratum remains that it is not primarily identified with ruralism, but rather with a type of agriculture that requires capital, larger holdings (over 10 feddan) and proximity to urban areas."

Binder's chapter 13 is an excellent summary and a useful critique of Nasser's efforts to develop a political party system which would legitimize his regime and mobilize his people to a new set of ideological goals. The short but well written analyses of Sadat's struggle with Ali Sabri and his eventual victory over his leftist opponents whets the reader's appetite for a more detailed and better documented discussion of those crucial months in 1971.

After having followed an imposing series of intricate arguments in this book, the average reader could be left with the feeling of incompleteness, partly because the author does acknowledge that there is still much to be done. But the sense of incompleteness may also be in some measure a product of the research strategy itself. The author spins such a fine and complicated methodological web that the conclusions tend to get lost in it. The findings are certainly substantial enough to merit greater delineation than they receive. But, minor flaws not withstanding, the book will perform a real service for students of comparative politics if it does no more than expose the complexity of reality found in rural Egypt.

JAMES B. MAYFIELD
University of Utah
Salt Lake City

FRANCIS MADING DENG. *Africans of Two Worlds: The Dinka in Afro-Arab Sudan.* Pp. xx, 244. New Haven, CT: Yale University Press, 1978. $15.00.

The Dinka are Nilotic pastoralists who, after Sudanese independence in 1956, revolted against the Arab dominated Khartoum government. The civil war that ensued lasted for seventeen years. This book is an attempt to examine the perceptions of some Dinka chiefs about Dinka history and Dinka traditions in the light of the situation they now find themselves in, as the leaders of a formerly disaffected people seeking integration and development in the Sudanese state. But it is written by an anthropologist with an axe to grind. Dr. Deng is an authority on the Dinka, his own people, but he has also been a diplomat and a minister in the Sudan government. He claims to find among his interviewees a yearning for national integration, and that yearning for unity seems to him to be mirrored in their current views about their creation myths, the history of their contacts with Egypt, Mahdism, and the British, and their aspirations in a postwar era. For him, this reflects the dynamic flexibility of an oral tradition that is always deeply rooted in attempts to understand the present and prognosticate the future.

It could be something else. Dr. Deng is the son of a Dinka paramount chief. He was also a member of the Khartoum establishment of President Nimeri at the time that he was researching this book. The Dinka chiefs knew what he wanted to hear. Their views might be less an expression of the dynamic flexibility of their own traditions than a rubbing-up of the perceptions of their interlocutor. Moreover, he seems to have flouted all the rules of interviewing technique. Some of the chiefs came to see him, putting them at an instant psychological disadvantage. Some were interviewed jointly. Some appear to have been interviewed with a quite considerable audience. The reader cannot help but feel skeptical about information elicited in this way, and expressed in such an impressionistic form.

Yet if this is an impressionistic book, Dr. Deng nevertheless presents an extensive range of views that run counter to his thesis. There seem to be some irreconcilables among the Dinka, particularly among the Ngok Dinka who inhabit the most sensitive area between North and South. Many express doubts about Deng's own notions of Afro-Arab unity, about the full willingness of the North to permit political expression in the South and provide the opportunities for rapid development there.

It is perhaps the economic dimension that is most lacking. We derive very little information in this book about the economic discontents that led into the war in the first place. Nor are we presented with any notion of the felt needs of the South in the new situation, apart from the vaguest of references to development. What sort of develop-

ment? To what end and for whom? There are one or two tantalizing glimpses of the true problem. For example, one of Dr. Deng's informants talks of the hostility to northern traders and entrepreneurs battening on the South. It is a lead Dr. Deng does not take up. Interestingly, one aspect of British policy up to 1955 was to ban northern traders in the South. It is one of the ways in which the southerners feel that the British abandoned them to the economic mercies of the more advanced North.

Inevitably the book is, in part, a celebration of the Nimeri regime which brought peace. Some of Deng's interviewees, we are told, see Nimeri as being endowed with supernatural powers. But the reality since this book was published seems to be somewhat different. Nimeri's divine attributes did not prevent the strike of 100,000 Gezira farmers in 1979, the banning of a threatened general strike in October, the resistance of students and teachers, and the obsession of the regime with vast prestige projects rather than encouragement to the peasant and pastoralist. The plain economic fact is that the Sudan exported in 1979 only 10 percent of its total 1956 exports in livestock and meat.

In his foreword to the book, Andrew Young describes securing from the interviews some "amazing insights into the dynamics of the Dinka culture," and finding the book "a deeply moving and human chronicle." American policy will surely never escape from its present disarray until policymakers abandon this sort of romantic impressionism and look at some of the hard economic facts of people like the Dinka in their new national setting. It is precisely those hard facts that this book so signally lacks. And those facts repose in the oral tradition of past and present just as powerfully as any of the material Dr. Deng chose to elicit for us.

JOHN MACKENZIE
University of Lancaster
England

M. NAZIF MOHIB SHAHRANI. *The Kirghiz and Wakhi of Afghanistan: Adaptation to Closed Frontiers.* Pp.

xxiii, 264. Seattle: University of Washington Press, 1979. $15.00.

Afghanistan's northeastern province of Badakhshan includes the mountainous panhandle which flanks the eastern effluents of the Oxus river. This corridor of the Wakhan and Afghan Pamir ranges and the narrow intervening valleys became a permanent part of the nation in the 1890s, when it served as a buffer zone convenient to the two great powers which bordered it—the Russian empire on the north and British India on the south. The Wakhan, difficult of access but useable as a communications route and a modest herding and agricultural base, qualified as a refuge area comparable to some areas of the Caucasus. Thus it is not surprising that the Wakhi, one of the ethnic groups considered in Dr. Shahrani's study, are the closest linguistic relatives of the first millenium A.D. Iranian speakers of the Tarim Basin of Central Asia. The second group, the Turkic Kirghiz, were seasonal nomadic visitors to Badakhshan from north of the Oxus before the Soviet Union established full control over its national borders.

Dr. Shahrani provides a clear introduction to the environment and recent history of the Wakhan before proceeding to the lives of the Wakhi and Kirghiz. The former are treated quite compactly, with concise description of the kinship system and major patterns of social organization and subsistence economy. It is the Kirghiz who furnish the chief theme, however. The fragility of their economy is not minimized, but there is precise delineation of their resiliency in managing the pastoral cycle within the harsh restraints of terrain, altitude, and climate, and in the face of a closed and threatening Soviet frontier and of the Afghan government's gradual extension of control and influence in the region.

Dr. Shahrani was perhaps the ideal researcher for such a problematic study. An Uzbek speaker from northern Afghanistan, he was little vexed by linguistic difficulties and brought to his subject a broad understanding of its background. With extensive survey data and graceful exposition, Dr. Shahrani presents Kirghiz activities (sheep and goat pastoralism, use of yaks, camels, and horses, pasturing patterns and market relationships), population (including consideration of the effects of cold and altitude, division of labor and authority patterns in the herding household unit), and identity (lineage traditions, kinship groups and their distribution, tribal structure and the role of the khan), and interdependence with the Wakhi.

Dr. Shahrani's study, providing valuable documentation of social patterns in a little known corner of the Muslim world, came none too soon. Since the establishment of the Khalqi regime in Afghanistan in 1978, an undetermined number of Kirghiz have taken their flocks and joined the more than 200,000 Afghan refugees (according to Pakistani figures) in Pakistan. The traditional or more recent adaptive ways of life in Badakhshan and all Afghanistan's provinces form part of the immense stake in that country's present internal war.

CHRISTOPHER J. BRUNNER
Encyclopedia Persica
New York

A. H. SOMJEE. *The Democratic Process in a Developing Society*. Pp. ix, 168. New York: St. Martin's Press, 1979.

This is an ambitious but disappointing attempt to link theory to empirical data in a discussion of political development in India. Its limitations are unfortunate because Somjee has a number of interesting things to say about the social dynamics of political behavior. His arguments are based upon a longitudinal study, 1967–1977, of elections and attitudes in the Gujarati city of Anand. Data were collected through interviews with 600 voters on their responses to five national or state elections held during the period.

Somjee pays much attention to critiquing recent theories of political change in non-Western societies. He claims that responses by primary groups— castes or their components, religious communities—are not adequately explained by Srinivas' stress on the politicalization of caste or by Weiner's or the Rudolph's use of caste associations to explain new form of group political activity. Instead, he argues that a variegated response within castes has permitted social controls to be retained while caste cohesion has unraveled in the areas of political and economic interests.

The force of this and other arguments is undercut by the weakness of the data and its presentation. Somjee offers a stream of impressions of the major, but not all, castes and religious groups in Anand, of some of the factors which marked each of the elections; and of the significance of his data for explaining political behavior. Voting patterns by social group, by generation, and by economic status are emphasized. Yet, in each case only the tersest statistical summary of his evidence is presented.

Such as it is, the evidence is also misused. For example, Somjee claims that support by the "Kshatriyas" of Anand, which are described in Shudra-like terms, for the Congress Party steadily declined (p. 61). In fact his data indicate that "Kshatriya" support for the Congress changed from 85–15 percent in 1967 to 76–24 percent in 1971, 74–26 percent in 1972 and 79–21 percent in 1975. The trend is neither steady nor pronounced. There are several other instances of overdrawing conclusions from the data. By not disclosing the nature of his evidence in any depth and by failing to describe his methodology in detail, Somjee reaches conclusions at the expense of credibility.

RICHARD S. NEWELL
University of Northern Iowa
Cedar Falls

WILLIAM B. TAYLOR. *Drinking, Homicide, and Rebellion in Colonial Mexican Villages.* Pp. 242. Stanford CA: Stanford University Press, 1979. $16.50.

This concise and carefully focussed study of social behavior in Mexican peasant villages during the colonial period is a contribution to Latin American

social history which combines to good effect the concerns and methodology of anthropologists with those of historians, and illustrates well the fruitfulness of such interdisciplinary cross-fertilization. The book deals specifically with three types of behavior about which documentary evidence is available because it involved breaches of colonial law—namely, excessive drinking and alcoholism, homicide, and occurrence of localized violent uprisings against political or religious authorities. Drawing primarily on extended records of criminal trials held in Central Mexico or in Oaxaca during the seventeenth and eighteenth centuries, Taylor attempts to discern patterns in the kinds of cases which were brought to the attention of the authorities during this period, and from these to draw inferences about the nature of the impact of Spanish colonial rule on peasant life and on the integrity of the Mexican village community.

An introductory chapter provides an overview of the necessary background on the Spanish conquest of Mexico and its aftermath, and discusses some of the current views about colonial Mexican social structure and political dynamics. Taylor then examines in turn each of the three categories of behavior on which he has chosen to focus and concludes with a chapter summing up the evidence, showing the interrelationships of the patterns he has discerned in each area of behavior with those in the other areas, and suggesting some of the implications of these for an interpretation of the role of the peasant and the nature of village-state relations in colonial Mexican society.

A recurrent theme throughout the book is how resilient the Indian and Indian culture are to the Spanish assault, and the highly persistent, cohesive, corporate communities at the village level, despite extensive economic exploitation by the colonial administration and its agents, and despite the political powerlessness of the Indian in the structure of colonial government.

Taylor tries to counter those views which see the Mexican peasant as having become thoroughly demoralized and culturally bereft in the wake of Spanish conquest, and uses the documentary evidence on certain kinds of "deviant" behavior to support his contention that the peasant response must instead have been one of adaptation and accomodation, enabling the survival of Indian communities without the complete loss of either cultural distinctiveness or local unity. Limitations of space prevent a more adequate treatment of Taylor's carefully documented and well reasoned study, but it is recommended that historians and social scientists with an interest in colonial Latin America or in peasant societies in general read it for themselves.

SYLVIA VATUK
University of Illinois
Chicago Circle

FREDERICK C. TEIWES. *Politics and Purges in China: Rectification and the Decline of Party Norms 1950– 1965.* Pp. xiii, 730. White Plains, NY: M.E. Sharpe, 1979. $35.00.

Until Mao Tse-tung launched the Cultural Revolution in 1966, it seemed clear that the Chinese Communist party had developed more subtle and effective means of institutionalizing correct behavior within its ranks than its Soviet counterpart. Did not Stalin liquidate party rivals and mercilessly purge dissidents, whereas Mao educated them to see the error of their ways, repent and be ideologically "born again?" The emergence of a distinctive Chinese doctrine of party rectification before 1949, and its increasingly controversial and problematic implementation in the fifteen years prior to the Cultural Revolution constitute the theme of this valuable study. In over six hundred pages of copiously documented text, Frederick Teiwes thoroughly explores the ramifications of what, in the light of recent denunciations of the "Gang of Four," obviously continues to be a salient feature of politics in the People's Republic.

Rectification theory and praxis were refined in the crucible of wartime Yenan, and contributed greatly to create and sustain the disciplined, dedicated revolutionary organization which gained national power in 1949. Teiwes establishes that a genuine normative consensus regarding the procedures and objectives of rectification existed within the party leadership from 1950 to 1957. He illustrates this point in case studies of rectification during the 1950–1953 era of power consolidation, the purge of the regional factionalists Kao Kang and Jao Shu-shih in 1954–1955, and the well-known Hundred Flowers episode and its denouement, the Anti-Rightist Campaign against suspect intellectuals in 1956– 1957.

Determination of what ought to constitute proper party behavior in the new socialist society, however, ultimately rested less upon objective Marxist-Leninist standards than on Mao's own charismatic political status and his frequently enigmatic ideological predilections. Serious policy conflicts during the ill-starred Great Leap Forward, 1957–1959, and the subsequent years of qualified retrenchment both fragmented China's leadership and confused or distorted the rectification process. Party morale did not thrive in an atmosphere where legitimate criticism of Mao's policies was interpreted as lese-majeste, as was the case in P'eng Te-huai's dismissal from power in 1959, or when party rank and file in the early 1960s were subject to nebulous charges of "revisionism." Teiwes depicts the Cultural Revolution as the fitting culmination of such political uncertainty, with Mao caste in the historically quixotic role of emasculating the organization he had done so much to create.

Politics and Purges amply rewards the persevering reader with fresh insights on the conduct of politics in Communist China, and the function of party hierarchs in formulating the groundrules for such conduct. At the very least, any serious reassessment of Mao Tse-tung's brilliant but paradoxical career must assuredly come to terms with the arguments in this book.

ROBERT P. GARDELLA
United States Merchant Marine
Academy
Kings Point
New York

RANDALL BENNETT WOODS. *The Roosevelt Foreign-Policy Establishment and the "Good Neighbor:" The United States and Argentina 1941–1945.* Pp. xiii, 277. Lawrence: The Regents Press of Kansas, 1979. $18.00.

For more than a century, relations between the United States and Latin America have centered around the possibility of intervention, intervention by the United States and from outside the hemisphere. After a very unhappy period in the early 20th century, Latin Americans were hopeful that Woodrow Wilson's views about self determination and the juridical equality of all states signalled a new era. Several specific improvements were made in the 1920s and 1930s, including the announcement of the Good Neighbor Policy.

But as Japan, Italy, and Germany revealed their expansionist plans, the United States became apprehensive about the security of the Western Hemisphere, and the Good Neighbor policy received its first real test. Argentina, above all, refused to regard an attack on one American nation as an attack on all. At a series of Inter-American conferences, the United States tried to get Latin America to agree to a continental collective security system, but Argentine opposition prevented this, and a nonobligatory consultative system was the only kind of agreement which could be reached. This was still true in early 1942, after Pearl Harbor; the Rio Conference decided that each government was to be free to do as it pleased, including the choice of neutrality.

Added to this international tug-of-war were domestic problems within the two governments. President Roosevelt stim-

ulated beaurocratic conflict and personal rivalries within his administration, hoping that the best answers emerged from conflict and compromise. United States–Latin American relations were no exception. Within the Department of State were two groups: first, the Latin Americanists, a group of career diplomats who had dealt almost exclusively with hemisphere policy for years, and who fought hard for an inter-American consultative system, believing that pressure on Buenos Aires would lead to common defense measures; and second, the Internationalists who were less regionally oriented and viewed U.S. relations with Latin America as part of a much larger whole, believing that the Latin American governments would trust Washington to make hemispheric policy towards the rest of the world. Thus, the Department of State was compartmentalized rather than unified under a single authority.

Other U.S. government agencies—the Treasury, the Bureau of Economic Warfare, the Office of Coordinator of Inter-American Affairs, and the military defense departments—some headed by very forceful personalities—complicated the making of policy still further. "The key to understanding Washington's response to Argentine neutrality was competition for control of policy between various individuals and agencies within the Roosevelt Administration foreign-policy establishment" (p. 210). Since there were somewhat comparable groups in the Argentine government, especially in the military, it is not surprising that the securing of agreement on these matters proved to be almost impossible.

Not until a series of personnel changes in the Department of State, in 1944, was this conflict ameliorated. The triumph of the Internationalists facilitated adoption of policies which brought all the Latin American states into the new United Nations and, ultimately, rapprochement between these two powerful governments. "The Good Neighbor Policy," Woods concludes, "emerged as a reaffirmation of Wilsonian internationalism" (214).

Professor Woods has worked very diligently to provide us with a lucid and interesting analysis of a very complicated topic. His research was painstaking and thorough; his extensive notes and a bibliographic essay are extremely helpful. This reviewer found his account of how original membership in the United Nations was secured for Argentina particularly fascinating. All who are interested in this part of American foreign policy will find this a book well worth reading.

DONALD G. BISHOP
Sun City Center
Florida

EUROPE

MICHAEL BALFOUR. *Propaganda in War 1939–1945: Organizations, Policies and Publics in Britain and Germany.* Pp. xvii, 520. Boston, MA: Rutledge & Kegan Paul, 1979. $37.50.

Among the many books on propaganda during World War II, Professor Michael Balfour's new volume will have a special place. It is a remarkably informative and objective "inside story." It is also based on extensive research in both England and Germany.

During World War II Professor Balfour had responsible positions in the British Ministry of Information, in the Political Warfare Executive, and the Psychological Warfare Division of SHAEF. From 1947 to 1964 he was Chief Information Officer of the Board of Trade, and from 1969 to 1974 he was a Professor of European History at the University of East Anglia. He is the author of several scholarly books on Germany.

Part I describes the organization of propaganda in both England and Germany, before and especially during World War II. Most of the 60 chapters (!) provide a detailed analysis of British and German propaganda efforts during the entire wartime period, with due attention to personalities and unfolding events. A new interpretation is given to the role and influence of Joseph Goebbels. According to Professor Balfour, Goebbels "was never able to establish exclusive authority in the propaganda field," and he was often frustrated by the influence on Hitler of his rival, Otto Dietrich, State Secretary and head of the Press Division in the Reich Ministry of Public Enlightment and Propaganda.

In his penultimate chapter Professor Balfour asks: "What difference did propaganda make?" His answer is rather surprising: "German propaganda to Britain had little practical effect," although "it is hard to think of another line, consistent with the Nazi mentality and the course of the fighting, which would have done better." "British propaganda in Germany must . . . be said to have failed," but this must be attributed to the Allied demand for Germany's "unconditional surrender," and "not to any lack of forensic or technical skill on the part of the propagandists."

The relevance of this detailed study to the postwar era is suggested toward the end of the work: "Nobody is ever likely again to base a government on the views of National Socialism. But there are plenty of signs that we have not heard the last of the authoritarian interpretation of the world which in the first half of this century took the form of National Socialism/Fascism."

It is unfortunate that because of its technical and detailed nature—and its extraordinary price—this remarkable volume will probably not receive the attention that it deserves.

NORMAN D. PALMER
University of Pennsylvania

JOHN GRIGG. *Lloyd George: The People's Champion, 1902–1911.* Pp. 391. Berkeley, CA: University of California Press, 1979. $25.00.

The feast of David Lloyd George Books continues. In this work, the second of a projected four volume biography, Grigg has written a book that can stand by itself without support from either the preceding volume or from the two which will presumably follow. Incorporating new material, Grigg has fashioned this volume around the theme announced in the subtitle: the People's Champion.

Though perhaps not as challenging as his years as Minister of Munitions and as Prime Minister of a coalition government, the period narrated here, 1902–1911, was arguably the most interesting and creative time in Lloyd George's political life. He rose from being a Liberal back bencher to being a member of the Liberal hierarchy as Secretary of the Board of Trade and then Chancellor of the Excheqor in the Asquith government. As a member of the Cabinet, he produced and guided precedent establishing legislation through an often critical Parliament. By 1911 he was unquestionably the Liberal Party's heir apparent.

It is a mark of Grigg's ability that he allows Lloyd George's scintillating personality to show through the narrative. All too often biographers allow themselves to be overly critical in their blame or too effusive in their praise with the result that the author's ego interferes with the presentation of the historical character. Such is not the case in this book. Grigg, while generously sympathetic to Lloyd George, stands in the wings while the protagonist stalks the footlights winning begruding administration from all.

Nonetheless, Grigg's balance and detachment do not prevent his engagement in the partisan and scholarly debates surrounding Lloyd George's career. For example, Lloyd George was heaped with invective by suffragettes and later criticized by scholars for what they perceived as his weaseling support of women's suffrage. Grigg carefully sifts the evidence and concludes that while Lloyd George did not deserve the suffragists' fulsome acrimony, he did blunder: "It must be said that he failed, despite seeing quite clearly what ought to be done, to rescue the Government from its crass mishandling of the women's suffrage issue" (p. 361).

Despite the overall strength of the book, one might snipe at Grigg for having relied on an overly cognitive explanation of Lloyd George's motivation. The author's interpretation tends to be in terms of a spectrum of motives that reads "Ideas" at one end and "Pragmatism" at the other. Lloyd George was more than a rationalist in his approach to politics and to life generally. Grigg could have provided more to help us understand Lloyd George's ambition, charisma, philandering, and success. This is not to suggest that he should have psychoanalyzed Lloyd George, but he might have probed deeper into the man who, like Disraeli before him, shinnied up the greasy pole more by impressing his character on the surge of events than by trading on social connections and material fortune.

NEAL A. FERGUSON
University of Nevada
Reno

EDWARD N. MULLER. *Aggressive Political Participation*. Pps. 305. Princeton: Princeton University Press, 1979. $17.50.

In this volume the author attempts to devise and test a multivariate theory of political aggression from an individual perspective. Muller contends that while aggressive political participation is a deviation from the norm it is still important to study because ". . . on occasion it can have dramatic consequences, contributing to major change in, or to the downfall of, established systems of government." Normal political participation is viewed as consisting of such actions as attending political rallies, voting, or joining a political party. The full range of political participation must, however, include aggressive actions such as seizing control of public buildings, conducting illegal strikes, or doing battle with law enforcement agencies. Muller contends that only by understanding unconventional political actions will we be able to comprehend ". . . collective political participation in general. . . ."

To measure aggressive political participation objectively at the micro level the author uses personal interviews of

2,662 adults in 1974. Approximately half of the respondents were reinterviewed in 1976. The survey was conducted at two urban, four rural, and six university areas in West Germany. These sites were selected because they had, during the five preceeding years, demonstrated a higher than average level of opposition to the ruling regime.

Muller presents a thoroughly adequate review of the literature and presents the reader with three motivational theories for aggressive political participation. These theories are called the "Expectancy—Value—Norms," "Utilitarian Justification," and "Relative Deprivation" models. All of these theories ". . . postulate psychological attributes of individuals as the direct antecedents of aggressive political participation." For example, the author's theory "Expectancy—Value—Norms" is made up of a set of sociopsychological motivational concepts such as utilitarian and normative incentives for forceful action as well as social acceptance of such actions.

Muller finds that 60 percent of the variation in aggressive political participation may be accounted for by components of the "Expectancy—Value—Norms" theory. On the other hand, the "Relative Deprivation" theory ". . . was found to bear no direct relationship to aggressive political participation independent of the variables in the Expectancy—Value—Norms model."

Professor Muller has presented us with a thorough empirical analysis of a long ignored but highly important aspect of political behavior. His work should be interesting to specialists in the area of German Politics, Political Psychology, and to those of us who are interested in the general field of man's political behavior. The volume is a superb example of professional scholarly work.

JOHN S. ROBEY
East Texas State University
Commerce

I. J. PROTHERO. *Artisans and Politics in Early Nineteenth-Century London:* *John Gast and his Times.* Pp. viii, 418. Baton Rouge, LA: Louisiana State University, 1979. $30.00.

Some fifteen years ago E. P. Thompson, in his significant book *The Making of the English Working Class*, pointed out that the social and economic history of England during the Industrial Revolution "now resembles an academic battlefield." The catastrophic view—economic crisis, repression of labor, misery, popular agitation—of the Webbs and the Hammonds was challenged by a new anti-catastrophic orthodoxy of Sir John Clapham, T. S. Ashton and others who concluded that, on the contrary, it was an age of improvement. However, according to Thompson, this latter group failed to understand "the whole political and social context of the period." Now Thompson himself is considered vulnerable in his concentration on politics and, thus, his preoccupation with tactics at the expense of ideas and, indeed, because of his own personal involvement.

It may well be a different outcome for Iorwerth Prothero. His book is primarily a contribution to knowledge. Thompson's persuasive notion that "the working class made itself as much as it was made by circumstance" has been clarified, extended and substantiated. But it is not the story of the modern factory worker. Prothero's theme is the role of the highly skilled and highly respected artisan class in London in providing working class leadership. Threatened by industrial change, the artisan class looked not back to a golden past but rather ahead to the future. The immediate focus of the Prothero study is the career of a typical artisan, John Gast, London shipwright, political radical, and trade union leader. Though Gast was attracted by the notion of balanced interests among ownership, management, and labor, he concluded, in time that they were irreconcilable and became committed to a united working class.

Gast's role provides human interest but it is the treatment of the articulate artisan class generally which gives this book significance. Prothero follows its ideas, its leadership, its activities through the Apprenticeship Campaign in the opening years of the nineteenth century, through the popular unrest and agitation which followed Waterloo, through doom and depression in the eighteen-twenties—establishment of trade unions, repeal of the Combination Laws, the *Trades' Newspaper* and the cooperative movement—and into the thirties, parliamentary reform, the *Working Men's Association*, and Chartism.

Prothero's book may not have as wide an audience as Thompson's but it is likely to win more general acceptance. *Artisans and Politics* is written with detachment, avoids facile generalizations, is thoroughly researched and fully documented. It is a major contribution to a broadening and deepening of our understanding of the English scene in the early decades of the nineteenth century, a period which until recent years has been relatively neglected by historians.

ALFRED F. HAVIGHURST
Amherst College
Massachusetts

GEORGE A. ROTHROCK. *The Huguenots: A Biography of a Minority.* Pp. xxv, 201. Chicago: Nelson-Hall, 1979. $16.95.

"Biography," according to Webster's, is "the written history of a person's life." In common usage we often broaden the definition to include the life history of a group. But, unless there is a specific delimitation—"The Early Years"—a reader expects that a biography will cover the full life span of the individual or group, up to the date of the writing. Rothrock's study of the Huguenots is deceptive in this regard. Unless he has paid close attention to the rather unpersuasive reasons Rothrock offers for ending his narrative in 1685 with the Revocation of the Edict of Nantes (pp. 177–78), a reader might well assume that there were no Huguenots in France after that date. This of course is not true. The Huguenots remain a powerful and influential minority in today's France; the number of

distinguished Protestants in business, banking, politics, the arts and letters far outweighs their percentage of the French population. One need but recall that the Peugeot family is devoutly Protestant, and has produced in addition to automobile magnates a number of *Pasteurs* (Protestant ministers).

One will learn nothing from Rothrock of the inglorious aspects of the history of the Huguenots after 1685, such as their extensive participation in the slave trade in the eighteenth century. For their moments of grandeur one must turn to works such as Philip Hallie's extraordinary account of the Protestant mountain village of Le Chambon, *Lest Innocent Blood be Shed* (New York: Harper and Row, 1979). The Chambonnais dedicated themselves wholeheartedly, and at great risk, to saving refugees, primarily Jewish children, during the Nazi Occupation.

These criticisms aside, Rothrock does a perfectly adequate job of what he in fact set out to accomplish. He has written a general work presenting a brief historical review of the Huguenots from their beginnings in the 1520s, through their formal organization as a church in 1559, down to the often vilified decision of Louis XIV in 1685, revoking his grandfather's edict of 1598 which had granted the Huguenots recognized minority status.

The major focus of this book is political and military rather than theological. The better part of a chapter is devoted to an account of how Henry IV consolidated his control over his realm after the hazard of an assassin's blade made him, in 1589, the first Bourbon king of France. A long section of military history deals with the siege of La Rochelle in 1627–28, which marked the end of the political and military power of the Huguenots.

Rothrock's style is clear and succinct and his narrative, unburdened by footnotes, is balanced and fair minded. The latter is no mean feat since he is portraying savage religious conflict, seemingly endless murders, assassinations, persecutions, and an enormous amount of intolerance. Rothrock's brief summary of the undying controversy over the linkages between Calvinism and capitalism is equally judicious. In sum, this book provides a perfectly adequate introduction to the first century and a half of the history of French Protestantism.

DAVID L. SCHALK
Vassar College
Poughkeepsie
New York

ANTHONY SMITH, ed. *Television and Political Life: Studies in Six European Countries.* Pp. x, 261. New York: St. Martin's Press, 1979. $22.50.

The working press in Western Europe is among the least restricted in the world. Television, in contrast, finds itself in one way or another under government regulation and control. How free are political broadcasters? How does government regulate and control television? The work under review answers these questions and more by examining the relationship between government and television in six Western European nations: Britain, France, Italy, Germany, Sweden, and Holland.

Each contributor to Anthony Smith's *Television and Political Life: Studies in Six European Countries* is a media expert. Specifically, Anthony Smith (Britain) is a television producer and the author of books dealing with modern media; Antoine de Tarlé (France) is a consultant on problems of finance and management in broadcasting; Fabio Luca Cavazza (Italy) is a newspaper publisher interested in television; Alfred Grosser (Germany) is a political scientist concerned with media and politics; Åke Ortmark (Sweden) is a writer, commentator, and television producer. In addition, five of the six contributors are citizens of the countries about which they write; the other is no doubt a knowledgeable, foreign observer. As a result, the reader is presented with six essays written by authors capable of understanding the subtle ways in which the nation's political culture has been affected by the medium of television.

What stands out from these essays is the similar experience each of the nations had with television. First, the free and international medium of television of the 1960s has in the 1970s witnessed a new sobriety in all six nations concerning its social impact. In Smith's own words: "The genie has been put back in the bottle" (p. 233). To be sure, this new soberness can be traced to the disturbing growth of terrorism, especially in Germany, Britain, Italy, and Sweden. Second, there is a realization in each nation that even when television has equal rights with the printed press, freedom of expression in television is far more difficult to locate. Third, television broadcasting retains the societal taboos in all the nations and, at the same time, has become the leading source of shaping and communicating these same taboos. And last, but not least, one nation's television industry is so like the others that broadcasters can easily switch places.

Television and Political Life is well organized, presented, and indexed. It is also well written and has the merits of both lucidity and succinctness. This edited volume is must reading for the social scientist concerned with the relationship between politics and television. In short, it should be perused by professionals, students, and anyone interested in good social science.

HARVEY W. KUSHNER
Long Island University
Greenvale
New York

UNITED STATES HISTORY AND POLITICS

KRISTI ANDERSON. *The Creation of a Democratic Majority, 1928–1936.* Pp. xv, 160. Chicago, ILL: University of Chicago Press, 1979. $13.

SIDNEY FINE. *Frank Murphy: The New Deal Years.* Pp. xi, 708. Chicago, ILL: University of Chicago Press, 1979. $42.

These two books deal with similar periods of American history from two distinct approaches: Professor Fine biographically and Professor Anderson analytically. Between 1928 and 1936 a fundamental shift occurred in American voting patterns, with the Democratic replacing the Republican as the majority party. Scholars have long recognized this change and debated the reasons for conversion of the Republican majority. Usually the answers offered have been dissatisfaction with Republican policies, the impact of the depression, and the emergence of an urban-labor oriented Democratic party.

Ms. Anderson looks deeper into this change, however, and finds not so much a shift of voter allegiences as an expansion of the electorate. Noting that participation, as a percentage of the eligible population, during the 1920s was significantly lower than the decades before or after, she searches for the reasons for change in this expansion.

During the 1920s, contends the author, immigrants, children of immigrants, the young, women, and the urban working class had only tenuous loyalties to political parties, often not participating in the democratic process. Towards the end of that decade, these "nonimmunized" voters were drawn into political action—mobilized—largely by the Democratic party and the popular appeal of Al Smith and Franklin D. Roosevelt.

The statistical data offered to support this theory is quite well presented and will convince most readers that it was this mobilization rather than shifting of already involved voters that accounts for the new Democratic majorities. The book is less convincing in its discussion of the reasons for this phenomenon. Most readers will find these arguments superficial and will wish the author had paid more attention to this issue.

Anderson's slim volume is written for a scholarly audience and will appeal, largely, to that group. On the other hand, volume two of Fine's projected three-volume biography of Frank Murphy will find a wider audience because it is well written, interesting, and highly readable. It is no less scholarly, 179 pages of notes, bibliography, and index, but its price will drive many to seek a copy at the library rather than purchase it.

Frank Murphy served as governor-general of the Philippines during the difficult period of the creation of the Comonwealth. He was an enlightened administrator who successfully balanced American and Filipino interests to establish the mechanisms which ultimately brought the Philippines independence.

In 1936 Murphy won the governorship of then largely rural, predominantly Republican Michigan. The Democratic forces in Michigan had temporarily united behind Roosevelt and Murphy, but labor difficulties—the Flint sit down strikes began in February 1937—and economic recession combined to make it a short lived victory, and the Republicans recaptured the governorship in the 1938 elections. Murphy gets high marks from Professor Fine, however, for his patience in mediating the strikes, and for administrative and social reforms. This book presents a balanced, well documented and informative account of Murphy's role in these predominantly local yet nationally significant events. Scholars who read this volume will anxiously await the third volume, covering Murphy's career as Attorney General and Supreme Court Justice.

DONALD B . SCHEWE
Franklin D. Roosevelt Library
Hyde Park
New York

STEVEN J. BRAMS. *The Presidential Election Game.* Pp. xix, 242. New Haven, CT: Yale University Press, 1978. $15.00. Paperbound $3.95.

The most serious activity of American politics is the quest for the presidency of the United States. A U.S. presidential campaign consists of hoopla, pageantry, and other dynamic activity, some of it frivolous. The stakes are high and the payoff worth the emotional and material investments.

Steven J. Brams attempts to apply some of the tools of modern decision theory and game theory to the whole process. Although he borrows from the prior works of William H. Riker and Anthony Downs, this book is a failure. Brams begins by developing models to analyze the three major phases of

the election process, the state pri-
maries, national party conventions, and
the general election. He then formulates
models around the theme of coalition
politics and how the candidates deal
with the various and often conflicting
interests within and without the party,
or within the general public.

The modeling is simple, and non-
mathematical, and is not the problem
with this work. The problem is three-
fold. First, there is very little postula-
tion between *real* campaign strategies,
real people (voters), and the model.
Second, there is a tendency to give
new meaning to such terms as mandate, voter behavior, popular vote,
uncommitted voters—and the creation
of a new term, "approval voting."
Third, Richard Nixon's confrontation
(debatable) with the Supreme Court
finds it way into the book as Chapter
5, and Brams's conclusion being that
an election mandate had been upset.
(Nixon was already President when
Watergate occurred). Lastly, Brams attempts to support his call for abolish-
ment of the Electoral College and its
replacement with his new system,
approval voting, with arguments that are
not consistent with his previous analysis.

Although this book has serious flaws,
it does point up certain problems
that may seriously threaten the American
system in future presidential elections.
What happens if 1824, or 1968 repeat
themselves. Brams raises these questions. Would it serve democracy in
the United States to have a president
elected by a small minority of the
popular vote but a plurality of the
Electoral vote? Or, if some voters have
trichotomous or multichotomous preferences, must the system be reformed
to provide what Brams calls "sincere
voting"?

Students of modern decision theory
and its application to the electoral
process may find this book of some
use. However, much work needs to be
done in this area before any reform of
the U.S. Electoral College is made.

FREDERICK M. FINNEY
Sinclair Community College
Dayton
Ohio

ROCHELLE JONES and PETER WOLL.
The Private World of Congress. Pp.
vii, 264. New York: The Free Press,
1979. $14.95.

This book takes exception to the
thesis of Mayhew's *Congress: The
Electoral Connection.* Jones and Woll
argue that the electorate is largely
irrelevant to the legislative activities
of members of Congress. Instead, these
members are motivated by the drive
to achieve and expand personal power
and status. Since the overwhelming
majority of Congressmen and Senators
have minimal re-election difficulties,
their most important constituency is
Congress itself and their major efforts
on Capital Hill are geared toward
favorably impressing their congressional
colleagues and aggrandizing their own
positions.

Jones and Woll trace the increase in
the prestige of a position in Congress
from the early beginnings—when five of
the twenty-six original Senators resigned before completing their first term
of office—to the present when turnover
is low and members rarely leave.
They then examine in detail the struggle
carried on by individual members of
Congress to further enhance that prestige.

Even the far-reaching reforms which
took place in both Houses of Congress
during the 1970s and which changed
those bodies so significantly must be
placed within this context. Rather than
constituting an attempt to improve the
effectiveness of Congress, those reforms
represented the outcome of a major
power struggle between congressional
haves and have-nots. In a number of
significant battles, the have-nots prevailed over the haves and Congress
became so democratized as a result
that it has become almost impossible
for the leaders in either chamber to
lead.

One of the strongest chapters in this
volume discusses the role played by
congressional staffs in the legislative
process. Members of Congress are kept
so preoccupied with their many committee and subcommittee activities that
they rely heavily on staff members for
advice—even for advice on which way

to vote on the floor. The size of a member's staff is viewed as a status symbol on the Hill and members fight for committee assignments that will afford them the largest number of staff members and the greatest possible budget.

Also, contrary to a widely held belief, Jones and Woll argue that members of Congress often seek Committee assignments not to enhance their re-electability back home but rather to enhance their personal power in Congress. For example, a Florida Congressman recently declined the Chairmanship of the Merchant Marine and Fisheries Committee whose legislative sphere directly touches the interests of his Florida constituency in order to retain the Chairmanship of the Health and Environment Subcommittee, whose legislative sphere only indirectly does so.

Jones and Woll present a strong case for their view that the legislative process is captive to the struggle for power and turf always being waged among members of both Houses. Their volume, however, should not be viewed as a refutation of Mayhew's work but rather as its complement. The importance of internal power and status, after all, is not always lost on the voters back home. Students of the legislative process would do well to read both books although admirers of Congress will be dismayed by the themes stressed in each.

ROBERT E. GILBERT
Northeastern University
Boston

LAWRENCE J. KORB. *The Fall and Rise of the Pentagon: American Defense Policies in the 1970s.* Pp. xvii, 192. Westport, CT: Greenwood Press, 1979. $19.95.

In this well researched, concisely written book, Lawrence J. Korb, Professor of Management at the U.S. Naval War College, charts the fortunes of the Pentagon between 1969 and 1979.

Korb sees the years between 1969 and 1974 as ones of darkness and decline for the U.S.'s defense establishment. He gives a number of reasons for this:

blunders in Vietnam plus the impact of the Tet offensive; ethical aberrations such as false reports to conceal unauthorized air strikes against the North, concern with military careerism in preference to making a real contribution in Southeast Asia, publicized atrocities by American troops; turmoil within the Pentagon under the autocratic rule of Secretary of Defense McNamara; massive cost overruns on new weapons systems; the attempt to counter domestic violence through the compiling of dossiers by Army intelligence on numbers of prominent men and women in business, public and academic life; and finally the coming Detente with the Soviet Union.

To meet the challenges of the new congressional mood which demanded large reductions in defense spending, and of rapid inflation, increased personnel costs, the great expense of replacing obsolete weapons, the Pentagon made a number of skillful adjustments. It responded with Vietnamization, reducing personnel levels and weapons inventories, adding missions to existing forces, reducing overhead costs, and improving management practices.

Korb gives credit for these innovations to a new breed of Secretaries of Defense —Melvin Laird, James Schlesinger, Donald Rumsfeld—who brought very different backgrounds and skills with them when compared to the first five Secretaries of Defense. Moreover, each was skilled in dealing with the political environment. These men, especially Laird and Schlesinger, also brought to the Joints Chiefs of Staff a new type of officer. All had experience and knowledge of the policymaking process prior to their selection. This was in sharp contrast to the pre-1969 Chiefs who were unable to operate successfully in the Washington environment because they had not spent much time at the higher levels of decisionmaking before their appointments.

All these events, plus the fall of South Vietnam and Cambodia, the Mayaguez incident, and the continuing build-up of Soviet arms led to a new mood and a new consensus on defense. President Carter, who had campaigned on a platform to reduce defense spending, actually continued the policies of President Ford to raise defense expenditure in real terms. And even Congress, which had made great reductions in the defense budgets between 1970 and 1976, treated the next three budgets much more gently. It cut spending by just 2.2 percent as compared to the 6 percent during the preceding six years.

Korb's last chapter deals with problems still to be solved. Most interesting is his charge that Congress has overreacted to its former passive role and is now at the point of "suffocating" the Pentagon. To substantiate his charge Korb points out that "Congressmen now send more than one million written and telephoned inquiries into the Pentagon each year. They put defense witnesses through some three thousand hours of questioning before seventy-two committees annually. . . . The legislature has subdivided the defense budget into some several thousand line items and has placed so many restrictions on each separate account that program managers literally cannot transfer funds or overspend individual accounts without 'an act of Congress'" (p. 174). Space does not permit listing all the other charges.

Some readers may consider this book a little one-sided in its approach, for there is little doubt that Korb is a friend and defender of the Department of Defense. But it is also true that his research is exhaustive, his arguments persuasive, and his scholarship meticulous.

Minoo Adenwalla
Lawrence University
Appleton
Wisconsin

Arthur Liebman, *Jews and the Left*. Pp. xiv, 676. New York: John Wiley, 1979. $17.95.

This study by Arthur Liebman is an effort to describe, largely in terms of institutions and social classes, the long and sometimes ambivalent relationship that has existed between the political left and the American Jewish community since the 1880s. While rarely covering new material the study constitutes a broad synthesis of earlier work and a somewhat different theoretical perspective.

Starting from the premise that initial Jewish response to Socialist ideas was largely a function of the occupational structure of the American Jewish community, with it's large concentration in the needle trades, Liebman analyzes the course of development this commitment took from its height in the years prior to World War I to its present largely vestigial existence. While mentioning in passing the assimilative character of American society and the attractions of political Zionism, he tends to trace this evolution largely in terms of the general upward mobility of the Jewish community and its large-scale entrance into the white-collar and middle-class strata, hardly an earthshaking or original insight.

While undoubtedly a highly detailed study of the American Jewish left, the book is singularly weak in two respects: firstly, an understanding of the importance of ideologies in the formation of political movements and, as has been frequently the case with Marxist studies on what used to be called "The Jewish Question," a serious lack of understanding of the relationship between national identity and social class. There is little or no discussion of the labor Zionist analysis of the "anamolous" character of the Jewish social structure and only a passing mention of the work of Ber Borochov, a body of doctrine that had a significant influence in drawing many Jews from Socialist to Socialist-Zionist ideologies. Again, in a book that makes a lengthy effort to understand the attraction of American Jews towards Communism in the 1930s, there is not a single mention of Biro-Bidjan, the Soviet Union's own effort, in opposition to Zionism, to create a Jewish state, an effort that was of enormous significance in attracting American Jewish sympathy to the Soviet Union, just as it's failure was a major cause in the loss of that support.

The major failing, however, of Liebman's mechanistic and reductionist study occurs in his analysis of the controversy between Lenin and the Bund at the now famous, to historians at any rate, 1903 conference of the Russian Social-Democrats. Liebman views the matter purely in organizational terms and from Lenin's point of view and ignores what should be obvious; the derogatory nature of Lenin's characterization of the Russian Jewish community. Taken logically, Lenin's argument would read:

Major Premise: Religion is reactionary and contemptible.
Minor Premise: The Jews are only a religion.
Conclusion: The Jews are reactionary and contemptible.

An implicit argument that goes a lot longer towards explaining the ultimate rejection of communism in favor of Jewish nationalism on the part of Jews than Liebman's lengthy book.

MURRAY SMITH
Verdun
Quebec

WOODROW WILSON. *The Papers of Woodrow Wilson*, Vols. 29, 30: *1913–1914*. ed. Arthur S. Link et al. Pp. xx, 592; xx, 526. Princeton, NJ: Princeton University Press, 1979. $25, $27.50.

These volumes show Wilson as a veteran of the Presidency, delivering his addresses to Congress, coping with trust legislation and, less anticipated, the Mexican Revolution, and with the outbreak of the Great War in Europe. Since he looms larger in these volumes than in public retrospect, it becomes an historical task to balance the ephemeral and enduring aspects of his reputation.

The country, Wilson told Congress, December 2, 1913, "is at peace with all the world, and many happy manifestations multiply about us of a growing cordiality and sense of community of interest among the nations, foreshadowing an age of settled peace and good will" (29, 3). It is unfair to tax Wilson with fatuous optimism, but we already know his limitations of temper and foresight. He dubs the Mexican dictator

Huerta a usurper, and will ultimately contrive to rid Mexico of him. But whether he fathoms the deeper currents of South-of-the-Border society may be doubted.

The role of Colonel House in a democracy continues to want probing. He himself does not think it too ambitious to seek, personally, a reduction of armaments between France, Germany, England, and the United States, or to have it whispered to the Kaiser that he, House, is "the power behind the throne," in order to be effective as mediator.

Wilson is normally seen as a fulfillment of Progressive efforts and ambitions, but it is striking how few are the veteran Progressives with whom Wilson deals. There is no traffic with Charles Edward Russell, with Ray Stannard Baker, with those of Upton Sinclair's persuasion. Frederick C. Howe is made Commissioner of the Port of New York, on recommendation, and several journalist-Progressives are complimented for approving Wilson's work. But the Progressive tide is noticeable for its absence.

Moorfield Storey of an older generation welcomes reports that Wilson's segregation policy in government has been checked. But the Negro leader Bishop Alexander Walters (29, 204–5) warns Wilson's aide Tumulty that ten million Negroes "and a host of their white friends" are resentful of Wilson's footdragging. Wilson has his problems with blunt Democratic bigots but he, himself, having once as an academic been cautious in such matters, tells a Negro joke in dialect at a press conference (29, 386).

With the women, in a gathering national suffrage fight, Wilson adopts a flat policy of representing his party platform, which does not call for suffrage. In a sharp confrontation with the Progressive Rheta Childe Dorr (30, 226–8) Wilson is driven to the wall by her persistent constitutional argument and all but loses his aplomb.

In the tragic Colorado miners strike, in the Tampico crisis where American sailors suffer arrest and humiliation, and on other issues, Wilson labors amid careless public assumptions. As telling a remark as any is a journalist's query in a press conference: "Is there any prospect or has any progress been made in the efforts to send the—to send Americans to Haiti?" (30, 319). Wilson underscores democratic principles and is praised by diplomats and associates for eloquence and deportment. Yet a doubt remains. His declaration that "in no conceivable circumstances would we fight the people of Mexico" (29, 468) reads uncomfortably like a first draft of the later war message, and as a too-pat formula for a world seething with unrest. His open dependence on House, when growth and the opinions of diverse principals are necessary, shows a weak connection with reality.

House thinks British-German difficulties can be worked out as with individuals. His smoothness and charm in talking with Sir Edward Grey and Kaiser Wilhelm elicit the praise of American Ambassador to Great Britain Walter Hines Page, an Anglophile. But how egregious of House, when war has actually been declared, to tell Wilson that it would help for the world to know that Wilson has done all humanly possible to avert war, that is, by sending House to Europe to reconcile differences.

There are always, in this series, nuggets for the student of the era to cull. Bryan survives decades of derogation to look well in his conscientious role of Secretary of State. John Reed, in midpoint between his career as bohemian and revolutionary, writes with restraint of the President (30, 231–8). A charming letter from Carnegie, apropos of his gift to Berea College, is in reform spelling. And Secretary of the Treasury McAdoo writes to his new father-in-law Wilson about the new Federal Reserve Board, ending: "The real truth is that since you have given me this glorious girl, I don't care very much what you do with the Federal Reserve Board!" (30, 55).

LOUIS FILLER

Ovid
Michigan

PAULA STERN. *Water's Edge: Domestic Politics and the Making of Foreign Policy*. Pp. xix, 265. Westport, CT: Greenwood Press, 1979. $19.95.

The book under review is a narrative account of the controversial Jackson amendment to the Trade Reform Act of 1974. This legislation grew out of the reaction to the administration's attempt to grant to the Soviet Union the coveted most favored nation status in trade relations. As the law of the land today, it binds the president not to extend trade concessions to the Soviet Union or any other nonmarket nation until the congress is assured of free emigration from these countries. The legislation was initiated and championed by Senator Henry Jackson in conjunction with one of the most powerful interest groups in the country, namely, American Jewry. As a work exploring the intricacies of the making of the American foreign policy, the author uses the Jackson amendment to delineate the interplay of forces at work that eventually lead to foreign policy decisions. The study, therefore, can be conceived of as a vehicle for describing in minute detail the making of foreign policy in the United States.

Paula Stern rejects the conventional wisdom that has held for generations that "politics stops at the water's edge" in the realm of foreign policy. The notion that foreign policy is the "calculated product of a complex balancing of international power blocs or the expression of traditional policies or ideas" (p. xi) is both erroneous and misleading, according to the author. In fact, the author claims, the politics of the formulation of foreign policy does not much differ from the politics of domestic issues. The creation of foreign policy is characterized by high domestic political involvement, in which competing economic, ideological, ethnic, and other types of interest groups play significant, or even decisive roles.

The central theme of the Stern volume is that foreign policy decisions are arrived at through complex interaction involving policymakers, elected politicians, prominent individuals, the mass media, interest groups, and most of all the legislative and executive branches of the government. The intricate relationships among various actors of the foreign policy process are painstakingly traced out, giving a wealth of data on the events that made the Jackson amendment a reality. Unfortunately, while the book is suffused with vivid particulars, the early beginnings of the amendment and how Senator Jackson became interested in sponsoring it are not clearly spelled out. There are additional points of confusion. At one juncture the author says that Jackson went to Jewish groups to seek their support for his bill (p. 32) but we already witness in the preceding chapter (p. 11) that activist Jews were concerned about Soviet emigration and one legislator was prevailed upon to introduce a bill (p. 12) on this issue in the House.

One of the most interesting aspects of this work is the documentation provided on the influence of legislative aides on policymakers. In this particular instance the impetus for Jackson's amendment seems to have largely emanated from Jewish staff aides. Through a variety of channels they were instrumental in translating a particularistic concern of theirs into the law of the land. The other even more intriguing part of this study is the impact of the world Jewish establishment on the foreign policy process of the United States. On the domestic front, the entire Jewish community was mobilized to ensure the passage of this legislation. The Jews constitute a powerful force in America and as a political interest group "have disproportionate influence and power" (p. 212). In a pluralistic democracy such as ours, where access to decisionmakers is relatively easy, it is likely that policy may reflect "not the will of the majority, but the will of highly leveraged, well placed minorities" (p. 212). The work by Stern is a testimony to this fact. Whatever may be thought of as rational goals, by groups and individual politicians, may not necessarily be rational for the nation as a whole, or even be in the

national interest. The Soviet displeasure at the Jackson amendment is a case in point.

Author Stern, in fact, advances an interesting theoretical proposition through her work that departs substantially from the traditional idea on the making of foreign policy. Through a case study method she succeeds in verifying her hypothesis, and in the process writes a very appealing and a worthwhile volume on a subject of perennial concern. This is a very balanced and a readable work which gives a good picture of the workings of the American political system in general and mechanics of foreign policy making in particular.

GHULAM M. HANIFF
St. Cloud State University
Minnesota

RICHARD L. STROUT. *TRB: Views and Perspectives on the Presidency.* Pp. 526. New York: Macmillan, 1979. $14.95.

BARRY GOLDWATER. *With No Apologies.* Pp. 320. New York: William Morrow, 1979. $12.95.

Journalism has been described as the first rough draft of history. Writing weekly in the *New Republic* as TRB, Richard L. Strout's journalism has been far more than a rough draft. It is an often eloquent and perceptive analysis of America's social and political institutions. TRB is a collection of the best of those articles with a special emphasis on the American presidency.

Strout's book is valuable for several reasons. First, his articles show how an intelligent, informed, and contemporary observer viewed some now historical figures. Like everyone else, TRB thought that Dewey was going to beat Truman, and he wrote that Johnson could lose in 1964 and that the Eisenhower-Stevenson race in 1952 was going to be close. He also felt that "Adlai Stevenson is having the time of his life, doing his most important service at the U.N.," a belief thoroughly destroyed by John

B. Martin in his 1977 biography of Stevenson.

There are excellent articles on the phenomenon of Joe McCarthy. An early McCarthy opponent, Strout wrote in 1950 that J. Edgar Hoover in effect attacked a McCarthy probe. What was the basis for McCarthy's power? "He is the most formidable figure to hit the Senate, we think, since Huey Long. He has the galleries with him. The Republicans around him beam."

TRB has a second major function. It shows that nothing really much has changed in recent American politics.

Strout's first column in 1943 was about an indifferent nation. "What the country craves is a moral tonic," he wrote. Congressional inaction is a favorite theme and there is a pattern about American presidents: the nation goes from hope that a new president will bring the vision and skills needed to solve problems to frustration at the lack of specific accomplishments. The presidential leadership issue was not discovered in 1979, according to these articles.

Political theorists will be interested in Strout's favorite remedy for solving our political ills. He wants a parliamentary form of government in the United States.

Barry Goldwater covers much the same ground as does Strout. There are naturally some major differences. One is most obvious: Goldwater is a conservative politician, Strout a very liberal political writer. There are others. Strout is willing to let mistaken ideas and his flaws appear in the public record. Goldwater is far less candid, taking a defensive posture in some cases and ignoring other embarrassments such as the Watergate-related actions of Attorney General Richard Kleindiest, a close professional friend.

Both writers have high regard for Harry S. Truman's now legendary toughness and honesty. Goldwater strongly endorses the Eisenhower presidency but Ike, for Strout, was a virtual total failure, an extremely harsh view in this reviewer's opinion.

One final difference must be cited. Strout writes extremely well; his book is a joy to read. In comparison, Goldwater's book is done in pedestrian style, lacking not only color but unity. This style is unfortunately the norm for much political autobiography, but it is not a norm that makes for eager reading.

FRED ROTONDARO
Congressional Affairs Press
Washington

MAURICE VAN GERPEN. *Privileged Communication and the Press: The Citizen's Right to Know Versus the Law's Right to Confidential News Source Evidence.* Pp. 239. Westport, CT: Greenwood Press, 1979. $22.95.

Once when I defended one of the Warren Court's flimsier decisions, Wallace Menselson warned me that I would live to regret this most recent revival of judicial policymaking. He was correct, for the Nixon Court is providing us with judicial policymaking at its worst.

Professor Van Gerpen's book is packed with solid information and with the exception of the first chapter or two, is interestingly written. He begins with the historical background of the concept of newsmen's privilege, from the case of John Peter Zenger to the latest federal and state court rulings. He develops the concepts of privileged communication as they affect attorneys and their clients; physicians and their patients; husbands and wives; clergymen and their parishioners; and jurors with other jurors.

Only two of these pairs, the attorney-client and the juror-juror have privileged communication based in the common law. The others have been legislatively defined. The author warns us, too, about attempting an analogy between the attorney-client relationship and the relationship between the newsman and his confidential informant. The first is purely private and the second is undertaken with the intention that it will result in public disclosure. There are two basic principles of democratic government in conflict here: the public right to know and the public right to every man's evidence.

Van Gerpen shows us how the United States Supreme Court has refused to extend First Amendment protection to a reporter's confidential sources when criminal activity is involved. He tells us that the Supreme Court, and other courts as well, see the claim of privilege as a matter of personal benefit to the reporter rather than one of public benefit. While the courts minimize the chill on the flow of information that will result when reporters have to reveal confidential sources, Van Gerpen is convinced that the public will be deprived of information that it requires to make reasoned judgments on certain kinds of issues. The courts seem bent on exercising their authority in the face of what they seem to regard as challenges to that authority. If the press can be converted into a law enforcement agency, then damn the consequences.

Van Gerpen is not optimistic about our prospects for protecting newsmen's confidential sources from forced revelation, but he is convinced that if a newsmen's privilege can be devised, it must come out of the First Amendment and the recognition that news gathering and news dissemination are inseparable.

CHARLES P. ELLIOTT
East Texas State University
Commerce

MARJORIE FALLOWS. *Irish Americans: Identity and Assimilation*. Pp. xii, 158. Englewood Cliffs, NJ: Prentice-Hall, 1979. $9.95.

PAUL WROBEL. *Our Way: Family, Parish and Neighborhood in a Polish-American Community*. Pp. xv, 186. Notre Dame, IN: University of Notre Dame Press, 1979. $12.95.

Irish Americans and *Our Way* represent two major streams within modern ethnic studies. Both are brief, readable, and intelligent books which reflect scholars' current emphasis on family, community, and religion as underpinnings of the American social experience. But Marjorie Fallows and Paul Wrobel approach their subjects in significantly different ways.

Irish Americans is part of the Prentice-Hall series on ethnic groups and follows a fairly traditional format. It opens with a look at the group's background in Ireland, continues with the general history of the Irish in America, then focuses on social mobility, the family, politics, the Church, and assimilation. The book is occasionally repetitious and sometimes confusing. For example, the author claims that the Irish "may already have moved beyond the point of no return" with regard to the loss of a distinctive ethnic identity and subculture (p. 148), yet she asserts that the group demonstrates that "American life can encompass difference without . . . eradicating it" (p. 150).

Fallows is frankly misleading on the matter of the Protestant vs. the Catholic Irish experience. She seems to suggest that the two groups shared the same secular heritage, ignoring the significance of the Scottish origins of most of the northern Irish immigrants. Later, in commenting about the Catholics' apparently superior educational and economic progress in America, she fails to confront the implications of the two groups' distinctive settlement patterns: north vs. south, urban vs. rural. Fallows notes the differences, but never analyzes their obvious impact on her socioeconomic profiles of the Irish.

Such imprecision is disturbing, as is the skimpy treatment accorded to significant topics such as nineteenth century nativism. However, these are by no means fatal flaws. On the whole, *Irish Americans* is a competent, balanced, and interesting portrait of a very important ethnic group. The author makes a commendable effort to compare the experiences of immigrants settling in different cities, and she integrates sociological concepts into her narrative more fluidly than most. Fallows also includes an entire chapter of first person narratives, which add a warmth and immediacy to her monograph.

Our Way is based almost entirely on personal evidence. Anthropologist Paul Wrobel moved into St. Thaddeus Parish in Detroit, Michigan and spent eighteen months observing, interviewing, and interacting with the largely second and third generation Polish-American residents. Throughout his study, he is intensely conscious of his own behavior and role within the community, and while this is useful in alerting the reader to possible biases in his findings, Wrobel goes too far. He gives us an elaborate account of his problems in finding a house and being accepted in the neighborhod before we're really introduced to that neighborhood, and he discusses his research methods so thoroughly we even get a description of his note card file. Wrobel's constant use of the first person is not impalatable in this highly personal study, but when compounded by frequent digressions and mechanical "Now I will discuss" transitions, this style makes the book seem less profound than it is.

Wrobel has actually done careful field work and provides considerable insight into the Polish-American experience. After a brief overview of the previous literature on this subject and a physical description of St. Thaddeus Parish, the author turns to the family, including relationships between husbands, wives, and friends. Most of the patterns he discerns seem to derive more from class than ethnicity, but they nevertheless illuminate the lives of these people, as do the chapters on the parish and the neighborhood. Some of Wrobel's analysis is vague, such as his description of the network linking those who do not participate in parish activities with those who do. But he is a keen social observer, and his study is both interesting and enlightening. Thus *Our Way*, like Marjorie Fallows' *Irish Americans*, adds to our understanding of this nation of nations.

LAURA L. BECKER
Clemson University
South Carolina

SOCIOLOGY

ANNELISE GRAEBNER ANDERSON. *The Business of Organized Crime: A Cosa Nostra Family*. Pp. 179. Standord, CA: Hoover Institution Press, 1979. $10.95.

Crime may pay, but organized crime, it appears, does not pay as well as one might think. Nor is its reach so pervasive, nor its effects so pernicious as one might fear. This is the main lesson to be learned from Annelise Graebner Anderson's study of one of the twenty-four "core" criminal groups in the United States.

Mrs. Anderson studied the "Benguerra" family and its seventy-five members in order "to be able to relate alternative public policies and practices with respect to law enforcement against organized crime to their costs and benefits in controlling and reducing the harm done by organized crime" (p. 6). Her findings are presented thoroughly and their implications drawn soberly; Mrs. Anderson is a model social scientist.

Her careful and conscientious investigation, like much good social science, tends to confirm the judgments of moderate common sense: organized crime is not as fearsome as it is often made out to be by journalists and scriptwriters; nor is it a figment of our imagination, as some debunking social scientists have argued. Her findings are along the lines of those of other recent capable investigators of organized crime such as Jonathan Rubinstein and Peter Reuter. Her conclusion—duly qualified by the acknowledged fact that she studied one family in one city—is that we are spending more than enough to fight organized crime, and that "it is especially doubtful that fears of organized crime should be used to justify legislation involving incursions into privacy and the potential for abuse . . ." (p. 141). Given the vulnerability of our public policies to enthusiasm and trendiness, it is a pleasure to see social science research serving a sobering and moderating function.

Would it be churlish to add that my pleasure could not but be tempered by the absence of any sprightliness in Mrs. Anderson's presentation of her findings, an absence made especially noticeable by the colorfulness of her subject? And more than style is at issue. Mrs. Anderson's earnest style is accompanied by, and reflects, a stern refusal to lift her eyes from her research and from rather narrow questions of public policy, to consider any of the broad and fascinating questions raised by the phenomenon of organized crime in American life. It is hard to criticize an author for failing to do what she did not intend to do; but can even apparently narrow issues of public policy be dealt with satisfactorily without some consideration of broader developments and some attempt to take a more general perspective? Mrs. Anderson "uses concepts from the fields of sociology and political science as well as economics" in treating her subject (p. 136); reading her book impressed upon me, in about equal parts, the utility of these social science disciplines, and their limits, at least as they are commonly understood.

WILLIAM KRISTOL
University of Pennsylvania

ARCHIE J. BAHM. *The Philosopher's World Model.* Pp. xi, 295. Westport, CT: Greenwood Press, 1979. $22.95.

A book in print may profess to have one aim in view and yet establish its value in the fulfillment of yet another aim. This book professes to attempt to "revitalize philosophy" and to create both *the* world model as well as a variety of world models to help mankind survive what the author pictures to be a threat to the continued existence of mankind. In the eyes of this reviewer, however, the value of the book is Archie Bahm's panoramic review of the variety of intellectual disciplines throughout the arts and sciences of human thought. He attempts to clarify definitions of the various disciplines in the field of Philosophy such as Philosophy itself, Epistomology, Logic, Being, Ethics, Religion, Economics and Political Science as well as History and Science.

The favorite theme of his solution seems to be what he refers to as a "Quantum Leap" into a world Universal model. His Quantum theory is, of course, the later theory of a balance between the "wave" and the "particular." It seems to this writer that he is paralleling the existentialist "leap of faith," con-

ditioned by the Hegelian" dialectic." He wants mankind to refrain from limiting itself to particulars and swing into a global state of mind. Yet, the particulars are not to be left behind.

A serious attempt is made by the author to show how and why other world models previously attempted have failed. He blames them for having been too particularistic and not universal enough. In some respects he underestimates the contributions of philosophers and religious leaders. Indeed, the classical Greeks made a serious attempt to develop an honest philosophy of Universalism. This is actually what the original Greek philosophers were looking for. Religions of the classical world also attempted to understand the world as a whole through the eyes of religious principles which they tried to establish as universal modes. On the one hand, Bahm states that all religions have a common theme—that is, the search for ultimate values. On the other hand he blames them for their narrow outlook. He makes a far too sweeping assessment that a "belief in God" is not necessary for religion. He ought to know that *the* global idea in religion is the universal God toward whom the "Quantum Leap" can be made. A number of references in his end-notes are from his own books on religion and other secondary sources instead of from primary sources. The same is true in some of the notes on philosophic ideas.

The aforementioned criticisms are not meant to deter one from the real value of the book. It is a splendid review of many trends in various fields of human thought. The three appendices show that there exist a number of societies of thinkers and analyzers who have global interests in their determination to bring the world around to positive and beneficial achievements. Current world events do seem to be narrowing the distances between the peoples of the world. A world outlook, therefore, indeed seems necessary. However, one should bear in mind that the particulars in human life should not be lost in the wave of global movement. A real quantum leap will look both ahead as well as behind in order to develop a better world order.

SAMUEL J. FOX
Merrimack College
North Andiver
Massachusetts

JAMES LEWTON BRAIN. *The Last Taboo: Sex and the Fear of Death.* Pp. 264. Garden City, NY: Anchor Press, 1979. $8.95.

The avowed purpose of *The Last Taboo* is to link the anxiety associated with the fear of death with a similar uneasiness surrounding human sexuality. Using a variety of biblical, cross cultural, historical and scientific references, Brain, a cultural anthropologist at SUNY-New Paltz, documents the prevalent place of both sex and death in human life. The underlying theme of discussions on diverse subjects such as incest, pornography, womb envy, sexual abuse, violence, blasphemous language, and ritual ceremonies is an assertion that the fear of death and the anxiety over sexuality are the results of cultural shackles which prevent unrestricted openness but permit societal stability.

This is basic anthropology or sociology since we know that biological needs are circumscribed by culture in order to manifest societal homeostasis. Chaos in economic and social institutions would be prevalent if women were still in an oestrous cycle and incest were permitted. We are taught from birth to fear and repress our animal instincts. Should they manifest themselves, we must feel shame and guilt. Brain's observation is essentially correct as it is a well-documented fact that sexual behavior, sexual images, and sexual expectations are significant sources of interpersonal altercations, self degradation, and social anxiety.

Humans, then, according to Brain, deny their link to an animal heritage. Sex is threatening because it reminds us of our mortality and of the "possibility of the dissolution of the security conferred on us by ordered society were we not to have very strict rules about how we have sex" (p. 79). Death is also a constant reminder of our finiteness

and of the fact that demise produces odor and decay which we find unpalatable. Even the funeral industry tries to evade reminders of this fact by endorsing the clothing of the deceased in the finest of garb and coffin so he or she will not depict any degeneration which accompanies death. Our generalized fear of sex arises out of our subconscious aversion to death, filth, and promiscuity. Women, usually being viewed as sexual objects, suffer the greatest as a result of these culturally created anxieties. They are the carriers of the sexual attributes and temptations which can bring the downfall of males.

Brain's somewhat hidden secondary purpose is to show that authoritarianism or rigid cultural restrictions on behavior, particularly sexual activity, produce undesirable side effects such as bigotry, tyranny, cruelty, and conservatism. In reality, sexual proscriptions and the defacement of death represent systemic efforts at social control. This fact is reflected particularly in traditional sex role arrangements where man has authority. Man possesses authority largely because of his physical superiority, not because of any unusual intellectual or emotional prowess. Women, being denied power, seek to manipulate men through sexual politics. The author's true colors come from this discussion. His elaborate effort to associate death and sex, documented more by imagination than fact, is really an extension of his belief that more sexual freedom is necessary to alleviate anxiety. The less regidity, the less anxiety, and, perhaps, the less cruelty and violence.

JAMES H. FREY
University of Nevada
Las Vegas

ROBERT A. BURT, *Taking Care of Strangers: The Rule of Law in Doctor-Patient Relations.* Pp. vii, 200. New York: Free Press, 1979. $15.95.

This book should be viewed as a contribution to the critique of benevolence, since it directly addresses current attempts to reform civil commitment statutes and to devise legal safeguards for patients and others subject to professional caretakers. It is also a tour de force of applied psychoanalytic and sociological theory.

Attempts to delineate rights and remedies in various treatment settings are based on the legal and philosophical assumption of separate, autonomous selves, a static model of self/other relations which underlies the norm of consensuality applied in recent judicial rulings. The only role allocations possible for the involved parties are those of omnipotent choicemaking or impotent choicelessness.

Whether the choicemaker role be assigned to the patient, the physician, or the judge, Burt contends that such an allocation of power, based on an absolute distinction between self and other, unleashes destructive impulses in both parties, impulses that lead to conceptual obliteration of the other and, often enough, from conceptual to physical obliteration. The libertarian tradition characterizes social relations as either voluntary or coerced, but these are all false disjunctions that obscure the mutual coercions framing *all* relations. It is only the ambiguous and dynamic relationship between self and other and the inherent ambivalence of all relationships that hold such destructive impulses in check and define equality between persons.

Burt develops a dynamic model of self by integrating a number of psychoanalytic and symbolic interactionist concepts, illustrating the model with several case studies: Lake v. Cameron, Karen Ann Quinlan, Milgram's obedience experiments, and others. His analysis follows the confusion of self and other, and the fantasy of omnipotence and impotence, to infancy, and then traces the persistence of these infantile modes of relatedness in adult social relations and especially in those interactions in which the infant/adult relationship is most nearly recapitulated.

Burt's intent is to make the law a more nurturant than abusing caretaker, not by reforming or abolishing the commitment statutes but by redefining the role of the court. Its function is not to abrogate to itself the choicemaker role, nor to end dispute, but to "ensure dispute rather than join the parties' delusive belief that dispute between them can be conclusively ended." The judicial writ would be viewed as

a time-limited expression which will be confirmed, modified, or abandoned in further negotiations between the parties themselves. . . . The law should keep the parties . . . uncertain about the precise measure of their power or impotence regarding one another, in order to counterbalance the impulse toward destructively stereotypical choicemaking/choiceless role allocations.

Burt's inferences from the case material are highly speculative, but they are well grounded theoretically and are, finally, convincing. The value of the analysis is easily illustrated if one considers other cases, such as the extremely problematic policies of deinstitutionalization of mental patients. We now have a compelling explanation of the "deep structure" of benevolence.

JOEL S. MEISTER
Amherst College
Massachusetts

GEORGE COMSTOCK, ET AL. *Television and Human Behavior*. Pp. xviii, 581. New York: Columbia University Press, 1978. $16.95 cloth. Paperbound $9.95.

During the past 25 years, television and social and behavioral science research about television have become growth industries. In the academy, people from political science, sociology, psychology, mass communications, speech, business, and education have produced 2,500 books, articles, and reports concerning television's influence on the way people behave. This valuable, important book seeks to consider "the entire relevant scientific literature in English"—all 2,500 surveys, experiments, case studies, content analyses, reviews, and commentaries—as well as offer an elaborate model and suggestions for future research. The authors' goal is indeed ambitious—a herculean attempt to treat something many consider a modern-day Cyclops—but, in most respects, they admirably accomplish what they propose to do.

Reviewing the existing research, the authors explain the rapid ascendancy and dominating role of what they say "may be the ultimate mass medium." They discuss in detail the ways television has affected viewers, other types of media, and political and social institutions. The picture that emerges from the words, numbers, and charts emphasizes television's pervasiveness and its power to preoccupy. Watching television now takes up 40 percent of an average person's leisure time; sleeping and working are the only activities consuming more time. What prompts such attention? "The medium is fundamentally perceived as the *entertainer*. Television is highly rated as a news source, and it is used to fill vacant time, yet its principal role from the viewpoint of the public is to provide entertainment and relaxation."

The book demonstrates that the effects of this *"entertainer,"* which periodically informs us about what's happening away from the studio and set, are significant, especially on the young. Evidence, for example, supports the hypothesis that viewing violent programs increases the "likelihood" of aggressive behavior in children and adolescents. The authors, however, take pains to point out that this finding and others require consideration within the context of other possible contributing factors so that inconsistency and ambiguity can be reduced. Much more research needs to be done. To further this necessary work, the authors propose a "model of the psychological processes behind any effect television may have on a viewer's behavior." Unfortunately, for the sake of this excellent book, the model is murkily explained in some places, making it difficult to understand and evaluate. Such lapses in clarity are uncharacteristic and the specific suggestions for future research following the model's presentation are clearly stated and imaginative.

As comprehensive as *Television and Human Behavior* is, it makes no claim to being the last word on social and behaviorial science research about television. It is, rather, a most serious effort to examine the first words and data of this empirical research and to chart the direction for future study.

ROBERT SCHMUHL
Indiana University
Bloomington

ANTHONY GIDDENS. *Central Problems in Social Theory: Action, Structure and Contradiction in Social Analysis.* Pp. 294. Berkeley: University of California Press, 1979. $20.00.

Central Problems in Social Theory leaves the reader with feelings of expectation and hope; expectation that Giddens is in the process of preparing a truly great opus in social analysis and hope for the future of an integrated perspective in sociology, or more broadly within the social sciences. The volume consists of seven essays in which Giddens, who is Fellow of King's College and Lecturer in Sociology at the University of Cambridge, develops what he refers to as a "theory of structuration." The essays have value as individual pieces but also hold together as part of a comprehensive attempt at theorizing and exposing trends in social analysis.

The author not only draws on traditional sources in sociology and the social sciences, but also brings a fresh perspective through his reliance on related theories and concepts from disciplines not normally addressed by sociologists or included in their writings. Giddens displays an in-depth knowledge of traditional approaches such as Marxism, structuralism, functionalism, and symbolic interactionism. He develops a lucid portrayal of their strengths and weaknesses, as well as the prospects for their integration or further development. The role of the discipline of history and its potentially relevant conceptual and methodological contributions to social analysis is highlighted.

The central theme of the book develops around the idea of the duality of structure. It includes the belief that the reflexive monitoring of action both draws from and reconstitutes the institutional arrangement of society. Members of society are viewed in a comprehensive active role. The main basis of the concept of the duality of structure rests in Giddens belief that to be a competent member of society means being an active participant, thus knowing a great deal about the society itself.

Traditional approaches to society have heretofore neglected the conception of action developed by Giddens and failed to develop fully concepts connected with the active role of the individual in society. Giddens gives much attention to the importance of time-space relations and their importance in social change. The distinction between synchrony and diachrony is rejected. The reader is forced to rethink a number of basic social concepts including: structure, system, power, domination, conflict, and contradiction.

The way in which the author illustrates and develops the basic concepts in his theory of structuration should prove quite valuable. Evaluation of his future work will depend on a thorough understanding of the framework outlined in the essays reviewed here.

WILLIAM A. PEARMAN
Millersville State College
Pennsylvania

JOACHIM ISRAEL. *The Language of Dialectics and the Dialectics of Language.* Pp. xi, 263. Atlantic Highlands, NJ: Humanities Press, 1979. $23.00.

The development of radical scholarship in the Seventies has been as remarkable as the outburst of left activism which marked the Sixties. The efflorescence of Marxian writings during this period in both book and journal form has spanned almost every field of the human sciences. It has been characterized by a sloughing off of orthodox rigidities and a willingness to rethink old dogmas and seek solutions in external perspectives. This renaissance has been most profound in its efforts to develop a critical theory of consciousness.

Part of this renewed interest in subjectivity has been the critical redefinition of the function and content of modern social psychology. Professor

Israel, over the last decade, has been in the forefront of this task and has established a solid reputation in both Europe and the United States as a leader in this critical movement. What gives his writings in this area special weight is that during his career he has demonstrated his proficiency both as a research social psychologist and as a knowledgeable commentator on issues confronting contemporary Marxian scholarship.

The content of the present volume reflects Professor Israel's dual commitments to a practicing social psychology and to the Marxian reconstruction of that practical activity. However, this work does not concern itself with a critique of particular empirical studies. Rather, its preoccupations are philosophical and apodictic. It seeks to establish a sound grounding for future studies critical social psychology.

The title of the book sufficiently sums up its contents. It is interested in a dialectical approach to the study of the person and society: it explicates a perspective which sees the social from a concrete and total perspective, and seeks the genesis of the social in the productive ontology of human praxis. Thus, Israel devotes a major part of his work to an explication of dialectics as a method, as a constituting social process, and as a language game.

What is unique, however, is the dialectics of language element of his work. Most attempts in the past to develop a Marxian theory of subjectivity have grounded the person and his intrasubjective processes in substantive or existential philosophies or metatheories. Israel rejects this approach and, instead, seeks his image of the person and human subjectivity in British Analytic Philosophy. He attempts to create a social psychology which is concrete, dialectical, and grounded in revolutionary praxis, while drawing upon the behavioral and theoretical insight of analytic philsophy's language analysis.

The structural key to this work is the author's attempt to reconcile Marxian theory and analytic philosophy. On the one hand, he presents and reinterprets dialectical method so as to preserve its critical thrust while at the same time reshaping some of its key concepts in order to make them amenable to the needs of the analytical language. On the other hand, Israel restructures the meanings of many of analytic language's concepts in order to demonstrate their latent dialectical structure. Key to both efforts and bridging them is Israel's reliance on an integrating conception of language and its function in human praxis.

How successful is Professor Israel's theoretical synthesis? It is difficult to say. Some readers will be uneasy with his rejection of empirical experience as an ontological and epistemological foundation for a critical social psychology. Others will criticize, undoubtedly, his application of the dialectic, feeling that his analysis falls short of a full dialectical integration of the two disparate traditions in which he writes. However, any final judgement of such an audacious theoretical effort should be held in abeyance. In that this book has articulated a novel synthesis and perspective, it must be judged on its ability to generate new insights and research concerning the structure of consciousness in Capitalist Society. There is, at the same time, no doubt that Professor Israel has penned an important and exceedingly clear work which can instruct both critics and champions of this position. The groundbreaking nature of this excellent volume will make it required reading for all serious students of social psychology in general and critical Marxist thought in particular.

DAVID L. HARVEY
University of Nevada
Reno

SHULAMIT REINHARZ. *On Becoming a Social Scientist.* Pp. xviii, 422. San Francisco: Jossey-Bass, 1979. $15.95.

This narrative of the author's professional socialization is a curious hybrid. It is exceedingly personal; recounting Reinharz' sequential consideration of the theoretical and methodological alternatives available within sociology was an agonizingly painful process of personal identity formation. Yet, the author recognizes, her experiences are hardly unique.

Other nascent sociologists have recognized the deficiencies of results obtained by ostensibly objective, "scientistic" methods, such as survey research techniques. But the use of such techniques is a defense against the problems inherent in supporting conclusions reached by more subjective methods, such as the approach she calls "experiential analysis." She is quite right to observe that in their efforts to achieve what they imagine to be scientific objectivity sociologists have adopted truly absurd strategies. The sociologist who assumes that his research is uncontaminated by any personal biases because he has managed to study a phenomenon for several years without ever observing it directly is utterly deluded; under such circumstances, his research procedures can reflect nothing but his preconceived notions.

Nevertheless, Reinharz' case against "scientistic" methodology—the use of standardized instruments to gather quantifiable data which can be summarized by some measures of association—is ultimately unsatisfactory, because she cannot prove that the methods themselves can never be useful, merely that they can be unintelligently applied.

Some of the most damning evidence against the misuses of survey techniques—evidence she herself presents—was itself gathered by methods she would have us condemn altogether; we cannot accept this evidence unless we assume that such methods at least occasionally yield meaningful data. Her methodological alternative—"experiential analysis"—poses problems which cannot be explained away. Such an approach requires the sociologist to be a highly involved "participant observer" in the situation she is studying, assuming her own personal reactions to the phenomena to be helpful in explication of the problem. Yet there is no reason to assume that the social scientist can translate personal reactions to circumstances into those of subjects, as the author herself recognizes. Used uncritically, such a subjective methodology seems to belie the basic axiom of social scientific inquiry, the assumption that through collective definition of a variety of gauges we may achieve mutual intelligibility and reliability.

In sum, Reinharz' account provides materials necessary for the construction of a plausible social science, but fails to synthesize them because she is still a convinced witness to the very "scientistic" faith she attempts to discredit. The quest for the perfect method, applicable to all situations and practicable for all researchers, is bound to be futile. And whether the social scientist adopts the method of "experiential analysis" or any other, he will not thereby be transformed into a camera, recording required data without distortions shaped by preconceptions.

Reinharz presents her book as a brief against "scientistic" social science, yet defends her own method in the terms she condemns. As social scientists, we can only conclude that we must gather an abundance of materials to support our claims, present them fully so that we are publicly accountable for our conclusions, and let others judge their adequacy.

Reinharz is at her best when she suspends efforts to make her own experience testify to universal methodological law, and describes her own field experiences. She writes persuasively and engagingly about the social world of the mental hospital and the Israeli border settlement but, alas, her ethnographic observations are subordinate to the general purpose of the book and occupy all too small a fraction of its pages.

As a technical product, the book leaves much to be desired. Many of its points are reiterated to excess and the text is littered with multiple quotations making identical points. A good editor should have prevented quoting the same lengthy passage twice (p. 167 and pp. 296–7) and excised some of the extraordinary grammatical blunders. Nonetheless, the final responsibility for the form as well as the content of this book must be the author's.

HENRIKA KUKLICK
University of Pennsylvania

JAMES RIORDAN. *Sport Under Communism*. Pp. x, 177. Montreal: McGill-Queens University Press, 1978. $14.95.

The success of Communist countries in international sport competition has been astounding in recent years. East Germany (GDR) and Russia have dominated the Olympic Games since World War II; the Cuban presence has been prominent in the Pan American Games and the Montreal Olympics; and China is reentering the Olympics in 1980 and will surely be a contending force in the future. Despite the success of Communist athletes, Westerners know very little of the particular sport systems which produced these athletes. Riordan and a team of qualified international observers have put together a highly descriptive and fairly readable comparative account of the organization and operation of the sport systems of five Communist countries—U.S.S.R., Czechoslovakia, the G.D.R., China, and Cuba.

Each country is described in terms of five basic themes: history and development, the emergence of new themes since the most significant political event in their history, Castro's seizure of power in Cuba in 1959, the organization of physical education in the schools, the organization and structure of contemporary sport, and the main goals of sport and physical education. The U.S.S.R. and China are reviewed because they are the largest Communist countries. Cuba and the G.D.R. were selected because their athletic success has been disproportionate to their size. Czechoslovakia is included because it is representative of the smaller Communist states. The material presented in each article exhibits more detail on these sport systems than has been found in any other previously published source.

There are several characteristics which are common to all of the Communist sport systems described in the text. In each case sport is: centrally operated and organized by government authoritis; oriented to the utilitarian goals of military preparedness, international prestige, and fitness for productivity; directed at dichotomous emphases on mass

participation and elite-athlete preparation; compulsory activity in schools; and
in the context of physical culture, sport
is viewed as a right, not a privilege, for
all. Every success of a Communist
sportsman is viewed as a success for
the socialist way of life whether it be
Russian, Chinese or Cuban.

The five accounts are rich in descriptive detail but each is sterile in analysis. Allusions are made to political
struggles between sport organizations,
to dissent by athletes, and to the use of
drugs by athletes but their implications
are neglected. None of the studies reports
data gathered from athletes or the
general public. None of the studies is
very critical of the systems each describes. They overlook, for example,
the fact that the emphasis on physical
fitness for the masses in these countries
is largely superficial. The real concentration is on the development of the
elite athlete who can bring fame and
glory to the motherland. As such, the
book falls short in its original purpose
to provide insight to the dynamics of
Communist sport.

JAMES H. FREY
University of Nevada
Las Vegas

JOHN SLAWSON, *Unequal Americans:
Practices and Politics of Intergroup
Relations.* Pp. xiii, 249. Westport, CT:
Greenwood Press, 1979. $22.95.

A variety of perspectives have been
employed to explain the subordinate
position of specific social groups. The
most popular theoretical frameworks
have indicated that the circumstances
of minority groups can be attributed
to: cultural variables, Culture of Poverty;
competing values and interests, Pluralism; and a social structure which is
designed to oppress particular elements
of the population, class-based or socialist
analyses. The most widely accepted
analyses of this phenomena are steeped
in pluralist belief. Pluralism is based
on the presumption that the relative
standing of a group in the social order
is a direct function of its capacity to
pursue and achieve specific objectives.
Each group's unique capacities are

perceived as being a product of intragroup and interorganizational forces.
This framework and the analyses it
nurtures implicitly accept as given the
value presumptions of the social order.
Quite clearly, such research emphasizes
microscopic forces and, in general,
ignores or relegates to a lesser status
the effect of the larger social structure
on individual and group behavior. John
Slawson and Marc Vosk have produced
a monograph, *Unequal Americans: Practices and Politics of Intergroup Relations,* which relies almost exclusively
on Pluralist explanations of group behavior. This emphasis has significant
implications for both the utility and
generalizability of their work.

This volume has been designed to address a very broad range of issues that
have affected intergroup or minority
group relations between the years 1930
and 1975. The breadth of this analysis
is most impressive. The authors touch
upon many of the important legislative
and judicial decisions which have
emerged in this area. In addition, they
address many of the pitfalls associated
with such decisionmaking; for example,
the enforcement of official decree and a
backlash by the majority group. Just as
importantly, the organization of their
work is most effective. The authors
developed chapter and section headings
which provide a newspaper like summary of the events and issues which
affected specific American minority
groups over an approximate thirty-five
year period. Finally, the volume is
written in a clear and simple manner.
The authors rarely, if ever, rely upon
social-scientific jargon to present or
elaborate upon an idea.

The monograph, however, does suffer
from a number of analytical and methodological weaknesses. The authors' almost exclusive reliance upon the Pluralist perspective has contributed to an
almost naive faith in particular institutions and reform measures, and an indifference toward the larger social
structure's effect upon the socio-economic standing of particular minority
groups. Slawson and Vosk presume that
the media, particularly television, has
seved to reduce intergroup tensions

(page 37). In addition, they indicate that government programs accelerated "group equality of opportunity" (page 8). Finally, the authors note that knowledge, particularly social science research, can serve to ameliorate many of the social problems that have affected minority groups (pages 12 and 122). The authors offer little, if any, evidence to substantiate their assertions. Just as importantly, each of these points could be disputed on the basis of recent experience and social research.

Slawson and Vosk almost entirely ignore those socio-economic forces which have contributed to inter and intragroup tensions. The authors' indifference or insensitivity toward these issues has spawned a series of reform proposals which rely upon psychoanalytic technique to affect attitudes both within and between groups. The authors' clear emphasis upon such measures is at best misplaced and at worst socially destructive. In addition, this void reflects the volume's inability to grapple with the economic and class-based issues which have functioned to oppress particular groups and ultimately increased the level and intensity of intergroup tension.

Finally the authors have developed much of their analysis from interviews with approximately 120 national leaders in intergroup relations. The status of the respondents provides the authors with the necessary springboard to use specific quotes as evidence to support very broad assertions. In effect, Slawson and Vosk have attempted to construct an analysis which is national in scope on the basis of the professional position of their sample. Unfortunately, the extent to which this subpopulation is representative of the leadership in the field is not clarified in either the text or appendices of the volume. The degree to which particular quotes are idiosyncratic or representative of a group's perspective, is also not apparent. As a result, the reader simply does not have the information necessary to determine whether the data underpinning the analysis can be generalized.

This book does not make a particularly unique or scholarly contribution to the literature on intergroup relations. Instead, it provides a succinct summary of many of the events and issues which have had a special relevance to minority groups during the past thirty-five years. The monograph is particularly useful in highlighting the pluralists' perspective on these social problems. Consequently, Slawson and Vosk's work should be of interest to a general audience and a particularly valuable supplemental reading in introductory policy, urban studies, and minority relations courses.

MICHAEL FABRICANT
Community Service Center
New York City

ECONOMICS

R. ALBERT BERRY and WILLIAM R. CLINE. *Agarian Structure and Productivity in Developing Countries.* Pp. x, 248. Baltimore: The Johns Hopkins University Press, 1979. $17.50.

This study is intended to throw light on an issue of great importance in many less developed countries: the relationship between farm size and the productivity of agriculture. Its importance stems from the fact that with the recent heightened concern to satisfy the basic needs of the population of poor countries, land reform and land redistribution have been suggested as means to achieve this end. In response, opponents of such schemes argue that only large scale farms are competent to use modern inputs efficiently and thus redistributing land to peasants would limit long-term growth.

Two basic tests of the farm size/productivity relationship appear in this study. First, Berry and Cline present data from twenty countries which carried out agricultural censuses in 1960 and for which data were compiled by the Food and Agriculture Organization (FAO). Second, specific case studies are presented for six countries for which extensive data are available: Brazil, Colombia, the Philippines, West Pakistan, India, and Malaysia. In addition, less comprehensive data and analyses are presented for six other countries in appendixes. In general, the statistical analyses presented here point to a clear conclusion: "the small farm sector makes better use of its available land than does the large-farm sector largely through applying higher levels of labor inputs (family labor) per unit of land" (p. 131–4). Furthermore, there is at least some evidence that total factor productivity as well as land yields are inversely related to farm size.

The contribution which this book makes is that it provides a firm empirical foundation for a hypothesis which, as the authors suggest, students of agrarian structures have long suspected. Less convincing and much less well supported empirically is the author's principal policy conclusion that "land redistribution into family farms is an attractive policy instrument for raising production. . . ." (p. 134). The problem is that very little evidence is presented on the question of advances in productivity over time by farm size. As a result, the possibility that a shift to small scale agriculture and more intensive cultivation might produce only a one time increase in agriculture, followed thereafter by sluggish growth, cannot be rejected. Since growth in agricultural output depends principally upon advances in technology, the hypothesis that long-term growth might adversely be affected by the kind of land reform suggested here remains unscathed.

Despite this reservation, however, Berry and Cline have made a welcome and valuable addition to the empirical literature on agriculture in poor countries.

JAY R. MANDLE
Temple University
Philadelphia

ROBERT J. GORDON and JACQUES PELKMANS. *Challenges to Interdependent Economies.* Pp. xii, 149. New York: McGraw-Hill, 1979. $9.95.

This book is the sixteenth volume of the 1980s Project sponsored by the Council on Foreign Relations. It is an assessment of the complications of macroeconomic management and the new economic nationalism that strain international economic cooperation. International cooperation has not filled the vacuum created by the diminished leadership of the United States in international economic affairs. The upsurge in international transactions coupled with a lack of leadership and meaningful economic cooperation have created uncertainty and increasing national vulnerability in the global economy.

The short volume is divided into two distinct sections. In the first part, Professor Gordon has outlined the macroeconomic policy problems that beset the American economy. Emphasis has been placed on the U.S. economy with the view that stability and growth of this economy will have favorable implications for the world economy. Gordon has outlined the dilemma faced by policy makers when confronted with divergent economic advice, for example, monetarist versus nonmonetarist activism. The failure to achieve an accurate record of forecasting and the unsuccessful price/wage control program of 1971–1974 has tended to undermine the case for policy activism.

In an analysis of inflation, Gordon suggests that inflation tends to be higher in countries with more aggressive trade unions, nationalized industries, and political control of central banks. He is somewhat optimistic about a slow down of inflation due to oil induced supply shocks. "But the major damage of higher prices has been done." Unfortunately, the book was completed just prior to the major boost in oil prices in 1979 which indeed have created serious stabilization problems for the American economy. Professor Gordon contends that the U.S. government has introduced "legislated inflation," analytically similar to supply shocks—increases in social security taxes, energy taxes, and a higher minimum wage.

Two additional "time bombs" will be the effects of dollar depreciation and the abysmal productivity record of the U.S. economy during the 1970s. The author does support a series of measures that would help alleviate some of America's economic ills. The selection of policy instruments would be based on the encouragement of saving and investment rather than government induced recessions to cure inflation which further erode the country's ability to achieve long-run stability and growth. These steps would include government-indexed bonds and tax brackets, easier money coupled with tighter fiscal policy, a Swedish-type countercyclical investment fund, government stockpiling of raw materials during recessions and the stockpiling of agricultural surpluses.

Gordon concludes that, "the impotence of the small countries and the need for austerity in the group of large 'invalid' nations leaves the responsibility for world recovery with the United States, Germany, and Japan." It is therefore essential to prevent a major downturn in the American economy in order to avoid dragging the global economy into another worldwide recession.

In the second half of the book, Professor Pelkams analyzes the success of economic cooperation among Western nations. Overall, Pelkams is very pessimistic in his outlook for the achievement of unified common leadership among them. Part of the problem is the politicization of international economic policy. This has led to the formulation of short-run policies within a governing period which seek to improve an incumbent politician's election prospects.

The populace of Western countries have shown an increasing preference for economic security which has moved policies away from international economic adjustment and cooperation. "The achievement of individual economic security eventually increases resistance to market adjustment processes," according to Pelkams. In addition, the quest for national economic security has become politicized which has eroded prospects for economic cooperation. The new economic nationalism has been directed toward increasing national autonomy to control domestic economic policies. This has slowly eroded the postwar structure of Western economic cooperation.

Although many organizations (GATT, IMF, OECD) have achieved some degree of cooperation in the past, Pelkams finds limited hope for future cooperation. Since the barriers to positive cooperation are prohibitive, only the hope of preserving the achievements of negative economic cooperation, removing discriminatory treatment against goods, can be accomplished. Western nations ". . . have generated a glut of conferences, sessions, and summits about economic cooperation but at the same time have yielded few, if any, improvements in economic cooperation." Examples of today's cooperation include economic summits that merely produce powerless communiques or new agencies that barely have constitutions. In fact, Pelkams finds that the multiplication of these international economic organizations may complicate cooperation and dilute any results.

Overall, the book is a frank appraisal needed at this time to critically review international economic cooperation. It does not pay lip service to the facade of cooperation, but provides a basis for new directions in international economic affairs. Perhaps there might have been a closer integration of the two sections of the book, but this did not detract from its impact. However, the book did not give enough attention to an analysis of the dilemma of oil policy —probably the greatest challenge to international economic cooperation at this time. While the potential positive avenues of new cooperation may not have been accentuated in the book, the main theme of the dangers of the further erosion of economic cooperation were clear.

RUSSELL BELLICO
Westfield State College
Massachusetts

JAMES C. HITE. *Room and Situation: The Political Economy of Land-Use Policy*, Pp. x, 340. Chicago: Nelson-Hall, 1979. $18.95. Paperbound $9.95.

ROBERT W. LAKE. *Real Estate Tax Delinquency: Private Disinvestment & Public Response*, Pp. xviii, 263. New Brunswick: The Center for Urban Policy Research, Rutgers University, 1979. $17.95.

Is private ownership of real property the root cause of both environmental and urban fiscal problems in the United States? There are at least two schools of thought which say that it is, judging from these two recent studies. *Room and Situation* by James C. Hite takes its title from a phrase in an 1893 book by John R. Commons, a prominent institutionalist. *Real Estate Tax Delinquency* by Robert W. Lake comes from that persuasion which regards "monopoly capital" as the bane of our social existence.

Hite takes a very long look at the origins of property laws and related institutions in the United States. His argument runs approximately thus: American colonial leaders saw unlimited opportunity for land speculation on the frontier and were forced to instigate rebellion when the British crown curtailed that practice; the successful new republic wrote its laws to favor nearly absolute rights of private ownership and used the powers of government to encourage massive infrastructure development; privately owned land increased in value even through the suburban boom of the 1950s; private ownership, however, is inherently likely to destroy environmental amenities and create adverse neighborhood effects, which early city planning and latter-day environmental measures have not sufficed to correct. Hite tentatively explores a more effective planning scheme involving transfer of development rights, but seems to back away after considering recent theory on the quandary of democratic decisionmaking.

The book is unpersuasive primarily because it omits so much that is obviously relevant and because the approach is very unspecific. The glaring omissions are any reference to the von Thuenen's basic contribution to the subject, discussion of the role of mortgage lending institutions, and a realistic examination of the income tax system— all of which might do Hite's argument more good than harm. The strong part of the book is a concise legal history, unfortunately very cursory. Hite is a professor of agricultural economics at Clemson University.

Robert W. Lake is an Assistant Research Professor at the Center for Urban Policy Research, Rutgers University. His book is occasioned by statistical and survey studies of property tax delinquency undertaken by the city of Pittsburgh, studies which Lake effectively summarizes.

He first presents a thesis, however, which runs about as follows: capitalists realize that profitable private investment in urban real estate depends on public investment in infrastructure which in turn requires that private investors pay property taxes; since capitalists control local government there is no conflict so long as basic private business activities flourish; as a city ages and acquires a population with need for public services, investors begin to withdraw capital from central city for reinvestment in the more promising suburbs; no longer needing central city infrastructure capitalists simply stop paying property taxes; the government of the central city is unprepared to manage erstwhile private land and buildings, having been created simply to serve capitalist ends, so the central city suffers physical decay and fiscal disaster and retrenches on services rather than expanding them to meet growing needs. Lake suggests that a new style in urban government might so effectively manage property acquired for taxes that fiscal and economic health could be restored.

The survey material and statistical experiments involving Pittsburgh fall very short of supporting this thesis. Much tax delinquency is on vacant land or properties already under public control. The average owed on delinquent residential properties is only $74, a good portion of which seems to be merely "slow pay" by low-income homeowners.

Lake does not provide a microeconomic decision model for an investor contemplating non-payment of property tax. Nor does he examine the eminently practical question suggested by his thesis, namely whether government should indeed act to constrain private investment so as to shore up declining regions or declining industries. Absent these specifics, Lake's text is only rhetoric.

There may be yet another school of thought with a more rigorous and effective approach to this set of subjects still waiting in the wings. In fairness to Lake and Hite those superior works have yet to be published.

WALLACE F. SMITH
University of California
Berkeley

JOSEPH G. KNAPP. *Edwin G. Nourse: Economist for the People*. Pp. xvi, 544. Danville, IL: Interstate Printers and Publishers, 1979. $11.95.

When a writer undertakes the biography of a figure who is or who has been very close to him, he inevitably is both to be commended for his intimate knowledge of subject and to be read cautiously for his uncritical praise. The reader of Joseph G. Knapp's life of Edwin G. Nourse must both feel satisfied with the awareness displayed therein of details of the great economist's life and must be cautious in seeing the book as a tribute to an admired friend.

Nourse is known to the economics profession principally for his service as the first chairman of the Council of Economic Advisers. He was named by President Truman to undertake that pioneer task after Congress created that body in 1946. He was the author of twelve books on economics and of dozens of articles. He served a term as president of the American Economics Association and was active in many other professional organizations. Knapp quotes numberless speeches which Nourse gave before professional and business groups and conventions.

Nourse was born in Lockport, New York on May 20, 1883 and spent much of his childhood in Downer's Grove, a suburb of Chicago. He was a descendant of a woman who was hanged as a witch in Salem, Massachusetts in 1691. He studied at the Lewis Institute in Chicago

and at Cornell University, and later earned a doctorate at the University of Chicago. He taught in a high school in Ogden, Utah, as well as in such institutions of higher learning as the University of Pennsylvania, the University of South Dakota, the University of Arkansas, and Iowa State College.

During his service in a high school and on several university and college faculties, he wrote extensively and enjoyed a rapidly expanding reputation as a specialist in agricultural economics and in marketing. In particular, he became known as an advocate of farm cooperatives. Throughout his life he was a supporter of private enterprise, low prices for industrial products, and of competition.

In 1922 Nourse was named to the Institute of Economics, one of the several bodies which Robert S. Brookings financed. The several groups which Brookings founded were later combined in the Brookings Institution. Nourse remained with Brookings, while his reputation as an economist grew, until President Truman named him chairman of the Council of Economics Advisers in 1946. Nourse remained in Washington from 1923 until his death at the age of 90.

Leon Keyserling, who had a background in both law and economics, and John D. Clark, who had taught economics at the University of Denver and had held public offices in Colorado and Wyoming, were the other two members of the first trio of heads of the Council. In his three years with the body, Nourse felt that it should keep clear of politics and only act as economic advisers to the president. Keyserling and Clark both had strong ties to the Democratic party.

This situation created strain which Knapp treats with care, but naturally from a pro-Nourse position. This disagreement is discussed at some length. Nourse resigned in 1949, to be succeeded by Keyserling. Nourse then spent the rest of his life speaking and writing on economics.

Knapp, who was himself employed as a government economist in Nourse's final years, tells of the period in which the economist's physical powers and his eyesight declined. Up to his death, Nourse worked on a book, which was left incomplete.

Much of the biography is devoted to extensive quotations from Nourse's books, speeches and articles. It is a study that belongs on the reading list of students of the history of the Truman administration as well as of students of the development of American economic theory.

F. B. Marbut
Sarasota
Florida

Leo McGee and Robert Boone, eds. *The Black Rural Landowner—Endangered Species: Social, Political, and Economic Implication.* Pp. xxi, 200. Westport, CT: Greenwood Press, 1979. $17.95.

Leo McGee is the Assistant Dean for Continuing Education at Tennessee Technological University and Robert Boone holds the position of Director of Public Service at Tennessee State University. They have compiled ten pioneer studies as the 44th title for the *Contribution in Afro-American and African Studies* series.

The first paper by Manning Marable relates the historical background of the post-Civil War transition of a plantation-slave agricultural system to one based on sharecropping. Frank Pogue explains how because of the poverty and discrimination, a migration began from the rural South to the urban Northeast. James Lewis describes the economic plight of black farmers whose small farms only yield an annual income of $3,400. The co-editors contributed the fourth paper which analyzed black farmers' favorable attitudes towards land ownership—it provides security, prestige,—in contrast to their correlative lack of expertise.

The fifth and sixth papers were written by Charles Nesbitt and William Nelson. They describe the sociological values of black rural communities and the positive relationship of political activism and land ownership. The next three papers attempt to suggest some strategies for solving the problems associated with the decline in black land ownership. Carl Marbury believes the Land Grant Colleges can play a much more significant role than they have heretofore. Joseph Brooks wants more education of black farmers via the Emergency Land Fund Program. Finally, James Lewis suggests more research regarding the unfairness of tax delinquency laws throughout the South.

In the concluding paper, Lester Salamon predicts that only the intervention of the federal government can halt the drastic decline in black ownership. From 1910, the peak year in black ownership, there has been a decline in acreage from 15 million to the current 6 million. Thus, in the past 70 years blacks have lost 9 million acres of farmland. The remaining 6 million average 52 acres per farm. It does seem obvious that federal financial and technical assistance is required to solve this problem.

This small volume is exceedingly valuable as the first in-depth look at the problems surrounding black land ownership. Thirty percent of the black population still lives on the land but unless they are given some needed assistance, they will be driven to the urban ghettoes. The implications, then, are serious.

Frederick H. Schapsmeier
University of Wisconsin
Oshkosh

John D. Owen. *Working Hours: An Economic Analysis.* Pp. xiii, 206. Lexington, MA: Lexington Books, 1979. $21.00.

John D. Owen, an economist who has focused his career on the work-leisure dichotomy in twentieth century American society, here presents a lucid examination of the past and present and a reasoned peek at the future. There are 134 pages of text in clear English supported by seven largely mathematical appendices. The purpose of work and income throughout is treated solely as the ability to acquire and consume. Unemployment and underemployment are not seriously considered.

His basic conclusions (pp. 133–34) are:

There is less leisure than is generally believed. Hours of work have leveled off for males while female labor force participation has increased.

This is, in large part, the price of continuing affluence.

The quality of consumption has increased, but "rigid work schedules, combined with higher labor force participation rates of women and the inflexible schedules of schools and other institutions, yield a difficult situation for families which must allocate limited resources of time and money to pursue a variety of consumption goals."

Some easing comes from flex-time or voluntary part-time work, now involving about one worker in three. Broader use of these alternatives will "very likely improve the quality of time by giving individuals more choice in planning their work, household production, and leisure schedules."

Reduction of hours is the most obvious way to increase leisure, but would be very expensive.

Owen warns against the approach— since taken by Rep. John Conyers, Democrat of Michigan, of a statutory reduction to a 35 hour work week with double time for overtime, as likely to increase the quantity of consumption time while reducing its quality as spendable income declined.

A greater familiarity with the work of historians would have enriched this work. Owen seems not to be aware of how close we came to a legislated 30 hour week in the early New Deal (the Black bill) and some of the insights of John Garraty, *Unemployment in History* could have added a dimension. Withall this is a clear, no-nonsense if somewhat one-sided approach to a universal problem. It should be consulted by anyone concerned with this basic question.

ROGER DANIELS
University of Cincinnati

TERUTOMO OZAWA. *Multinationalism, Japanese Style: The Political Economy of Outward Dependency*. Pp. xiii, 289. Princeton, NJ: Princeton University Press, 1979. $16.50.

Japan's multinational enterprises differ markedly from the U.S. model, both in motivation and support behind the corporations and in their basic character. Not too surprisingly, Japanese multinationals are the offspring of a rather limited group of factors which in large part produced the Japanese economy today. One of these, with a history as old as Japan's participation on the world economic scene, is her paucity of resources. With a very heavy resource demand, she is the least self-sufficient of industrialized nations. Other factors, more recent phenomena than the first, include a dwindling labor force whose standards of living and of demand have risen steadily, and an increasing and widespread concern in Japan about the effects of home industries on the ecology. A final consideration is the difficulty in obtaining industrial sites in a land poor country. These factors have spurred the search for new methods of obtaining raw materials, fuels, and cheaper labor pools, and have led to moves to establish the fuel consumptive and dirtier industries abroad.

The truly distinguishing features of Japan's multinationals, however, are their group orientation and interdependency and the degree of governmental support underwriting them. The move into multinationals for Japan has not been the result of oligopolistic and spontaneous decisions on the part of individual corporations to expand, and in doing so to conform to dominant Western theories of multinational development. These theories, Professor Ozawa notes, while valid perhaps in describing Western multinationals, have little relevance to Japanese development. The government and not the individual competitive concern led the way into multinationalism in Japan, and the degree of cooperation among the participants in her investment activities abroad contrasts sharply with Western models. This is particularly noticeable in relation to the services offered other Japanese enterprises by the great trading companies.

Mr. Ozawa's work is carefully researched, lucidly presented, and praiseworthy in its objective utilization of the data. He devotes considerable attention to Japanese investment in the Asian home area and in more distant lands. Of particular interest is his chapter on conflict with local interests as Japanese multinationals seek to establish themselves. He sees a Japan no longer viewed abroad as the product of an economic miracle, but rather one with the deteriorating image of the pollutor and even the "economic animal" in its quest for resources, labor, and industrial sites.

The book is a most solid and valuable addition to the growing shelf of literature on multinationals.

R. KENT LANCASTER
Goucher College
Baltimore

ERIK OLIN WRIGHT. *Class Structure and Income Determination.* Pp. xvii, 266. New York: Academic Press, 1979. $21.00.

As a Marxist sociologist, Wright sees "Marxism (as a) re-emerging . . . serious theoretical force" to deal with economic and social equality in modern capitalist society. In what is described as the first attempt to test Marxist theory empirically with modern econometric techniques, Wright attempts to reconcile theoreticians' concepts of class in income determination with the growing body of empirical studies and quantitative data on status attainment and educational inequality. In a detailed review of various definitions of "Classes in Advanced Societies," Wright opts for updated Marxist classes as a base; discusses in detail "three categories of positions within those class relations that are generally designated 'middle class.'" He regards as especially important clusters: Managers and supervisors, semi-autonomous employees, and small employers; he also discusses other locations in the class structure which he says do not fit neatly into the traditional Marxist theory of class structure. He devotes a chapter each to race and sex in determining incomes.

Wright concludes that class "consistently and significantly affects income of people in different class positions but who have the same level of education and occupational status, age and seniority, social background, and working hours a year." He adds that otherwise comparable individuals in different class positions get fewer benefits in income from increased education. In treating how race and sex per se affect income, Wright cites concentration of blacks and women in worker and lower managerial classes as an example of how class position enters into income determination.

Having dealt with other variables in class and income relationships where adequate data are, or are not, available, Wright suggests areas for future research. He includes: More specific measures of class, for example, managers, supervisors, and semi-autonomous employees; degree of control over ones own labor; class structure in monopolies, franchises, and other enterprises; family and class especially related to women, as they affect family production.

Illustrating the scope of influences on income, Wright also touches on hiring and promotion practices and other factors. Perhaps with equal validity, one might extend Wright's refinements of elements in achievement and income into areas as diverse as: breast-fed vs. bottle-fed babies; mother vs. surrogate mother, vs. day-care tended children; and TV vs. non-TV reared children—or performance of "TV Zombies."

Moving beyond income determination, Wright proposes studying how class affects political-governmental forms; and class and non-class struggle. Finally, as a "critical next step" in the study of Marxist theory of income determination, Wright proposes examining cross-society patterns. In reminding us that, "Marxism is, after all, a theory of social change, of the role of classes and class struggle in the transformation of societies, rather than an analysis of structural determinations within a given system of class relations," we hope that he and other social scientists will re-examine Marx's theories of transformation. Do Cambodia, China, Cuba, Nicaragua, and Stalinist Russia offer useful models for classless societies for Third World Countries? Are terrorism, violence, mass murder, imprisonment, idea control the only realistic tools for change?

While the thousands of professional developers, with their billions of dollars, are finally beginning to murmur audibly about political will, a working majority still approach the subject academically. With much of the world still in turmoil, they, in effect, tend simply to wait passively for the revolution.

DANA D. REYNOLDS
International Center for Dynamics
of Development
Arlington
Virginia

OTHER BOOKS

ALLEN, LOUIS. *Singapore 1941–1942: The Politics and Strategy of the Second World War.* Pp. 343. Cranbury, NJ: University of Delaware Press, 1980. $12.00.

BERES, LOUIS RENÉ. *Terrorism and Global Security: The Nuclear Threat.* Pp. xii, 161. Boulder, CO: Westview Press, 1980. $18.50.

BERNHARD, VIRGINIA, ed. *Elites, Masses and Modernization in Latin America, 1850–1930.* Pp. viii, 157. Austin, TX: University of Texas Press, 1979. $9.95.

BERRY, R. ALBERT, RONALD G. HELLMAN, and MAURICIO SOLAUN, eds. *Politics of Compromise: Coalition Government in Columbia.* Pp. xii, 488. New Brunswick, NJ: Transaction Books, 1980, $29.95 Paperbound.

BLAIR, ROGER D., and STEPHAN RUBIN, eds. *Regulating the Professions.* Pp. viii, 328. Lexington, MA: Lexington Books, 1980. No Price.

BOND, BRIAN. *France and Belgium 1939–1940.* Pp. 206. Cranbury, NJ: University of Delaware Press, 1980, $12.00.

BRUYN, SEVERYN, T., and PAULA M. RAYMAN, eds. *Nonviolent Action and Social Change.* Pp. xix, 316. New York: Irvington Publishers, 1979, $18.75.

BURCH, WILLIAM R. JR., ed. *Long Distance Trails: The Appalachian Trail as a Guide to Future Research and Management Needs.* Pp. 172. New Haven, CT: Yale University, School of Forestry & Environmental Studies, 1979. $11.50 Paperbound.

CALLAHAN, RAYMOND. *Burma: 1942–1945: The Politics and Strategy of the Second World War.* Pp. 190. Cranbury, NJ: University of Delaware Press, 1980. $12.00.

CHURCHILL, SALLIE R., BONNIE CARLSON and LYNN NYBELL, *No Child is Unadoptable.* Pp. 173. Beverly Hills, CA: Sage Publications, 1979. $7.00.

COMBS, JAMES E., *Dimensions of Political Drama.* Pp. vii, 215. Santa Monica, CA: Goodyear Publishing Co., 1980. No Price Paperbound.

CROPSEY, JOSEPH. *Political Philosophy and the Issues of Politics.* Pp. ix, 329. Chicago, IL: University of Chicago Press, 1980. $7.50 Paperbound.

CROWELL, JOHN, and STANFORD J. SEARL, Jr., eds. *The Responsibility of Mind in a Civilization of Machines: Essays by Perry Miller.* 224 Pp. Amherst, MA: University of Massachusetts Press, 1979, $14.50.

CURTIS, MICHAEL. *Totalitarianism.* Pp. vi, 128. New Brunswick, NJ: Transaction Books, 1979. $5.95.

DENITCH, BOGDAN, ed. *Legitimations of Regimes: International Frameworks for Analysis.* Pp. 305. 1979. $16.00. $7.95 Paperbound.

DE WEYDENTHAL. JAN B, vol. 72, *The Washington Papers, Poland: Communism Adrift.* 88 Pp. Beverly Hills, CA: Sage Publications, 1979. $3.50.

DIGGINS, JOHN P. *The Bard of Savagery: Thorstein Veblen and Modern Social Theory.* Pp. xiii, 257. New York: The Seabury Press, 1978. $14.95.

EINER, S. E., ed., *Five Constitutions: An Annotated Edition of the Complete Texts of the U.S.A., U.S.S.R., West German and French Constitutions.* Pp. 349. Atlantic Highlands, NJ: Humanities Press, 1980. $28.95.

FISHER, CHARLES F. and ISABEL COLL-PARDO. *Guide to Leadership Development Opportunities for College and University Administrators.* Pp. xvii, 197. Washington, DC: American Council on Education, 1979. No Price.

FOUNTAIN, ALVIN M, II. *Roman Dmowski, Party, Tactics, Ideology, 1895–1907.* Pp. xiii, 240. New York: Columbia University Press, 1980. $16.00.

GERMANI, GINO. *Marginality.* Pp. viii, 99. New Brunswick, NJ: Transaction Books, 1980.

202   THE ANNALS OF THE AMERICAN ACADEMY

GIBERT, STEPHAN P. *The Washington Papers: Vol. 71. Northeast Asia in U.S. Foreign Policy.* Pp. 88. Beverly Hills, CA, Sage Publications, 1979. $3.50.

GIBSON, WELDON. *SRI: The Founding Years.* Pp. xii, 212. Los Altos, CA: Publishing Services Center, 1980, No Price.

GOODMAN, PAUL S., JOHANNES M. PENNINGS, et al., *New Perspectives on Organizational Effectiveness,* Pp. ix, 275. San Francisco, CA: Jossey-Bass, 1977, $12.95.

GOUDSBLOM, JOHAN, *Sociology in the Balance: A Critical Essay,* Pp. v, 232. New York: Columbia University Press, 1977, $12.50.

GOUDWAARD, BOB. *Capitalism & Progress.* Pp. xxvii, 270. Grand Rapids, MI: Wm. B. Eerdams Publishing Co., 1979. $9.95 Paperbound.

GRAY, CHARLES M. *The Costs of Crime.* Pp. 280. Beverly Hills, CA: Sage Publications, 1979. $18.50. $8.95 Paperbound.

GRAYCAR, ADAM. *Welfare Politics in Australia: A Study in Policy Analysis.* Pp. viii, 231. South Melbourne, Australia: The MacMillan Company of Australia, 1979. $17.50. $8.95 Paperbound.

GRINDLE, MERILEE S. *Bureaucrats, Politicians, and Peasants in Mexico: A Case Study in Public Policy.* Pp. 239. Berkeley, CA: University of California Press, 1977. $12.50.

GROSSMAN, LAWRENCE. *The Democratic Party and the Negro: Northern and National Politics 1868–92.* Pp. ix, 212. Urbana, IL: University of Illinois Press, 1976. $9.95.

HALLMAN, HOWARD W. *Emergency Employment: A Study in Federalism.* Pp. ix, 207. University, AL. University of Alabama Press, 1977, $11.50.

HENDERSON, P. D. *INDIA: The Energy Sector.* Pp. v, 191. New York: Oxford University Press, 1976, $4.75.

HENRY, NICHOLAS. *Public Administration and Public Affairs.* 2d ed. Pp. xvi, 511. Englewood Cliffs, NJ: Prentice-Hall, 1980. No Price.

HILLS, STUART L. *Demystifying Social Deviance.* Pp. xiii, 210. New York: McGraw-Hill, 1980. No Price Paperbound.

HOLZER, HANS. *How to Win at Life.* Pp. x, 174. Los Angeles, CA: Pinnacle Books, 1980. $1.95 Paperbound.

HOROWITZ, IRVING LOUIS, ed. *Outlines of Sociology: Ludwig Gumpowicz.* Pp. 336. New Brunswick, NJ: Transaction Books, 1980. $19.95.

HOROWITZ, IRVING LOUIS. *Taking Lives: Genocide and State Power,* 3rd ed. Pp. xvi, 199. New Brunswick, NJ: Transaction Books, 1980, $12.95. $5.95 Paperbound.

HORTON, PAUL B. and CHESTER L. HUNT. *Sociology,* 4th ed. Pp. xvi, 526. New York: McGraw-Hill, 1979, $17.95.

HOWELL, ROBERT G. and PATRICIA L. HOWELL. *Discipline in the Classroom: Solving the Teaching Puzzle.* Pp. xviii, 221. Englewood Cliffs, NJ: Prentice-Hall, 1979. $13.95.

HUDDLESTON, BARBARA and JON McLIN. *Political Investments in Food Production: National and International Case Studies.* Pp. viii, 220. Bloomington, IN: Indiana University Press, 1979. $19.95. $10.95 Paperbound.

JACKSON, W. G. F. *'Overlord': Normandy 1944: The Politics and Strategy of the Second World War.* Pp. 249. Cranbury, NJ: University of Delaware Press, 1980. $13.50.

JACOB, HERBERT. *Crime and Justice in Urban America.* Pp. ix, 198. Englewood Cliffs, NJ: Prentice-Hall, 1980. $7.95 Paperbound.

JORDAN, AMOS A. and ROBERT A. KILMARX. *The Washington Papers, Vol. 70, Strategic Mineral Dependence: The Stockpile Dilemna* Pp. 83. Beverly Hills, CA: Sage Publications, 1979, $3.50.

KANTOWICZ, EDWARD R. *Polish-American Politics in Chicago 1888–1940.* Pp. xi, 260. Chicago, IL: University of Chicago Press, 1980. $5.50 Paperbound.

KATZ, ELIHU and GEORGE WEDELL. *Broadcasting in the Third World: Promise and Performance.* Pp. v, 305. Cambridge, MA: Harvard University Press, 1978. $15.00.

LARSON, ALLAN L. *Comparative Political Analysis,* Pp. x, 167. Chicago, IL: Nelson-Hall, 1980. $14.95. $7.95 Paperbound.

LEVITT, IAN and CHRISTOPHER SMOUT. *The State of the Scottish Working Class in 1843.* Pp. x, 284. New York: Columbia University Press, 1980, $15.00.

LAUFFER, ARMAND. *RESOURCES: For Child Placement & Other Human Services.* Pp. 192. Beverly Hills, CA: Sage Publications, 1979. $7.50 Paperbound.

MARGOLIS, MAXINE L and WILLIAM E. CARTER. *BRAZIL: Anthropological Perspectives.* Pp. xvi, 443. New York: Columbia University Press, 1979, $20.00.

MARSHALL, DALE ROGERS, ed. *Urban Policy Making.* Pp. 283. Beverly Hills, CA: Sage Publications, 1979. $18.50. $8.95 Paperbound.

MARTIN, JOSEPH, *A Guide to Marxism.* Pp. 157. New York: St. Martin's Press, 1980, $14.95.

MARX, GARY T., and NORMAN GOODMAN. *Sociology: Classic and Popular Approaches.* Pp. x, 436. New York: Random House, 1980. No Price.

McCARTHY, MELODIE A. and JOHN P. HOUSTON. *Fundamentals of Early Childhood Education.* Pp. xi, 366. Cambridge, MA: Winthrop Publishers, 1980. No Price.

McCAUGHEY, ELIZABETH P. *From Loyalist*

to Founding Father: The Political Odyssey of William Samuel Johnson. Pp. xiv, 362. New York: Columbia University Press, 1980. $22.50.

MILLER, ABRAHAM H. Terrorism and Hostage Negotiations. Pp. xvi, 134. Boulder, CO: Westview Press, 1980. $16.00.

MOE, TERRY M. The Organization of Interests: Incentives and the Internal Dynamics of Political Interest Groups. Pp. x, 282. Chicago, IL. University of Chicago Press, 1980, No Price.

NEWLYN, W. T. The Financing of Economic Development. Pp. vi, 374. New York: Oxford University Press, 1978. $24.00.

NYE, ROBERT D. What is B. F. Skinner Really Saying? Pp. ix, 198. Englewood Cliffs, NJ: Prentice-Hall, 1980. $9.95. $4.95 Paperbound.

PETTMAN, RALPH. State and Class: A Sociology of International Affairs. Pp. 270. New York: St. Martin's Press, 1980. $25.00.

PHILLIPS, DEREK L. Wittgenstein and Scientific Knowledge: A Sociological Perspective. Pp. vii, 248. Totowa, NJ: Rowman and Littlefield, 1977. $17.50.

PLIMPTON, PAULINE AMES, ed. Oakes Ames: Jottings of a Harvard Botanist. Pp. x, 403. Cambridge, MA: Harvard University Press, 1979. $12.95.

PORTER, JACK NUSAN, ed. The Sociology of American Jews: A Critical Anthology. Pp. vii, 282. Washington, D.C.: University Press of America, 1978. Paperbound.

QUANDT, WILLIAM B. Decade of Decisions: American Policy Toward the Arab-Israeli Conflict, 1967–1976. Pp. 321. Berkeley, CA: University of California Press, 1977. $14.95.

RABINOW, PAUL and WILLIAM SULLIVAN. Interpretive Social Science: A Reader. Berkeley, CA: Univ. of California Press, 1979. $6.95 Paperbound.

ROSENTHAL, DONALD B. The Expansive Elite: District Politics and State Policy Making in India. Pp. 361. Berkeley, CA: University of California Press, 1977, $16.95.

ROTHMAN, JACK. Social R & D: Research and Development in the Human Services. Pp. xiii, 290. Englewood Cliffs, NJ: Prentice-Hall, 1980. $10.95 Paperbound.

SAVAGE, HENRY JR., Discovering America: 1700–1875 Pp. xviii, 394. New York: Harper & Row, 1980. $6.95.

SCALAPINO, ROBERT A., The Washington Papers, Vol. 69, The United States and Korea: Looking Ahead. Pp. 88. Beverly Hills, CA: Sage Publications, 1979. $3.50.

SCAMMON, RICHARD M. and ALICE V. McGILLIVRAY, eds. America Votes 13: A

Handbook of Contemporary American Election Statistics, 1978. Pp. iv, 384. Washington, DC: Elections Research Center, 1979. $46.50.

SHADOIAN, JACK. Dreams and Dead Ends: The American Gangster/Crime Film. Pp. vii, 366. Cambridge, MA: The MIT Press, 1977, $15.00.

SINGER, J. DAVID. Explaining WAR: Selected Papers from the Correlates of War Project. Pp. 328. Beverly Hills, CA: Sage Publications, 1979. No price, Paperbound.

SKINNER, ANDREW S. A System of Social Science: Papers Relating to Adam Smith. Pp. x, 278 New York: Oxford University Press, 1979. $24.95.

SOHNER, CHARLES P. and HELEN P. MARTIN. American Government and Politics Today. Pp. x, 435. Glenview, IL: Scott, Foresman & Co., 1980. No Price Paperbound.

STAVE, BRUCE, M. The Making of Urban History: Historiography Through Oral History. Pp. 336. Beverly Hills, CA: Sage Publications, 1977, $6.95.

STIVERS, RICHARD. A Hair of the Dog: Irish Drinking and American Stereotypes. Pp. 197. University Park, PA: Pennsylvania State University Press, 1976. $13.95.

TOLL, NELLY, Without Surrender: Art of the Holocaust. Pp. ix, 109. Philadelphia, PA: Running Press, 1978, No Price.

WAGNER, JON, ed. Images of Information: Still Photography in the Social Sciences. Pp. 311. Beverly Hills, CA: Sage Publications, 1979. $17.50. $8.95 Paperbound.

WALICKI, ANDRZEJ. A History of Russian Thought: From the Enlightenment to Marxism. Pp. xvii, 456. Stanford, CA: Stanford University Press, 1979. $25.00.

WARNER, SAM BASS, JR and SYLVIA FLEISCH. Measurements for Social History. Pp. 232. Beverly Hills, CA: Sage Publications, 1977. $6.95.

WATSON, JAMES L., ed. Asian & African Systems of Slavery. Pp. vii, 348. Berkeley, CA: University of California Press, 1980, $20.00.

WEINTRAUB, SIDNEY, Capitalism's Inflation and Unemployment Crisis. Pp. iii, 242. Reading, MA: Addison-Wesley, 1978. No Price.

WILLIAMS, DONAVAN, UMFUNDISI: A Biography of Tiyo Soga 1829–1871. Pp. xx, 146. Cape Province, South Africa: Lovedale Press, 1978. No Price Paperbound.

WILLIAMS, PETER W. Popular Religion in America: Symbolic Change and the Modernization Process in Historical Perspective. Pp. xiv, 258. Englewood Cliffs, NJ: Prentice-Hall, 1980. $7.95 Paperbound.

INDEX

INDEX

INDEX

ACADEMIC TENURE: ITS RECIPIENTS AND ITS EFFECTS, Lionel S. Lewis, 86
Affirmative Action/Equal Employment Opportunity (AA/EEO), 103–104
Affirmative Action Guidelines (1979), 113
AFRICAN ACADEMICS: A STUDY OF SCIENTISTS AT THE UNIVERSITIES OF IBADAN AND NAIROBI, Thomas Owen Eisemon, 126
ALTBACH, PHILIP G., and Sheila Slaughter, The Crisis of the Professoriate, 1
Amalgamated Clothing Workers, 84
American Association of Colleges, 53
Conference Statement, 1925, 53–56
American Association of University Professors (AAUP), 47–48, 51–60, 78, 81, 82
Conference Statement, 1925, 53–56
Interpretative Comments, 1970, 59
Statement of Principles, 1940, 56–57, 59
American Civil Liberties Union (ACLU), 55
American Council on Education, 32, 43, 53, 71
Conference Statement, 1925, 53–56
American Economic Association, 48
American Federation of Labor (AFL), 81
American Federation of Teachers (AFT) 55, 81, 82
American Political Science Association, 48
American Sociology Society, 48
Andrews, Frank, 28
Association of American Colleges, 56
Statement of Principles, 1940, 56–57, 59
Association of American Universities, 23, 79, 80
Atelsek, Frank J., 32
Atkinson, Richard, 27
Autonomy and accountability, 11

Backman, C. W., 39, 42
Bakke case, 111–112, 113
Balch, Emily, 53
Beard, Charles, 53
Ben-David, Joseph, 31
Berea College vs. Kentucky, 106
Bergman, W. G., 55
Blackburn, Robert T., 34
BLACKBURN, ROBERT T., Careers for Academics and the Future Production of Knowledge, 25
Bohmer, Peter, 60
Bombay Study of college teachers, 144–146
Brawer, Arthur M., 67
Breneman, David W., 32

Brewster, James, 52
Brown vs. the Board of Education, 106, 114
Bury, John B., 23
Bushnell, David, 67

CAREERS FOR ACADEMICS AND THE FUTURE PRODUCTION OF KNOWLEDGE, Robert T. Blackburn, 25
Carnegie Commission, 32
Carnegie Council, 26, 34
Carr, Robert K., 91
Cattell, James McKeen, 53
CHITNIS, SUMA, The Indian Academic: an Elite in the Midst of Scarcity, 139
City University of New York (CUNY), 75, 78, 84
Civil Rights Act of 1964, 109, 112
Cohen, Florence B., 67
Cole, Jonathan R., 30
Cole, Steven, 30
Collins, Randall, 31
Commission on Civil Rights, U.S., 108
Community of scholars, 6
CRISIS OF THE PROFESSORIATE, THE, Philip G. Altbach and Sheila Slaughter, 1
Cross, Patricia K., 65

Dana, Henry W. L., 53
"DANGER ZONE": ACADEMIC FREEDOM AND CIVIL LIBERTIES, THE, Sheila Slaughter, 46
Davis, Angela, 60
Davis, Jerome, 55
De Lacy, Hugh, 55
Deutch, Karl, 28
DIALECTIC ASPECTS OF RECENT CHANGE IN ACADEME, Logan Wilson, 15
Dubois, W. E. B., 106

EISEMON, THOMAS OWEN, African Academics: a Study of Scientists at the Universities of Ibadan and Nairobi, 126
Equal Employment Opportunity Commission (EEOC), 113
Equal Opportunity Act of 1972, 109

FACULTY UNIONISM: THE FIRST TEN YEARS, Joseph W. Garbarino, 74
FAIA, MICHAEL A., Teaching, Research, and Role Theory, 36

207

Fashing, Joseph, 93
Federal Loyalty Program, 57
Feldman, S. D., 125
Fifth Amendment, 59
Freedman's Bureau, 105

GARBARINO, JOSEPH W., Faculty Unionism: the First Ten Years, 74
Garrison, Roger, 66
Glueck, William, 30
Gomberg, Irene L., 32
Goode, William, 100
Graham, Patricia, 117
Granbury, J. C., 55
Green vs. Board of Regents, 109–110
Griggs vs. Duke Power Company, 108–109

Hammond et al., 42
Hart, J. K., 52
Hatch Act, 57
HISTORICAL CRITIQUE OF AFFIRMATIVE ACTION IN THE ACADEMIC PROFESSION, A, Robert C. Johnson, Jr., 102
HORNIG, LILLI S., Untenured and Tenuous: the Status of Women Faculty, 115
House Unamerican Activities Committee (HUAC), 57
Humphrey, Hubert H., 113
Hunter, Dr. Carolyn F., 110–111
Hutchins, Robert, 19

IN BETWEEN: THE COMMUNITY COLLEGE TEACHER, Howard B. London, 62
INDIAN ACADEMIC: AN ELITE IN THE MIDST OF SCARCITY, THE, Suma Chitnis, 139
International Union of Electrical Workers, 84
Ives Laws, 56

Jauch, Lawrence R., 30
Johnson, Andrew, 105
JOHNSON, ROBERT C., JR., A Historical Critique of Affirmative Action in the Academic Profession, 102
Johnson vs. University of Pittsburgh, 110
Joint Committee on Academic Freedom and Tenure, 48–49
Jones, Edward, 104

Katz, David A., 101
Kirk, Wade R., 67
Kline, M., 39
Ku Klux Klan, 105

Ladd, Everett C., 26, 32, 38
Lazarsfeld, Paul L., 58
Lester, Richard, 125
LEWIS, LIONEL S., Academic Tenure: its Recipients and its Effects, 86
Lightfield, Timothy E., 29

Linskey, A. S., 43
Lipset, Seymour M., 26, 32, 38
LONDON, HOWARD B., In Between: the Community College Teacher, 62
Long, J. Scott, 29
Lynd, Staughton, 60

Machlup, Fritz, 28
McCarthy, Senator Joseph, 38, 60
McLean, G., 55
MacNaboe, Dies and Rapp-Courdet Investigating Committees, 56, 57
Mannheim's theory of generations, 30
Miller, John Perry, 93
Millet, John, 19
Morrill Land-Grant Act of 1862 and of 1890, 105
Murray, George, 60

National Academy of Science, 23
National Education Association (NEA), 81, 82
National Labor Relations Act (NLRA), 80
National Research Committee, 27
National Science Foundation (NSF), 27, 34
National Security Act, 57
Nearing, Scott, 51, 53
Nexus between publication and good teaching, 43
Nisbet, Robert, 100

Ortega's hypothesis, 30

Parenti, Michael, 60
Patten, Simon N., 53
Pelz, Donald, 28
Perrucci, Carolyn, 125
Planck's Principle, 30
Platt, John, 28
Plessy vs. Ferguson, 106
Powell, Justice, 112
Price, De Solla, 27

Rader, Melvin, 58
Report of the Committee on Academic Freedom in Wartime, 52
Research and teaching, 5–6, 18
Riesman, David, 12, 44, 64, 67, 72
Roosevelt, Franklin D., 55
Roueche, John, 67
Russwurm, John Brown, 104

Schaper, William A., 53
Seattle Central Labor Union, 56
Secord, P. F., 39, 42
Senghaas, Dieter, 28
Shils, Edward, 9
SLAUGHTER, SHEILA, see ALTBACH, PHILIP G., joint author
SLAUGHTER, SHEILA, The "Danger Zone":

Academic Freedom and Civil Liberties, 46

Smith Act, 57

Starsky, Morris, 60

Straus, M. A., 43

Student Nonviolent Coordinating Committee (SNCC), 107

TEACHING, RESEARCH, AND ROLE THEORY, Michael A. Faia, 36

Thielens, Wagner, Jr., 58

Tidball, M. E., 124

Unemployed Citizens League, 55

United Automobile Workers, 84

United States Merchant Marine Academy, 75

United Steelworkers of America vs. Brian Weber, 111, 112

Universities
as a social institution and enclave, 17
autonomy and heteronomy in, 18
egalitarianism and elitism in, 19

University of Ibadan, 127

University of Nairobi, 127

UNTENURED AND TENUOUS: THE STATUS OF WOMEN FACULTY, Lilli S. Hornig, 115

Van Alstyne, William, 56

Van den Berghe, Pierre, 128, 130

Wadkins, Charles, 111

Weber, Max, 52

Wheelock College vs. MCAD, 111

WILSON, LOGAN, Dialectic Aspects of Recent Change in Academe, 15

Zuckerman, Harriet E., 37

A History of Russian Thought
From the Enlightenment to Marxism

Andrzej Walicki. Translated from the Polish by Hilda Andrews-Rusiecka. This comprehensive synthesis of Russian intellectual history from the reign of Catherine II to the end of the 19th century emphasizes philosophy but also discusses the European political, social, and economic ideas that expanded Russian intellectual horizons. The period covered saw a superb flowering of literature and culture, and demonstrated an unusual cross-fertilization of ideas and influences. Professor Walicki cogently assesses the impact on the intellectual elite of European ideas on the one hand, and of rediscovered native forms on the other. A notable feature of the book is the author's reinterpretation of the two great controversies in Russian nineteenth-century thought: the clash between the Slavophiles and the Westernizers, and the struggles between the Populists and the Marxists. $25.00

Lionel Trilling
Criticism and Politics

William M. Chace. For fifty years Lionel Trilling was a critical presence in America. "He believed passionately," wrote Irving Howe, "and taught a whole generation also to believe, in the power of literature—its power to transform, elevate, and damage." In this first comprehensive study of Trilling's criticism and fiction, Professor Chace demonstrates the range of Trilling's influence and examines his part in America's search for a sense of its cultural self. "Reading Chace is rather like reading Trilling's essays for the first time: one experiences the same sense of a sinuous, resourceful mind at work upon concerns which are as central to our age as they are delicate, elusive, and resistant to simple formulation."—*Thomas Flanagan.* "A fine study, lucid and gracefully written, of one of the two or three critics in mid-century America that mattered the most."—*M. H. Abrams.* $12.95

 Stanford University Press

HOOVER

Traditional Authority, Islam, and Rebellion
A Study of Indonesian Political Behavior
Karl D. Jackson

Jackson's analysis of the Dar'ul Islam rebellion in West Java (1948-1962), takes the uprising as a laboratory for examining rarely tested theories of peasant political behavior, interviewing participants themselves, and in the process undermining many assumptions about peasant rebellion.
$20.00, illustrated

New in paper—
The Politics of the Chinese Cultural Revolution
A Case Study
Hong Yung Lee

"An intriguing study . . . For those interested in the social stratification of communist societies, this is one of the few books on China to even scratch the surface."
—*Foreign Affairs*

"(An) important contribution to an understanding of modern China." —*Annals*
$6.95

The Cult of Violence
Sorel and the Sorelians
Jack J. Roth

This book focuses on the intellectual and political movements inspired, both during and after his life, by the writings and activities of Georges Sorel. Although the Sorelian movement as such had disappeared by the end of World War II, the degree to which more recent advocates of violence owe something to Sorel has become a matter of much scholarly debate.
$25.00

Expanded Edition—
National Power and the Structure of Foreign Trade
Albert O. Hirshman

A new edition of this pioneering study of the connection between economics and politics in international relations.
$15.50 cloth, $4.95 paper

Public Policy in a No-Party State
Spanish Planning and Budgeting in the Twilight of the Franquist Era
Richard Gunther

This behind-the-scenes examination of decision making under Franco combines the approaches of both quantitative public policy and decision-making studies. Its analysis of the inner working of the Franquist regime will interest students of modern Spain, comparative government, public policy, and politics in general.
$17.50

University of California Press
Berkeley 94720

Origin and Purpose. The Academy was organized December 14, 1889, to promote the progress of political and social science, especially through publications and meetings. The Academy does not take sides in controverted questions, but seeks to gather and present reliable information to assist the public in forming an intelligent and accurate judgment.

Meetings. The Academy holds an annual meeting in the spring extending over two days.

Publications. THE ANNALS is the bi-monthly publication of The Academy. Each issue contains articles on some prominent social or political problem, written at the invitation of the editors. Also, monographs are published from time to time, numbers of which are distributed to pertinent professional organizations. These volumes constitute important reference works on the topics with which they deal, and they are extensively cited by authorities throughout the United States and abroad. The papers presented at the meetings of The Academy are included in THE ANNALS.

Membership. Each member of The Academy receives THE ANNALS and may attend the meetings of The Academy. Annual dues: Regular Membership—$18.00 (clothbound,

$23.00). Special Membership—contributing, $40.00; sustaining, $60.00; patron, $100. A life membership is $500. Add $2.00 to above rates for membership outside the U.S.A. Dues are payable in U.S. dollars in advance. Special members receive a certificate suitable for framing and may choose either paper or cloth-bound copies of THE ANNALS.

Single copies of THE ANNALS may be obtained by nonmembers of The Academy for $4.50 ($5.50 clothbound) and by members for $4.00 ($5.00 clothbound). A discount of 5 percent is allowed on orders for 10 to 24 copies of any one issue, and of 10 percent on orders for 25 or more copies. These discounts apply only when orders are placed directly with The Academy and not through agencies. The price to all bookstores and to all dealers is $4.50 per copy ($5.50, clothbound) less 20 percent, with no quantity discount. Orders for 2 books or less must be prepaid (add $1.00 for postage and handling). Orders for 3 books or more must be invoiced.

All correspondence concerning The Academy or THE ANNALS should be addressed to the Academy offices, 3937 Chestnut Street, Philadelphia, Pa. 19104.